A KENTUCKY ALBUM

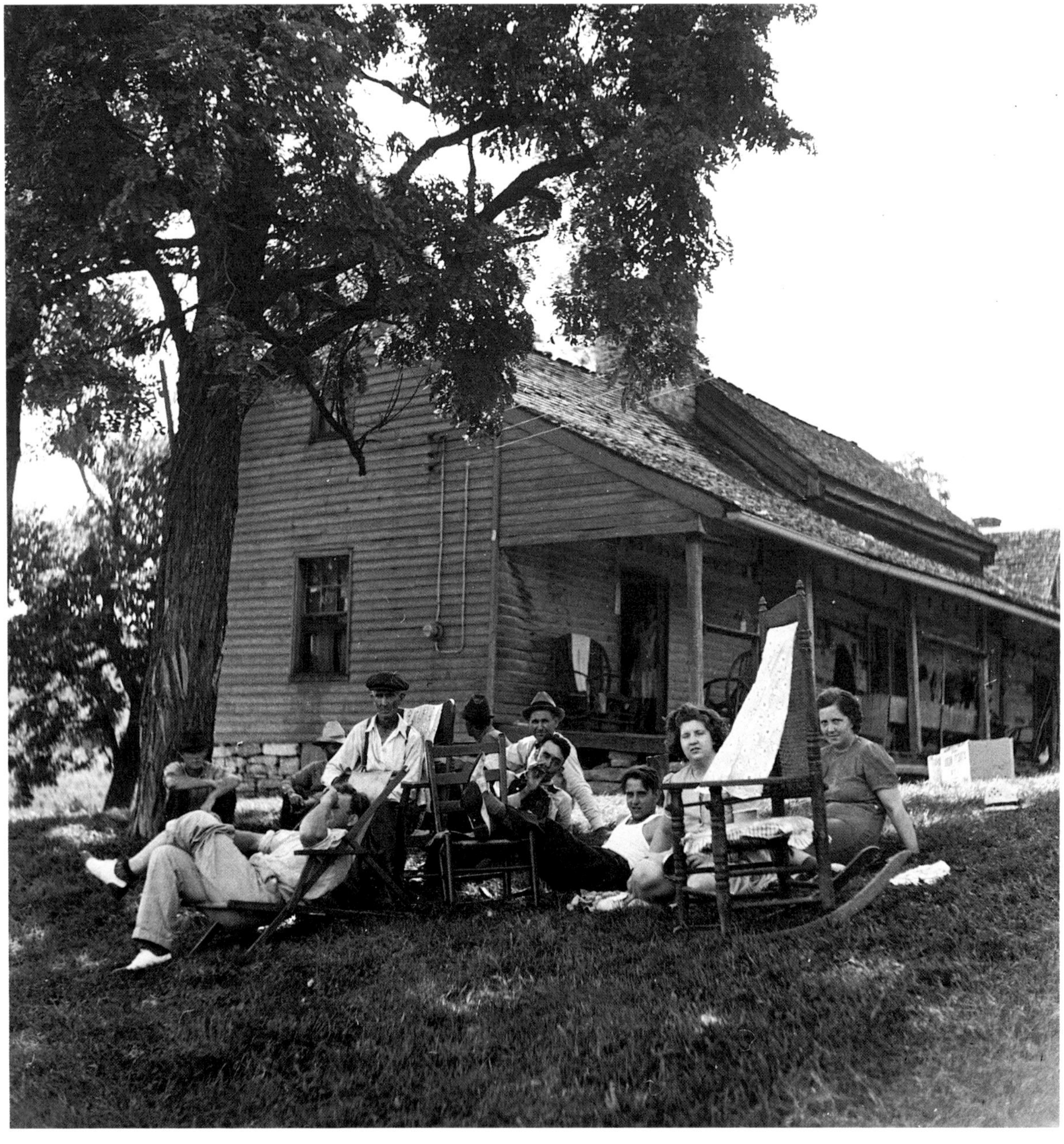

A KENTUCKY ALBUM

Farm Security Administration Photographs, 1935-1943

BEVERLY W. BRANNAN and DAVID HORVATH, Editors

With a Foreword by Jim Wayne Miller

THE UNIVERSITY PRESS OF KENTUCKY

For John Michael Vlach, who suggested considering the Kentucky images as a state portrait, and for those who share our love for Kentucky and FSA photographs.

Frontispiece: Sunday afternoon in the front yard. Near Lawrenceburg, summer 1940. MARION POST WOLCOTT. Of this photo, Wolcott wrote her boss: "Chief Stryker! Calling all cars. Caution all photogs! Never take a picture of pregnant woman sitting in rocking chair on sloping lawn. . . . Consequences are—lady doesn't want photograph taken in present state, starts hurriedly to get up & run in house, but chair tips over backwards dumping (& embarrassing, not seriously damaging) her. Photog. is surprised, sorry, tries to apologize, inquire after victim's health, etc. etc. & succeeds only in almost being mobbed & beaten & driven off by irate & resentful & peace loving members of family—*dozens* of them (P.S.) Camera was saved."

04 03 02 01 00 5 4 3 2

Scholarly publisher for the Commonwealth,
serving Bellarmine College, Berea College, Centre
College of Kentucky, Eastern Kentucky University,
The Filson Club, Georgetown College, Kentucky
Historical Society, Kentucky State University,
Morehead State University, Murray State University,
Northern Kentucky University, Transylvania University,
University of Kentucky, University of Louisville,
and Western Kentucky University.

Editorial and Sales Offices: Lexington, Kentucky 40506-0024

Printed in Japan by Dai Nippon Printing Co. Ltd. through DNP (America), Inc.

Library of Congress Cataloging-in-Publication Data
Main entry under title:

A Kentucky album.

Bibliography: p.
1. Kentucky—Social life and customs—Pictorial works.
2. Kentucky—Description and travel—Views. I. Brannan,
Beverly W., 1946- II. Horvath, David G.
F456.K35 1986 779'.99769042 85-16434
ISBN 0-8131-1563-9

Contents

Foreword by Jim Wayne Miller vii
Acknowledgments xi
Introduction by Beverly W. Brannan 1

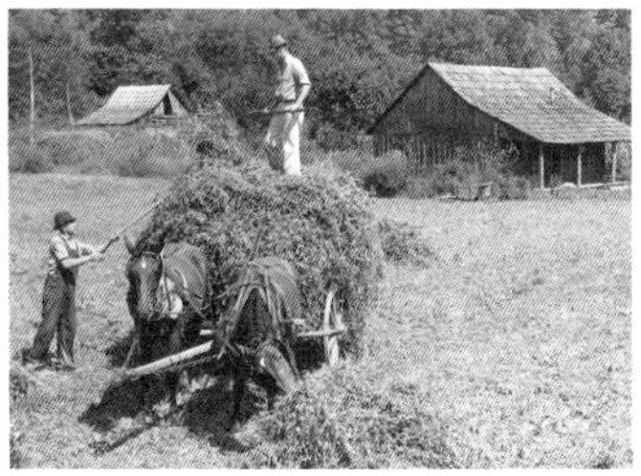

RURAL LIFE 9

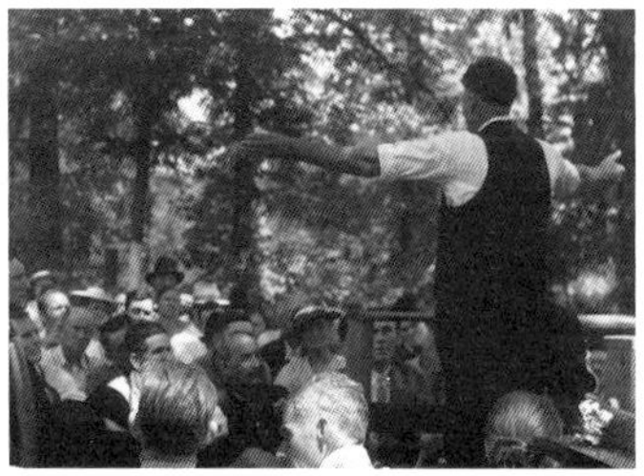

RELIGIOUS CUSTOMS 39

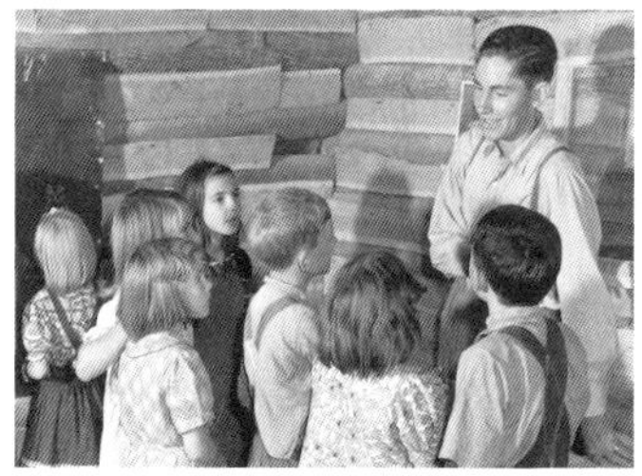

EDUCATION 53

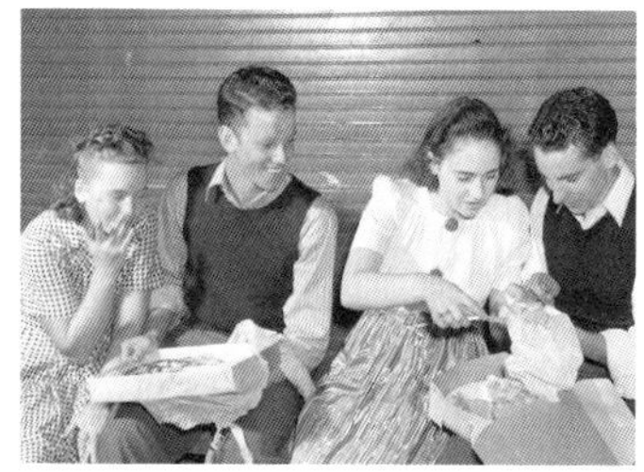

SOCIAL GATHERINGS 65

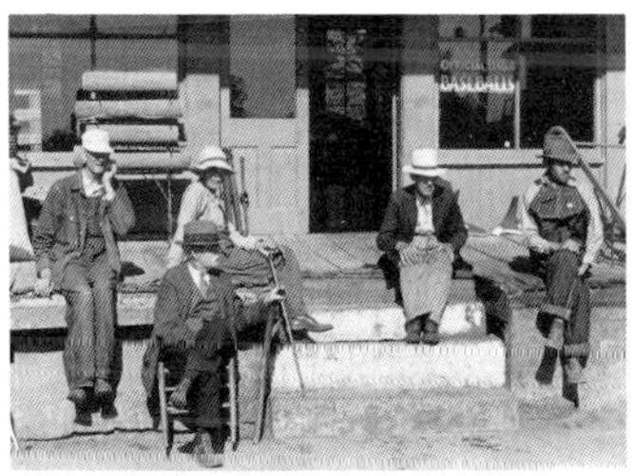

CITIES AND TOWNS 83

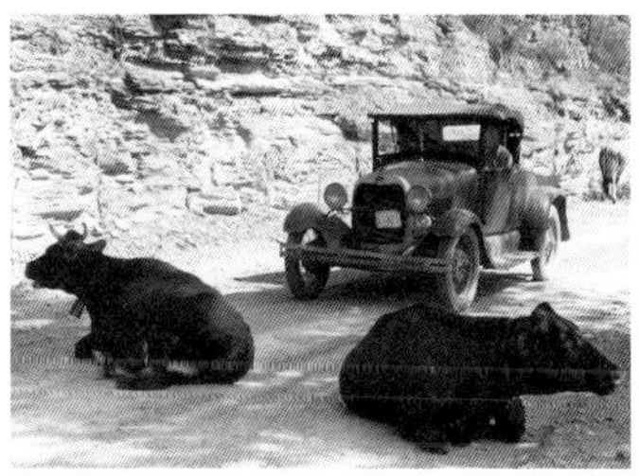

TRANSPORTATION 111

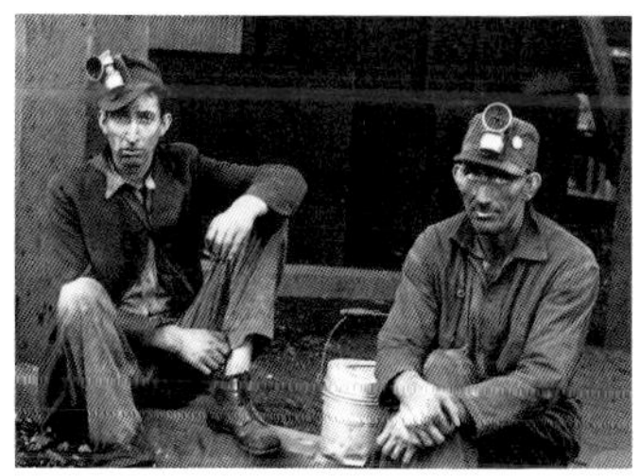

COAL MINING 125

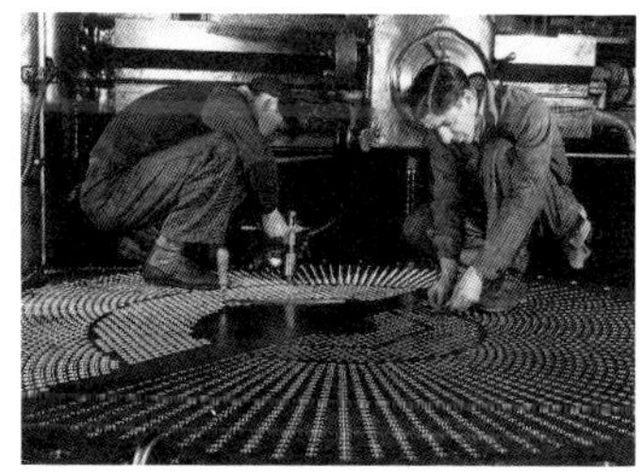

THE HOMEFRONT 135

Photo Negative Numbers 147
Bibliography 148

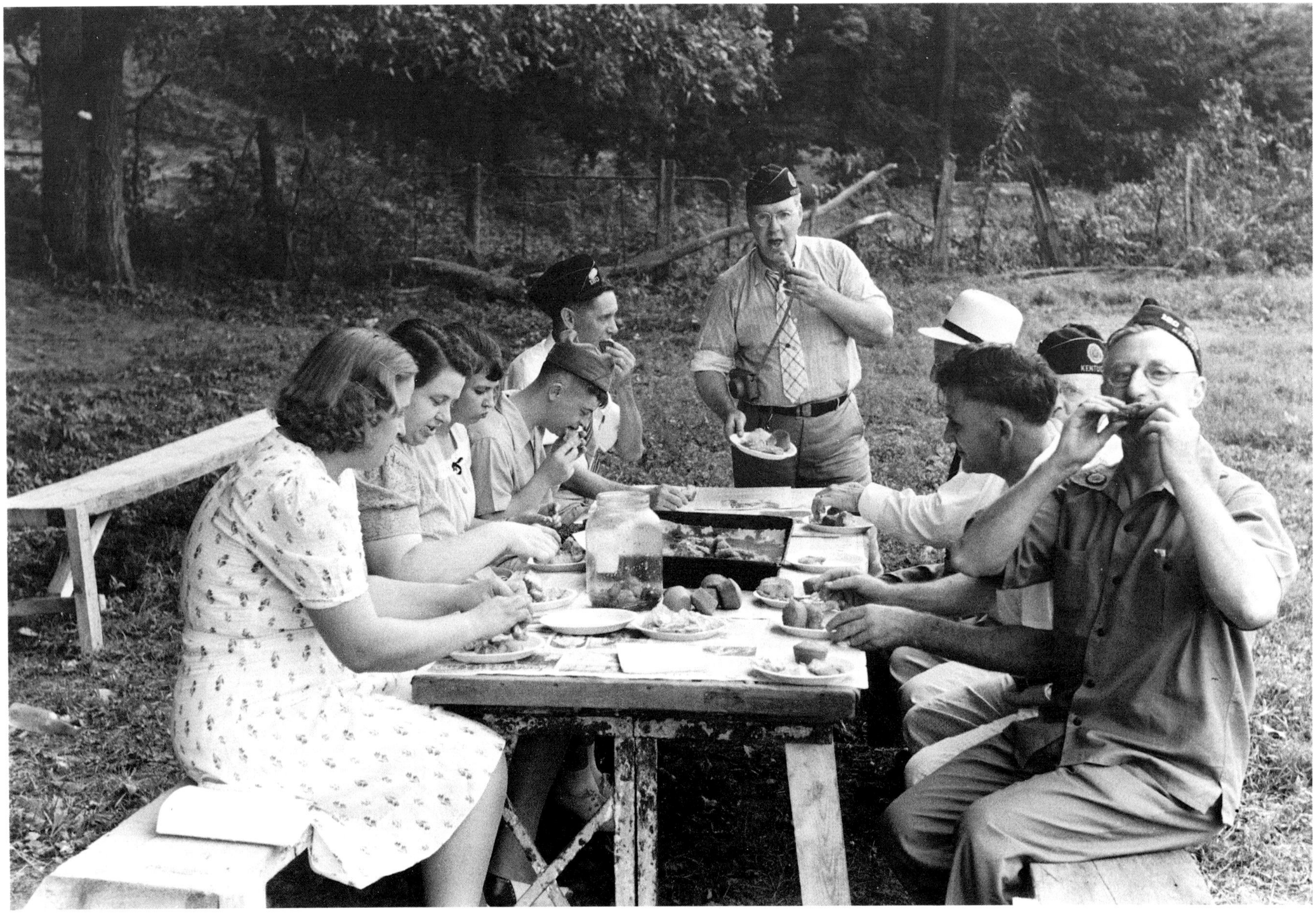

Fish and all the fixings. American Legion fish fry near Louisville, August 1940. MARION POST WOLCOTT.

Foreword

ANYONE WHO LOOKS at these photographs, anywhere in America, is apt to have the sensation of encountering people and places simultaneously strange and familiar, distant and near. We know these roads, cars, towns, and people to be somehow as typically American as legionnaires and their wives at a fish fry. Maybe this is because the photographs come from a border state which is neither north nor south, east nor west, exactly, but something of all of these—Kentucky. Where else would one find such a mix of horses, tobacco, coal mines, and distilleries, of mountains, river towns, and bluegrass?

Like photographs in our family albums or on the mantlepieces of relatives, friends, and neighbors, the faces and places in these photographs come out of a time—the 1930s—that seems both remote and recent. They remind us of someone remembered from childhood, or of someone we were talking to only yesterday—of some place we drove through a long time ago—or was it just last summer?

For some of us, many of the people in these photographs might be our grandarents in their prime. For others of us, they might be our parents at the age we are now. Still others will know why these photographs are at once strange and familiar: they are photographs of us! And of our children, our neighbors, our place, our labor, our leisure. They show us our lives. This is the way things were in a time so recent, yet already a part of history.

We Americans have not had much use for history. We repeat with relish Satchel Paige's advice: "Don't look back, something might be gaining on you!" We've preferred action to reflection. With our desire for the new and our often urgent need to accommodate change, we rearrange our houses and the patterns of our lives. We relegate things to the attic and forget them—a wooden churn, an old pie safe, a marbletop table—only to come on them years later and discover a new appreciation—and use—for them. Similarly, in our collective national life, distracted by urgent new priorities, we often relegate shared experiences, whole chunks of our history, to the national attic and forget them, only to come on them years later better prepared to appreciate their meaning and utility.

Such is the case with these photographs, part of a national self-examination that took place during the 1930s, a self-examination set aside by World War II and mostly forgotten, and certainly considered irrelevant during the postwar period. Now, poking around in the national attic, we come on these images made half a century ago. It is as if we'd discovered a trove of precious family mementos occasionally mentioned but long considered lost.

We come to these photographs better prepared to appreciate the value of historical memory and the uses of history. In past years it did not much matter to us who we had been or even who we were just then; we were more concerned with who we might become. But increasingly we have had a collective change of attitude. We are more and more inclined to try to understand who we are by looking at who we were, to think about where we are going by considering where we've been. We are not quite so ready to discard the past, for we have come to know that much in our heritage works. We figure a lot of things are not just good because they're old; they're old because they're good. They keep on working.

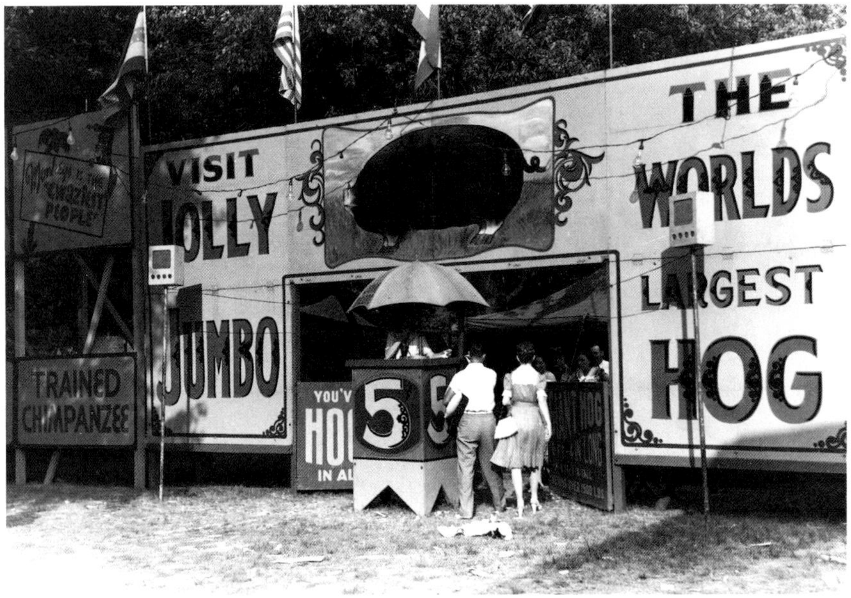

The midway and carnival at the Shelby County Horse Show and Fair. Shelbyville, August 1940. MARION POST WOLCOTT.

We are increasingly appreciative of the insights of writers and poets who help us see how knowledge of the past deepens our understanding of the present, how seeds of the future are buried in the soil of the past. Thinking about the presence of the past, novelist Thomas Wolfe writes at the outset of *Look Homeward, Angel:* "Each of us is all the sums he has not counted." And Kentucky poet Wendell Berry, paralleling Wolfe, suggests that it is not merely desirable but obligatory to understand the past because "We owe the future / the past, the long knowledge / that is the potency of time to come."

We can gauge the degree to which our attitudes have changed by reminding ourselves that there was opposition half a century ago to making these photographs. The Farm Security Administration, under whose auspices they were made, was considered by many to be another socialistic scheme out of Washington. It is ironic that today these photographs may have proved to be a long-term investment in freedom, functioning as a counter to the socialism and collectivization they were once suspected of serving and abetting.

For one of the uses of history is the maintenance of historical memory, which is crucial to the preservation of our freedom. Certainly this is not self-evident. But in countries having no democratic traditions or in which freedom and democracy are only weakly established or recently won, the importance of historical memory is better understood and appreciated. The Russian dissident Alexander Ginzburg makes vivid the connection between freedom and historical memory when he points out how, in Russia, it was absolutely necessary for the revolution to obliterate historical memory so that people could have no conception of an alternative to what the revolution offered. The revolution killed history, destroyed the past, so that the present would be tolerable.

Ginzburg's countryman Alexander Solzhenitzyn, author of *The Gulag Archipelago* and now a resident of the United States, quotes the proverb: "Dwell on the past and you lose one eye; forget the past and you lose both eyes." We Americans are coming more and more to the realization that a democratic future requires a vivid awareness of a democratic past. These photographs are a part of that past made visible; they constitute another kind of historical text contributing to the preservation and maintenance of historical memory.

Not everyone will agree that photographs are useful as historical texts, perhaps because our attitude toward photographs, and toward pictures generally, is contradictory. On the one hand, we say that a picture is worth a thousand words. On the other we consider pictures to be superficial, incapable of providing deep meaning. Photographs have been characterized as aids to misunderstanding, giving us only the surface of reality. Photography, we know, has often been the tool of propagandists and manipulators of our minds and thoughts. Photographs have even been faulted for their tendency to democratize experience.

But if photography—particularly documentary photography of the kind represented here—tends to democratize experience, this tendency hardly compromises the usefulness of the work found in *A Kentucky Album*, now or for the future. On the contrary, this characteristic may constitute one of the virtues of these photographs, for they present us—in a vivid and immediate way—with aspects of our common past.

Admittedly, these photographs were made for the purpose of propagandizing, but in the best sense of that word. They were intended to help educate two-thirds of the American people about the condition of the other third who were, according to President Franklin D. Roosevelt, "ill-housed, ill-clad and ill-nourished." And part of the pictures' original purpose was to help justify the need for an agency such as the Resettlement Administration and other federal programs. But this purpose was never secret, nor was this kind of propaganda illegitimate.

These photographs are useful as historical texts if we learn how to read them properly. We should not look here for a "balanced overview"; that is appropriate to another kind of text. We should not chafe that different parts of the state are not represented with equal numbers of photographs. The FSA photographers never attempted

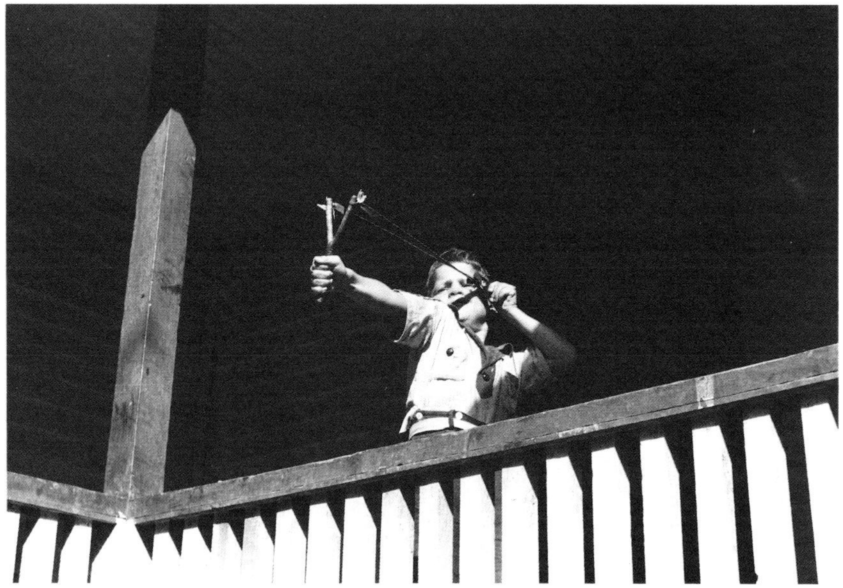

A mountain child shoots a homemade slingshot from the porch of his home near Buckhorn. September 1940. Marion Post Wolcott.

that sort of representation and should not be faulted for not having achieved it. Rather, we should read the photographs in their own language, for although they are accompanied by explanations, the images themselves are the main text here; they have their own meanings, their own grammar and syntax. We should read them with the same trust their makers had, a trust in particulars to suggest their own meanings.

Part of that meaning resides in contrasts, blends, juxtapositions: the contrast between the unusual and the commonplace, between deprivation and prosperity, between good husbandry and poor, between labor and leisure, between urban scenes and rural. We should note how the county seats and market towns have a rural accent no less than if the streets, buildings, and signs were a kind of silent language. We should note the evidence of blended urban and rural experiences where we see, for instance, Madison Avenue reaching all the way to the barnyard to hawk tobacco and cold medicine from the side of a barn beneath which cows take their ease.

The original reasons for making these photographs are compatible with the reasons why we should value them now, and with other uses they may come to serve. Half a century ago these photographs struck people with the stark insistence and timeliness of newspaper headlines. Today, while we recognize them as belonging to a particular time, what we value most about them may be their timelessness. They are no longer news but something closer to literature, which poet Ezra Pound defined as "news that stays news." We can think of the makers of these photographs as poets with cameras, seeking out "news that stays news"—the timeless and universal experience of people in all times and places.

These photographs celebrate not just the extraordinary and unusual but the commonplace and everyday. They help us to encounter the familiar and understand it as if for the first time. They add to our available reality, give us an expanded sense and heightened definition of now—not just a sense of the past but an uncanny sense of the past in the present, as real and close and dear as photographs of our grandparents, parents, aunts and uncles, brothers and sisters. Like good poems, these photographs present us with particular times and circumstances, particular people and places, but in such a way that the new is seen under the aspect of the unchanging, while the unchanging is forever renewed.

These photographs were originally meant to educate. Today they can teach us in ways profounder, perhaps, then they could half a century ago. They teach us how little we've changed in some ways and how much we've changed in others, and they suggest how much the change has been in our minds and hearts. They make us realize how easily similar scenes could be photographed today. They humble us when we recognize that urban America may be more ignorant of rural and small-town America today than ever before.

At the same time, these photographs challenge us—with images of people who have endured adversity and deprivation with spirit, humor, and even grace. They ought also to make us feel confident about our spirit as a people and the goodness of the land, to feel pride in the realization that we can heal hurt land and take better care of it whenever and wherever we want to.

Like older relatives who have endured calamity and indifference, these photographs help us to see beyond what is frenetic in our lives, suggesting a longer, steadier view of what is really important. Catching in a fraction of a second something timeless, they suggest connection and continuity, rooted diversity as an alternative to rootless uniformity.

We prize these photographs because they are a way of helping us count the sums we are, individually and collectively. They are a part of the past we owe to the future. They help us to understand who we are and who we might yet be by showing us who—not so long ago—we were.

JIM WAYNE MILLER

Acknowledgments

WE ARE GRATEFUL to those who made, posed for, and preserved the FSA photographs, and especially to Arthur Rothstein and Marion Post Wolcott for sharing their memories with us.

And we want to thank the many people who helped us on this project:

• John C. Broderick, Assistant Librarian of Congress for Research Services, and Stephen E. Ostrow, Chief of the Library of Congress Prints and Photographs Division; the University of Louisville Library, and James C. Anderson, Curator of the Ekstrom Photographic Archives, University of Louisville.

• Our colleagues Carol Pulin, Library of Congress, and William Carner and Barbara Crawford, University of Louisville.

• Those who supplied us with photoprints: Evelyn Nave, the Library of Congress Photoduplication Service printing lab staff, and the negative monitor.

• Our friends Jeanne and Truman Temple, Pete Daniel, Lynn Metcalf, Jane Hogg, and Judy Jennings.

• Our families: Beverly's parents, Ruth and Kenneth Wood, and our respective spouses, John Vlach and Mary Horvath, for their patient listening and reading.

Funds from the Kentucky Humanities Council and the University of Louisville Library made possible the exhibition "Things As They Were," from which this book originated.

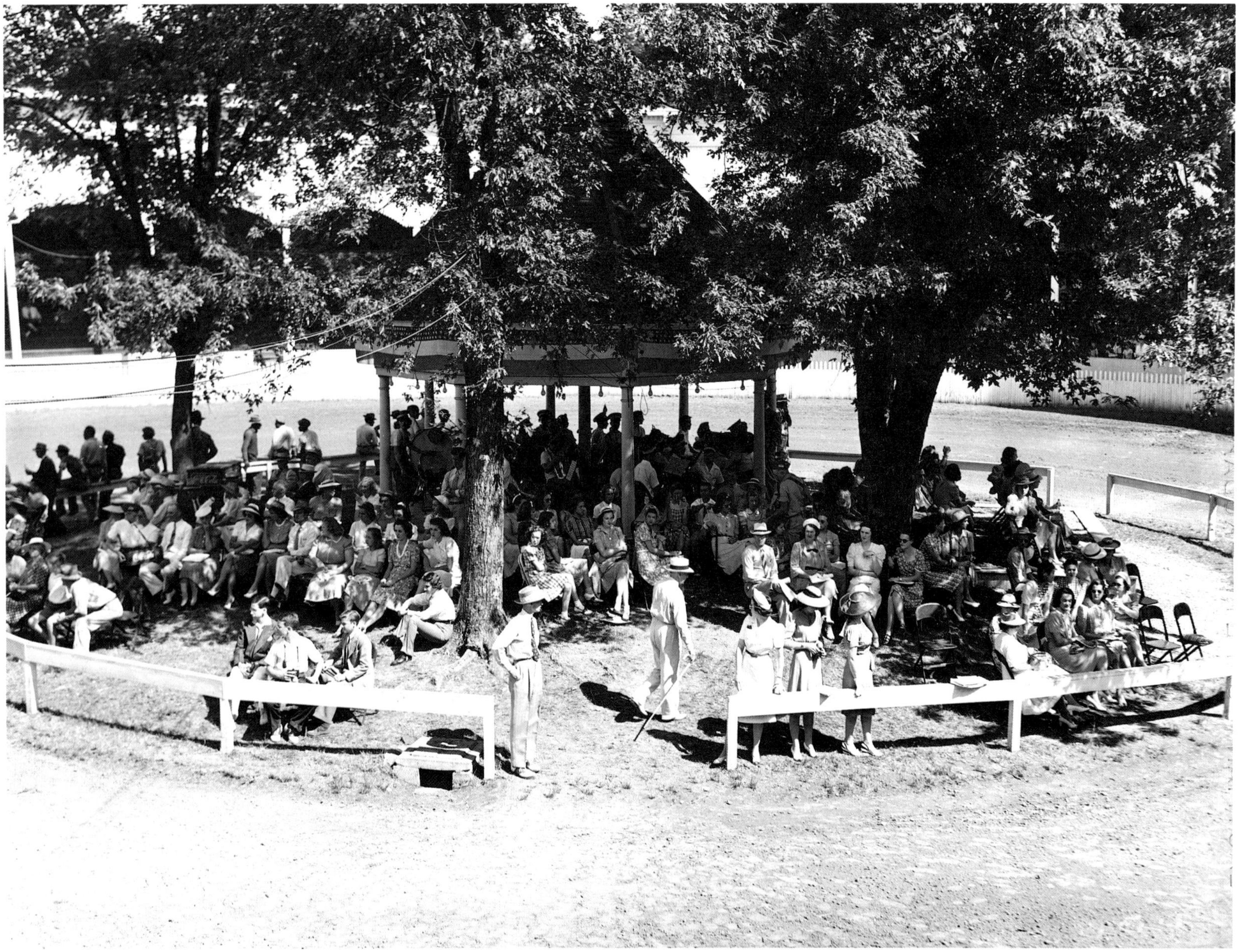

Spectators enjoy the shade in the inner circle at the Shelby County Horse Show and Fair. Shelbyville, August 1940. MARION POST WOLCOTT.

Introduction

LIKE MANY who have lived for a long time outside the Commonwealth, I still consider myself a Kentuckian. Ancestors on both sides of my family have made their homes in Barren County continuously since the 1790s, and it has been home to me all my life. I was born in Louisville, part of the huge baby boom that occurred when the soldiers came home from World War II, married, and started the families delayed by the war. My parents, like the millions of other couples who began marriage and formal education at the same time, had settled there so my father could begin his college education on the G.I. Bill.

Because my own Kentucky story starts only three years after the last photos included in this book, I feel somehow familiar with the Kentucky it shows. From my early childhood in the state and from a lifetime of hearing my parents' families talk about the "good old days," I grew up almost as profoundly influenced by the Great Depression and the wartime as if I had lived through them.

The pictures included here show Kentucky as it looked to federally-hired photographers who worked in the state between 1935 and 1943. The Farm Security Administration photos have long enjoyed tremendous popularity at the Library of Congress, where they have been housed since the end of the project. As curator of photographs in the Library's Prints and Photographs Division, I had occasionally browsed through this massive file alongside other curious researchers. The file took on new meaning for me when I realized that the thematically-grouped images could be brought together to form a portrait of my home state.

While considering such a project as a thesis topic for the advanced degree I am pursuing at The George Washington University, I contacted David Horvath at the University of Louisville, where FSA project director Roy E. Stryker's manuscripts are housed. When I proposed combining appropriate manuscript quotes with the Kentucky images, he suggested I serve as guest curator for an exhibition, eventually titled "Things As They Were," that hung at the University of Louisville from September 6 through November 9, 1984. It evoked so much interest that the Kentucky Humanities Council provided funding and later arranged to have the exhibition travel throughout the state. This book, inspired by that exhibition, contains many of those same images.

The picture survey by the FSA was one of the largest photographic projects ever undertaken in United States history. FSA photographers produced 75,000 black-and-white pictures with captions, and 140,000 negatives, as well as 1,600 Kodachrome color slides, documenting social and economic conditions in this country, Puerto Rico, and the Virgin Islands during the Great Depression and as the United States prepared to and entered World War II. The FSA photographs at the Library of Congress form one of that institutions best known and most frequently requested collections. People have looked at them for their enormous aesthetic appeal as well as for the depiction of broad themes in society.

The FSA project began as the brainchild of Rexford Tugwell, a New Dealer who pulled together the miscellaneous federal government projects designed to help those too poor to be assisted by the major legislative programs enacted by President Roosevelt and the Congress. Many of the people Tugwell set out to aid were farmers unable to sustain themselves or their families on their land. Project photographer Dorothea Lange encouraged people to tell her their stories as she took their pictures. From these interviews she learned of people whose farm income had been as little as $1.80 for the previous year. Even in 1930s dollars that certainly was not enough to sustain an individual for a year, much less an entire family. These people were desperately poor.

Tugwell appointed his former student and colleague from the Economics Department at Columbia University, Roy Stryker (1893-1975), to head the FSA Historical Section, which oversaw the photography project. At Columbia, Stryker had been an instructor who spent a good deal of time obtaining photographs for use in teaching economic concepts to undergraduate students. He came to his new job with experience in combining images and concepts, but he had not used them to educate and motivate whole masses of people. Working from well-organized scripts, which he continually revised and expanded as new ideas came to him from academics, politicians, and photographers in the field, Stryker managed to send his photographers all over the country to create visual documentation of broad themes in American life, such as agriculture, transportation, and social and political organizations.

What did the project accomplish in Kentucky? The catalog records in the Library of Congress prepared at the end of the FSA project show approximately 13,000 numbered negatives allocated to photographs of Kentucky. Although this is an imprecise count because it includes numbers not used and others assigned to images "killed" because of unacceptable technical quality or repetitive subject matter, it is the only existing way to estimate the number of pictures taken in the project.

Stryker hired good photographers to work on his project, starting in July 1935 with Dorothea Lange (1895-1965), whose photographs documenting the problems of agricultural workers in California received national attention as early as 1935. Although she never photographed in Kentucky for the FSA, Lange's influence is felt in the Kentucky pictures because her work set the style for the realistic documentary photography of the FSA project.

The Kentucky portion of the photo-documentary project began slowly as some of the better known photographers toured the state. Their work is influential on the picture file as a whole but not necessarily because of the photographs they took in Kentucky. From the Resettlement Administration artists program, Stryker acquired the services of Ben Shahn (1898-1969) as a photographer for short periods in 1935, 1936, and 1937. Although Shahn did most of his government work as a painter, in 1935 he took approximately sixty images in Eastern Kentucky, where he photographed miners, and in Western Kentucky, where he recorded scenes of small-town life.

Carl Mydans (b. 1907) served on the Historical Section staff from the end of 1935 until the fall of 1936, when he went to work on the initial staff of *Life* magazine, where he is still employed. He made one brief trip through Kentucky in March 1936, taking approximately seventy-five pictures of the Ohio River flooding Louisville and of water erosion control and reforestation projects in Western Kentucky.

Roy Stryker established close friendships with many of the photographers with whom he worked. In chatty letters usually sent to his home, they addressed him as an elder and esteemed counselor. He in turn seems to have regarded them as promising students whose full potential he was helping to develop, much as his boss, Rexford Tugwell, had helped him in earlier years. Thus with Stryker's encouragement, his former Columbia University student Arthur Rothstein (b. 1915) quickly expanded his duties in setting up the FSA laboratory to include photographic fieldwork. In his capacity as a photographer, Rothstein traveled throuh Kentucky several times, snapping random shots on his way to assignments, most of them in other states, for FSA and other federal agencies.

Russell Lee (b. 1903) was another photographer who passed through Kentucky. He worked for the FSA from 1936 until 1942. Lee concentrated on his native Midwest and later on the Southwest, although he did some work outside those areas during his long tenure with the project. All seven of the pictures he took in Kentucky in 1938 were made in the western part of the state, in Owensboro and Irvington, while he was en route to his native Illinois.

Marion Post Wolcott is the person responsible for the majority of FSA photographs available for Kentucky, since she was assigned more than 7,000 numbered negatives between the summer and early autumn of 1940. Most of her pictures were taken in Louisville, Lexington, and especially the Appalachian region of the state. The pictures she took in other parts of Kentucky were shot from alongside major highways as she traveled to assignments in various parts of the southeastern FSA administrative region, where she was assigned from 1938 through 1940.

In the late fall of 1940, John Vachon (1914-1975), who had worked in turn as a writer, FSA clerk, and photographer, took nearly 500 images in northern Kentucky and the Bluegrass area. Vachon brought a touch of Walker Evans to those Kentucky photos, for early in his career he had consciously modeled his work on Evans's. One of the most popular photographers of all time, Evans took no photographs in Kentucky, despite Stryker's directions to do so on at least three of his trips to the South. Vachon's was the last of the Kentucky work done by FSA staff before the office was transferred to the Office of War Information.

Because of the increasing opposition of citizens and commercial agricultural organizations to New Deal policies and the demand for more emphasis on America's rearmament, the FSA lost both political and financial support and was abolished in October 1942. The Historical Section was transferred to the OWI, where the photographic assignments focused on mechanization of agriculture and preparation for war. Only occasionally did OWI photographers add images to Stryker's uncompleted shooting scripts for the nationwide photo survey.

Although their photographs are of high technical quality, few of the OWI photographer are as well-known as their predecessors, and biographical information is not available for most of them. OWI photographers took several hundred pictures in Kentucky in this

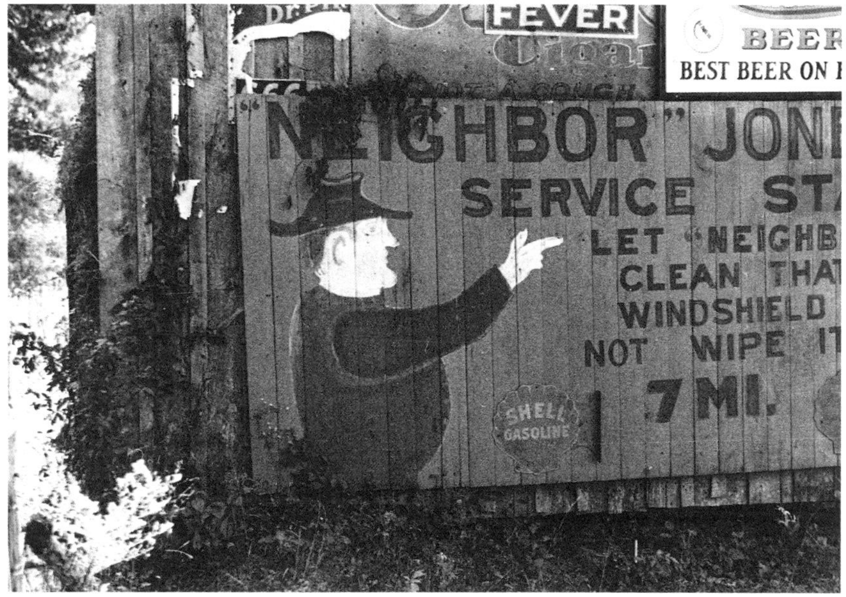

A billboard advertising a Middlesboro service station. October 1935.
Ben Shahn.

final phase of the project. Howard Hollem photographed extensively throughout the state, showing primarily military and civilian war preparations. Esther Bubley's pictures of passengers and stations, made while traveling through Kentucky on public buses, completed an agenda item long postponed on Stryker's shooting scripts. The Kentucky work of another OWI photographer, Alfred Palmer, consists largely of construction photographs of massive, publicly financed projects to build roads, houses, dams, and military installations. The nature of the pictorial project had changed drastically under the OWI and in 1943 it was disbanded.

Most of the photographers traveled alone by car, except for Ben Shahn and Russell Lee, whose wives accompanied them, at least on their Kentucky trips, and Esther Bubley, who traveled by bus. They were issued tripods, flashbulbs, and three cameras—a 35mm range finder, which they called "the miniature," a medium format roll film camera, and a larger format view camera, with which they generally preferred to work. But they relied on the government issue equipment only when their own broke down. All their work in Kentucky was done in black and white, with the exception of slightly more than two rolls of 35mm color transparency film that Wolcott exposed at a tobacco farm near Lexington, and miscellaneous scenes in the mountains of Wolfe County.

What does the picture record say about Kentucky between 1935 and 1943? In large measure it says what people outside the Commonwealth have always said about Kentucky—that it consists of the two cities of Louisville and Lexington, with their surrounding Bluegrass region, and the colorful mountain area of Appalachia. From earliest times these have been the areas of Kentucky talked and written about, while most other areas of the state have been barely mentioned. From the earliest folk narratives through today's literature and political tracts, these two cities and the mountain areas have continued to figure most prominently in the concept of Kentucky. The FSA photographs reinforce that image.

What factors influenced the subjects covered in the files? Stryker's concept of his assignment was undoubtedly a primary influence. Unlike directors of most other federal arts or information projects, he dominated the FSA project throughout its existence, maintaining careful control of his agenda, budget, and personnel. His initial task was to document nationally the need for and efficacy of Resettlement Administration projects to aid the needy. Stryker's skill as a bureaucrat, diplomat, and politician enabled him gradually to expand the coverage to include many subjects that satisfied his curiosity as a sociologist-historian. While the project's declared agenda called for documenting national rather than local phenomena, he did encourage the photographers to watch for aspects of local color. He incorporated suggestions from many sources, but his correspondence shows no evidence of his being in contact with Kentuckians while compiling his shooting scripts for the nationwide survey. Neither Stryker nor any of his photographers was from the South, much less from Kentucky, further restricting opportunities for an insider's suggestions of quintessential Kentuckiana that could be photographed. Wolcott's experiences in Kentucky illustrate many of the difficulties encountered in attempting to fulfill Stryker's plans for the file.

That Wolcott was able to complete as many of Stryker's shooting script assignments in Kentucky as she did is a tribute to her own dedication to duty, her willingness to endure mental and physical hardships, and her skills as a fieldworker. In 1940 her attempts to meet her schedule of assignments outside Kentucky kept her time so fragmented that she could rarely locate and follow through with the Kentucky resource people she and Stryker did identify. In addition, road conditions seldom permitted safe or speedy travel and uncooperative weather made crops late and productivity low. As a result, the little time that farmers spent harvesting was slightly off the schedule Wolcott had been told to expect, and she missed harvest altogether in some parts of the state. Like many workers in the federally administered Writers Project and the Post Office mural project, she often found her work rewarding in terms of the people she met but frustrating administratively.

In one instance, however, she did find an ideal contact person and many of the administrative details fell into place. Through the suggestion of someone at the *Louisville Courier-Journal*, where she went to get help fixing her camera, Wolcott found an ally who helped her get some of her best pictures of Kentucky. That person was Marie Turner, then Breathitt County school superintendent. Although Wolcott generally followed Stryker's suggested schedule, this time she took the initiative. She telegraphed him on September 5, 1940 saying: "Making 2 or 3 days trip into mountains with school superintendent. Cannot be reached very easily. No telephone or Western Union. Getting exciting material. Will wire you again on return. Continue to use Jackson [,Ky.] mailing address. Will answer your letter this weekend. Send case flashbulbs Jackson immediately."

When Wolcott returned to Jackson on September 9, she sent Stryker a wonderful letter describing some of her adventures, a number of which are depicted in this volume:

> I've been going out into the "back woods" with the county school superintendent. She's a wonderful woman & has helped me immensely. She was raised here & has more "kin folks" all over, & everyone knows & likes her. We borrowed an old car the first day—had to be pulled out of a creek by a mule, then later hauled out of the sand, & finally had a flat [tire] miles from everything & no jack! Tore down fencepost, & while our driver (a young kid who is the son of the school janitor) tried to prop the car up I was down on my belly in the creek bed piling rocks under it. But we finally got it fixed. We had to do some walking too, so that when we got back late I was one tired girl.
>
> Next trip we decided to take my car, after having no luck trying to rent or borrow a high truck. We did amazingly well over the worst and most dangerous roads & creek beds I've ever seen. Got a long way with it—only bent the running board a little & ruined one tire (which was almost worn out anyway) over a bad place in what is called a bridge. We took to mule back which is not *too* bad, & finally someone met us with a horse, so we rode over a tiny trail over a mountain just after dark. Two of us on little mountain pony, picking his way over & around rocks & up the steepest places. A mule that was tied to a fence we were passing got mean when our horse came close to him & hauled off & kicked Mrs. Turner (the sch. Supt.) on the foot. It

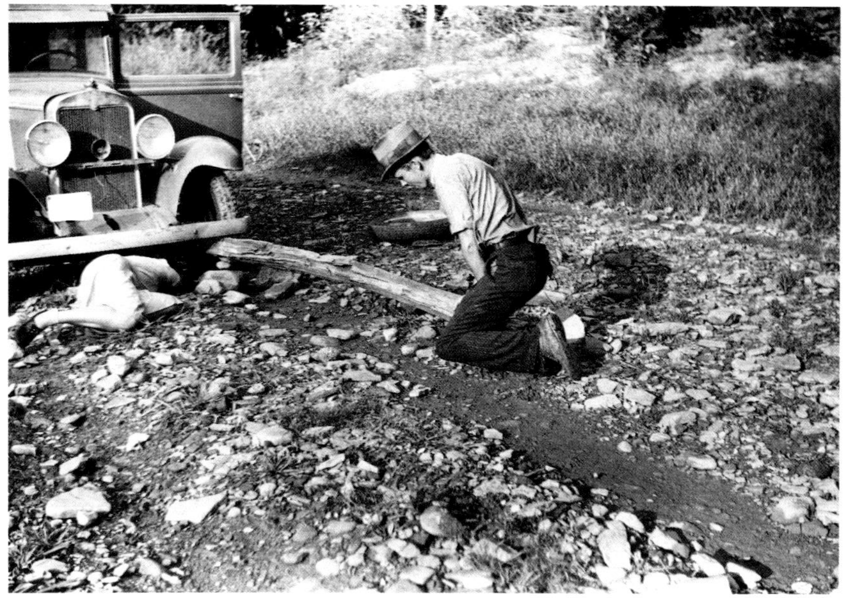

With the help of a fencepost and a local assistant, Marion Post Wolcott changes a tire along the South Fork of Quicksand Creek in Breathitt County. August 1940. MARIE R. TURNER, using Wolcott's camera.

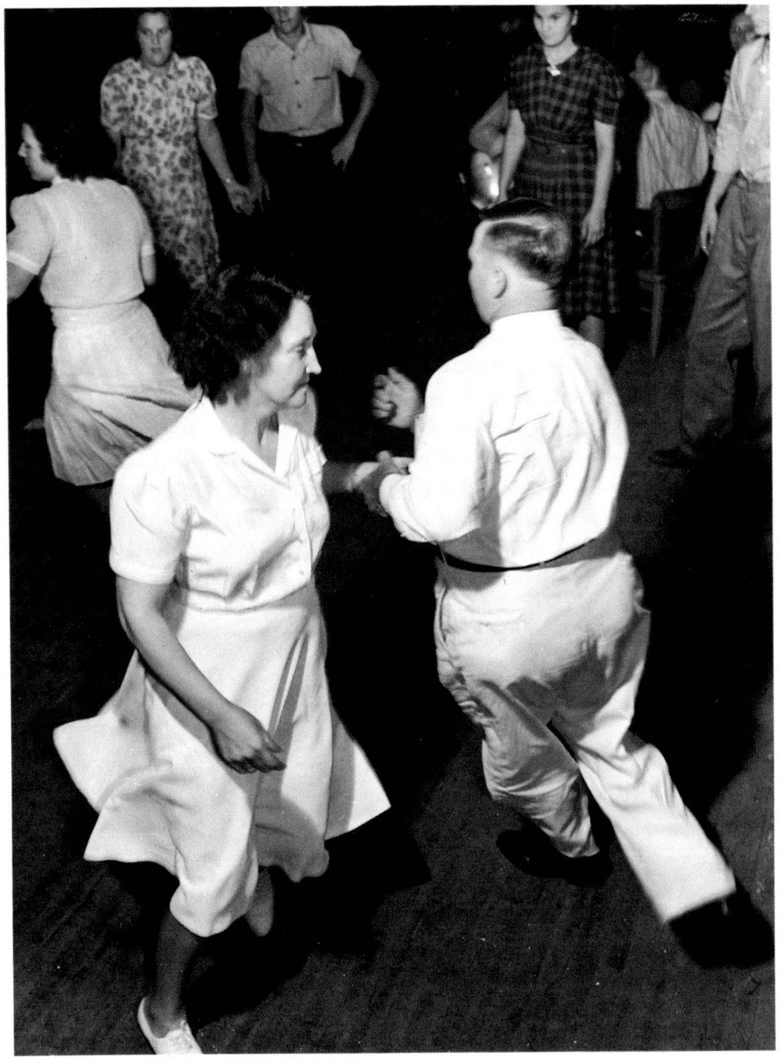

Marie R. Turner, superintendent of schools for Breathitt County, joins in square dancing at a school pie and box social. Jackson, September 1940. MARION POST WOLCOTT.

hurt her quite badly, but was just a bruise & she's better now. It was too narrow to avoid the damn animal.

Throughout her FSA work Wolcott encountered growing citizen distrust of documentary photographers, along with mounting war hysteria and fear of "foreigners" that led to her arrest in one Kentucky town. She described her arrest by a county sheriff because of suspicions that she was a Communist or a representative of the "Fifth Column," a World War II term for enemy agents undermining the war effort. She wrote:

> Got arrested the other day in a town in the next county, even after all kinds of precautions & after having gone to the F.S.A. office & walked all over town with F.S.A. people too. But there's a feud there between F.S.A. & triple A [Agricultural Adjustment Act], & that's where it all started. They just took me before the county judge who asked questions & looked at identification, etc.—it was just funny because the whole town was full of people (Labor Day) & got all stirred up over it & followed me in a big procession to the court house—all crowding around the judge afterwards to see my papers & getting into arguments about spies & 5th columnists, etc.

Wolcott's love for her work and her enjoyment of the people she met outweighed any second thoughts she may have had at the courthouse. Her letter continued:

> *Please, please please* let me stay this week at least. Right now is the most interesting season. Everything is happening—they're just beginning to make sorghum molasses & have "stir-offs" when all the neighbors & friends come to dip into the syrup with their cane sticks & hang around & talk & help each other, etc.
>
> Then there are community apple peelings & bean stringings—(like cornhuskings)—all the women neighbors get together to peel apples for drying & "sulphuring" & storing in barrels for the winter—a large dinner is cooked too & *sometimes* dance afterwards. Bean stringing is similar.
>
> It is wonderful country and the people are so simple & direct & kind if they know you, or if you're with a friend of theirs. I got some excellent school pictures I think, & some other things as we went along. It takes a great deal of time just to *get* anywhere & to make friends (& answer

questions) on one's first trip to see these people. I can do more next time as far as people are concerned. You see I've just really made these contacts here & gotten established & the confidence of the people.

They are having all these religious meetings & "memorials" too, some of them coming for miles on foot & horseback. I'm getting children walking to school up creek beds & teachers riding for miles—the mail carried by horseback, etc. people carrying heavy sacks of supplies, & so much else.

In a September 1984 conversation with me, Wolcott recalled that she took many more photographs than usual in Kentucky because she panicked, thinking that her camera might not be working and that she might not return. Her fears were well founded. The left side of many of her pictures were out of focus because of camera malfunctions, and, after a quick November trip to Barbourville in November 1940, she did not return to follow up on the contacts she had made that summer. In 1941 she married and requested assignment to the FSA western region, where she settled with her husband and began a family.

During the eight years the project lasted, far too many photos were taken to reproduce in one book, so several criteria determined the selection made here. Each photographer's assignment is represented here by at least one image, as well as by some taken "on the run" as staff traversed the state.

Because the intent of the original photographic assignments was thematic and generally related to specific federally-funded programs, the photographs omit many sections of the state. The selection includes nearly every area photographed in order to represent the widest possible coverage of Kentucky subjects and sites. The arrangement of images here is broadly thematic—from farms to community events to small towns to cities—and chronological—from traditional agricultural life to mechanization and industrilization for war. Images of tobacco growing, mining, alcohol production, and factory work appear. Gatherings around the courthouse, court days, and jockey days represent Kentucky's emphasis on the county political unit. Scenes of transportation and vehicles show a range of travel options. Religion, education, food preparation, hospitality, and leisure activities are also depicted, as well as the Bluegrass horse culture for which Kentucky may be best known. The volume concludes with glimpses of the ways America's participation in World War II changed the Commonwealth.

The FSA pictorial record for Kentucky is so rich that its omissions are noted not with criticism but with regret that the project could not have been totally comprehensive. With their declared intention of recording the activities of common people going about their daily routines, the FSA photographers provided a record rarely available from other photographic sources. Most pictures are taken to mark the extraordinary, nonrecurring events of life, such as birthdays, graduations, weddings, and funerals. The FSA images are unusual in that they capture the ordinary times that make up the major portion of our lives.

As documents of social history, the FSA photographs provide a collective snapshot of another time. Today we can look at these images to reminisce or to study a time we never knew. Often the pictures are of occurrences so common that their familiarity masks their significance. But in fact it is the everyday activities of people that form the pattern of our social fabric, its human warp and weft.

BEVERLY W. BRANNAN

Hay is loaded on a horse-drawn wagon on the farm of Edgar Back near Noctor. August 1940. MARION POST WOLCOTT.

Rural Life

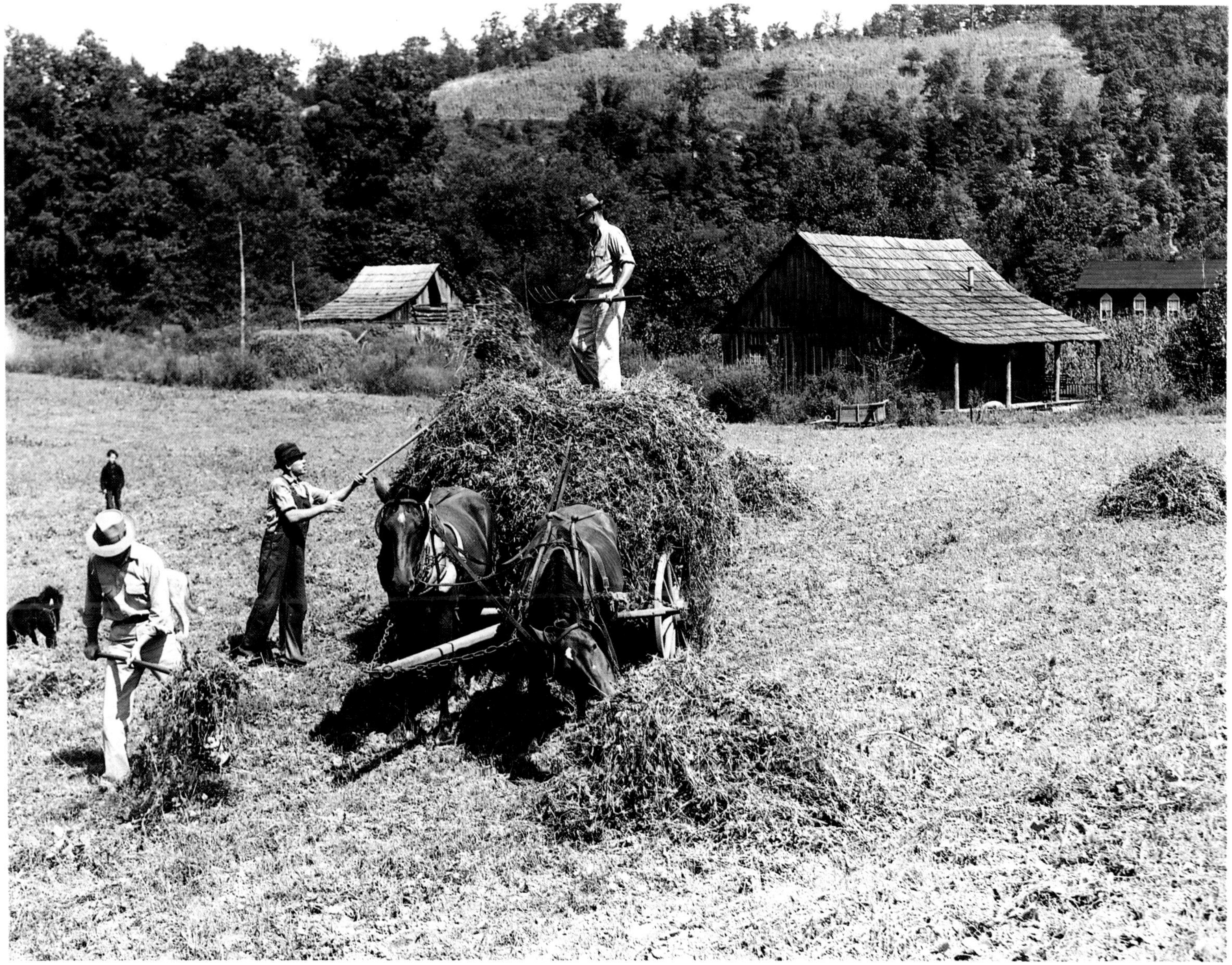

MORE CHANGES took place in American farming during the period of the FSA photographic survey—1935 to 1943—than had occurred in many decades before. Mechanized labor was rapidly replacing human and animal labor. Modern farming techniques, Extension agents, and increased government regulation and assistance were drastically affecting Kentucky's major economic unit, the subsistence farm.

Although the self-sufficient family farm was well on its way to extinction even as these pictures were being taken, the changes wrought by New Deal policies were not yet evident in many parts of Kentucky, especially the mountains. Many of the scenes depicted here could have come from earlier decades: children enjoying a "syruping off," a farm wife proudly displaying her home-canned products, milk buckets set in the sun to dry. Others illustrate the shift to modernization: one group of farmers using a traditional horse-drawn wagon for haying while another farmer feeds his wheat into a mechanical thresher.

Part of the FSA photographers' assignment was to document major industries, such as tobacco production, although they seldom stayed in one place long enough to show the whole story in a single locale. Marion Post Wolcott complained to Roy Stryker in the spring and summer of 1940 that Kentucky was having a bad tobacco season, with much of the crop ruined by cold and rust. She managed, nevertheless, to photograph that year's tobacco crop at various stages, especially in harvest season as the leaves were gathered and hung for curing. Among her pictures is a typical eastern Kentucky tobacco barn with its distinctive high roof and its ventilators opened for the curing season. Then, as now, tobacco was Kentucky's principal cash crop, enabling many subsistence farmers to survive the Depression.

Pictured here also are a wide range of farm homes, from the cabins found throughout the mountains to the mansions of the wealthy Bluegrass horse farms. Kentucky mountain homes of the period were similar to those found throughout the upland South—log or milled lumber houses of one or two rooms with shingled or occasionally tin roofs. Many of them sheltered extended, multigenerational farm families.

Many of the FSA photographs show farm homes in the context of the land and buildings that surrounded them. Some indicate good husbandry and productive land, others show worn out soil, the result of misuse and overuse. One particularly striking photograph, taken by Carl Mydans for testimony before a congressional hearing, shows severe soil erosion. It may have helped bring about federal support for soil conservation for Kentucky's farms.

Together, these documentary photographs give a sense of Kentucky's varied rural character in the late 1930s and early 1940s and of the close relationships between families, communities, and nature on which farm life was based.

Opposite: Mrs. Josh Calahan displays some of her home-canned goods in the cellar of her new home near Barbourville. November 1940. MARION POST WOLCOTT.

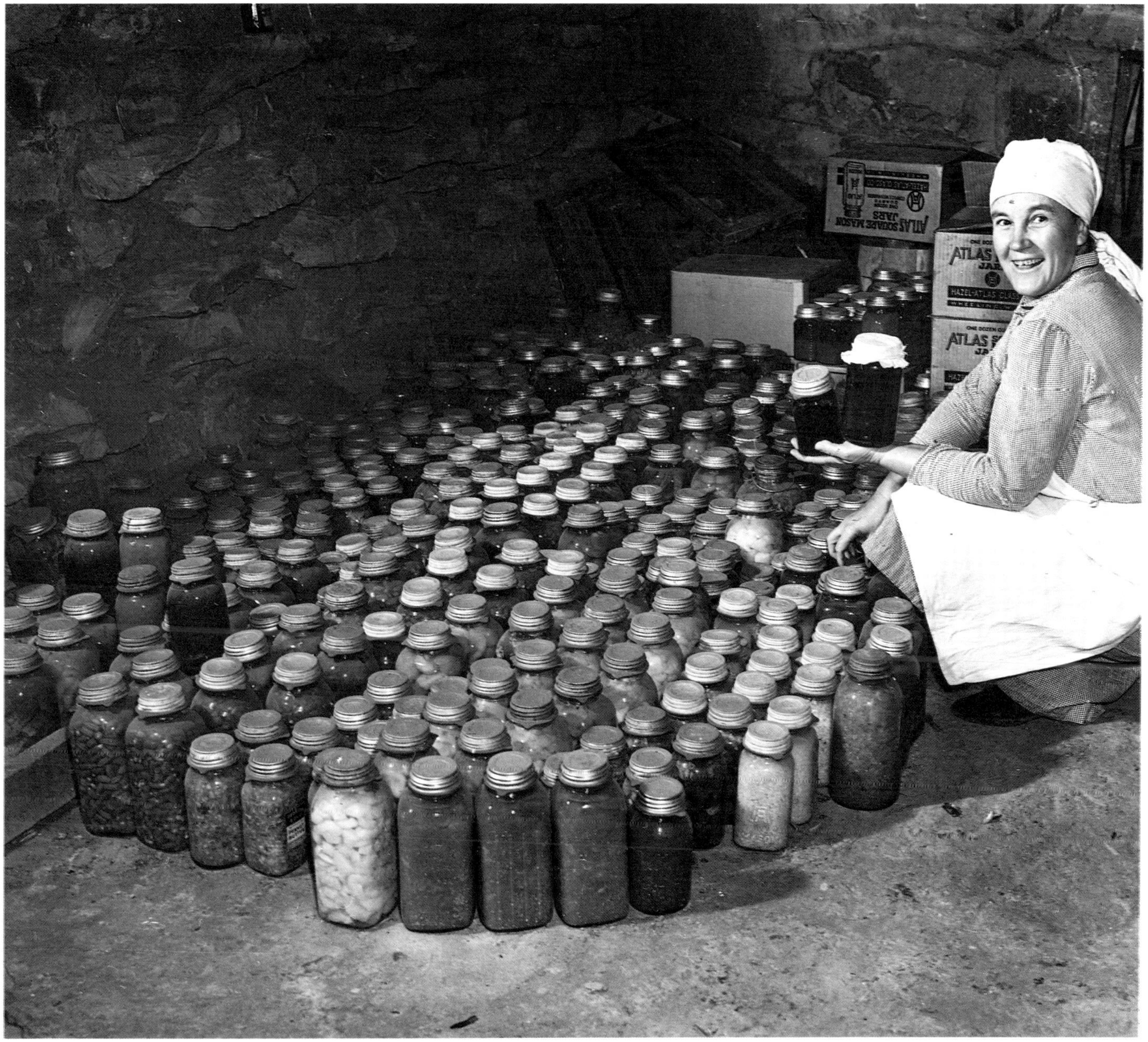
ATLAS SQUARE MASON
JARS
ATLAS
JARS

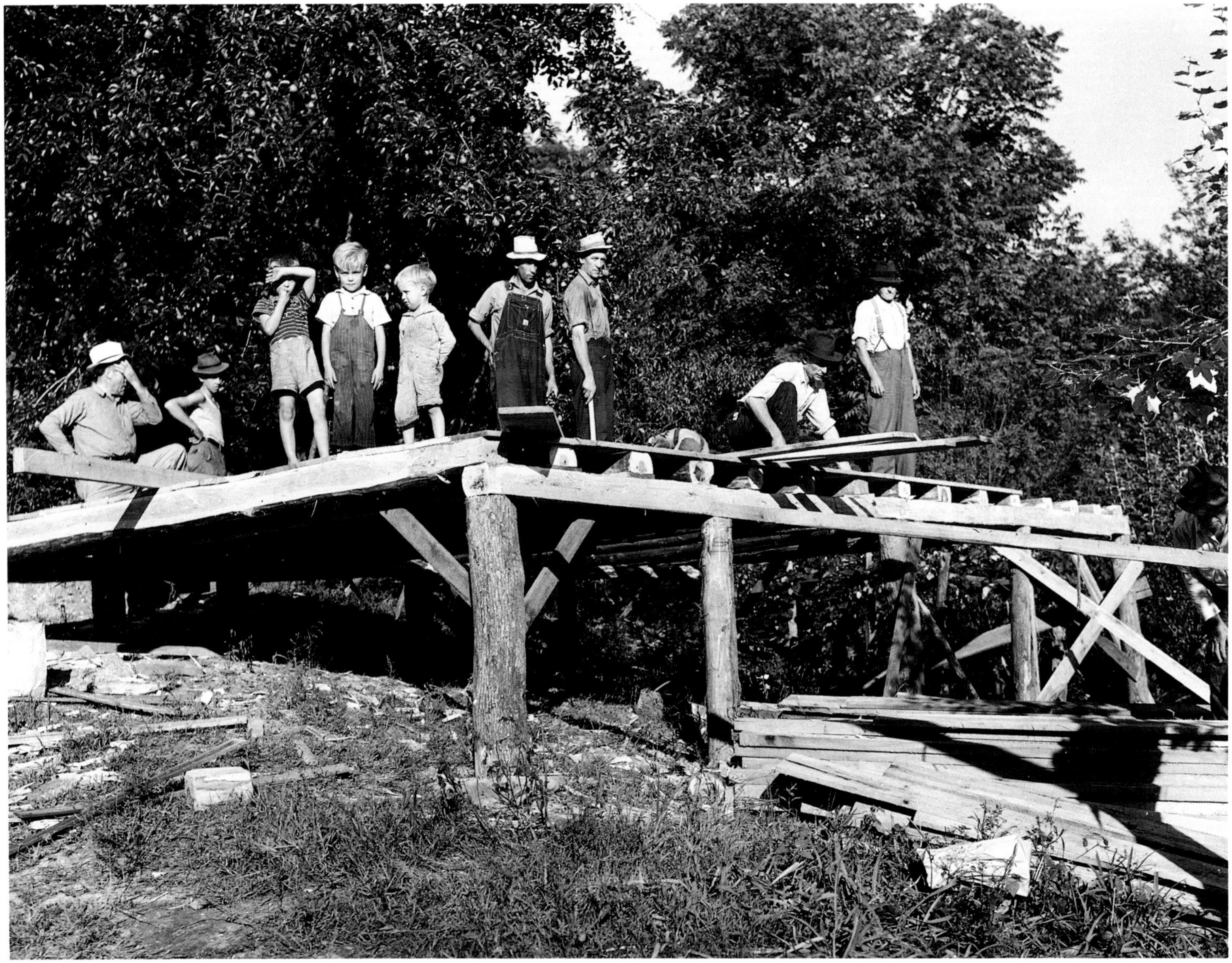

Neighbors pitch in for a house-raising. Near Jackson, September 1940. MARION POST WOLCOTT.

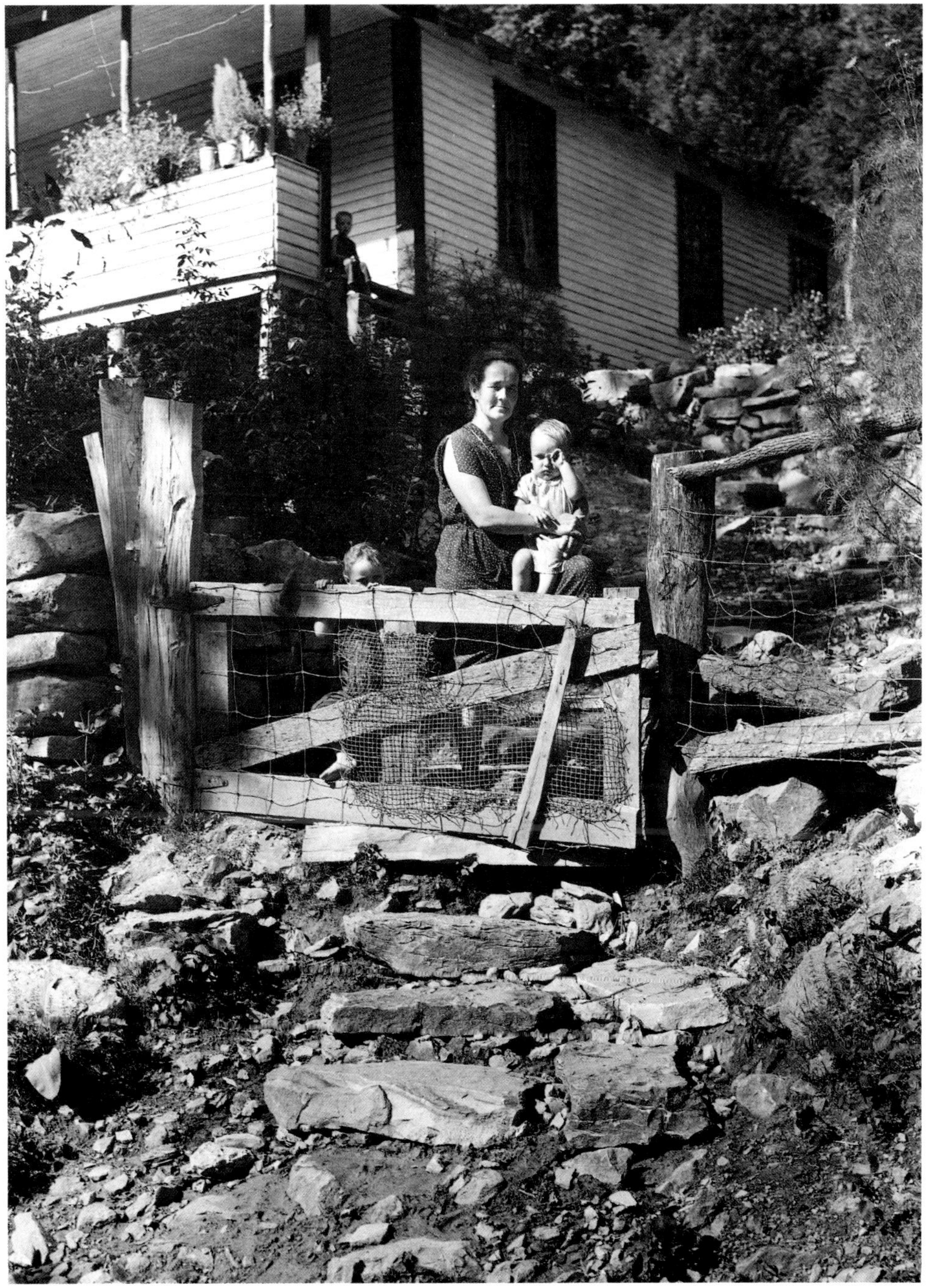

Mother and children.
Up Stinking Creek near Pine Mountain,
August 1940. Marion Post Wolcott.

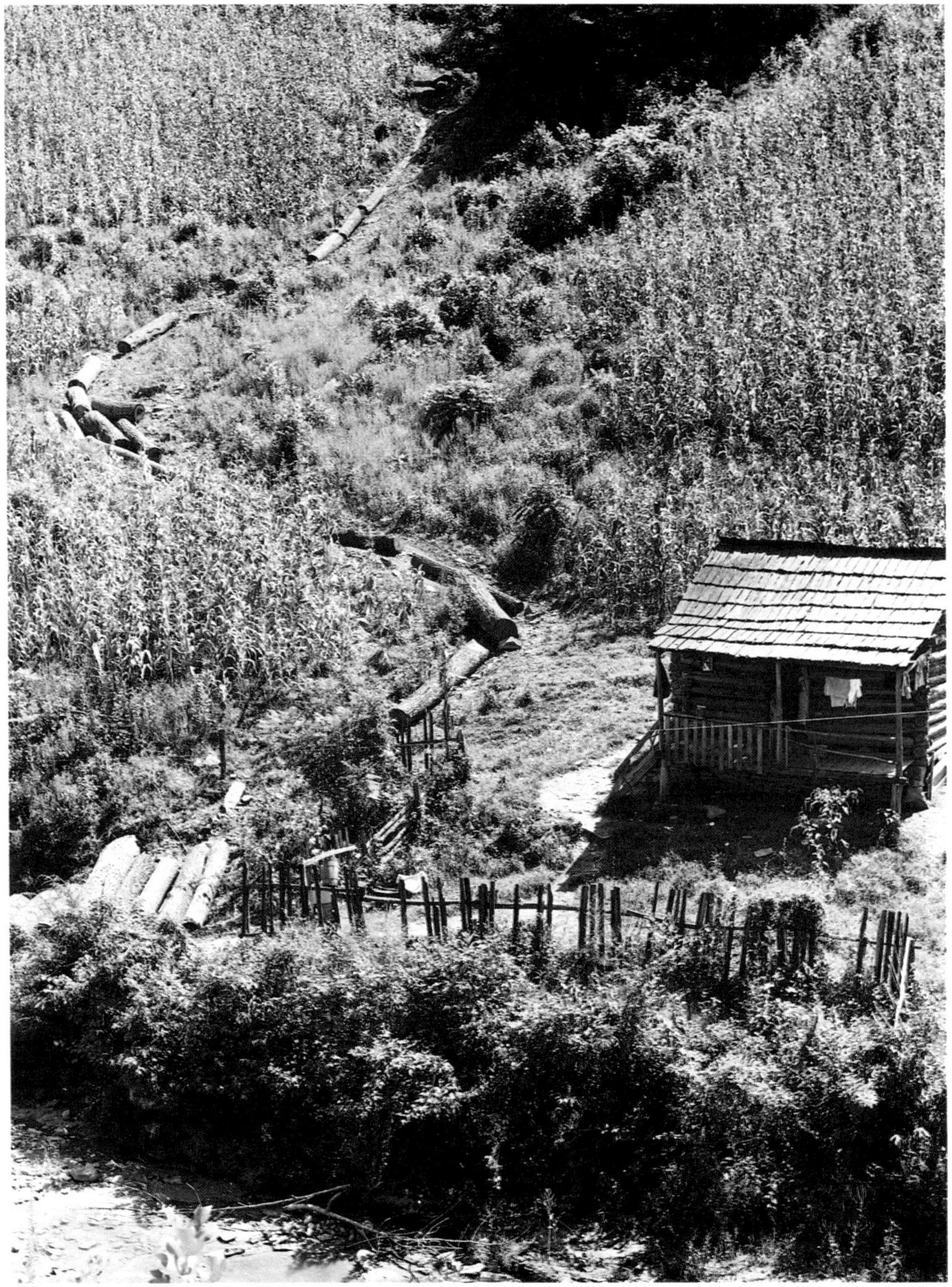

Logs—the chief source of income for many Eastern Kentuckians—lie on a hillside farm near Hyden, waiting to be marketed. August 1940. MARION POST WOLCOTT.

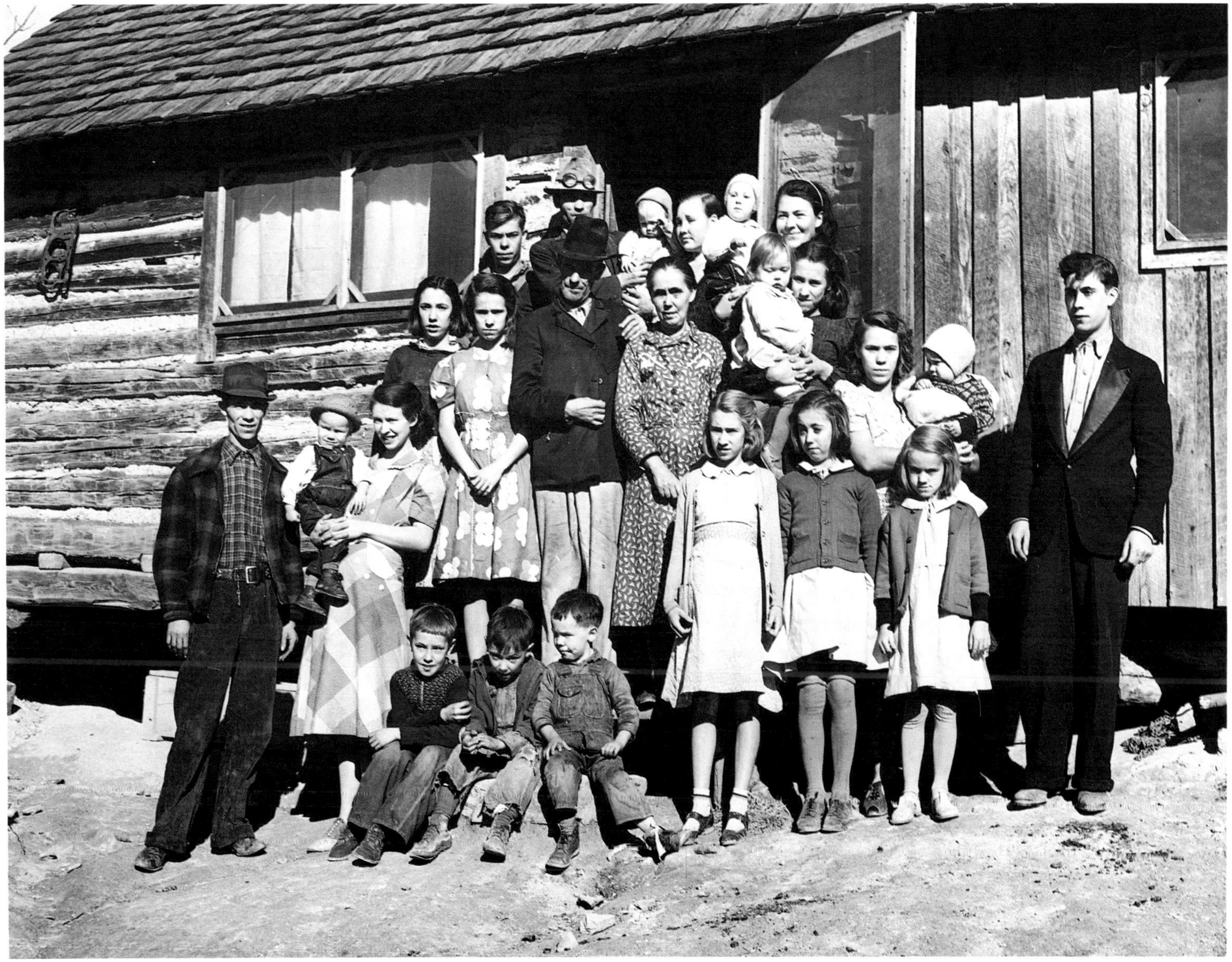

Three generations of the Noah Garland family pose beside the home they share near Barbourville. November 1940. MARION POST WOLCOTT.

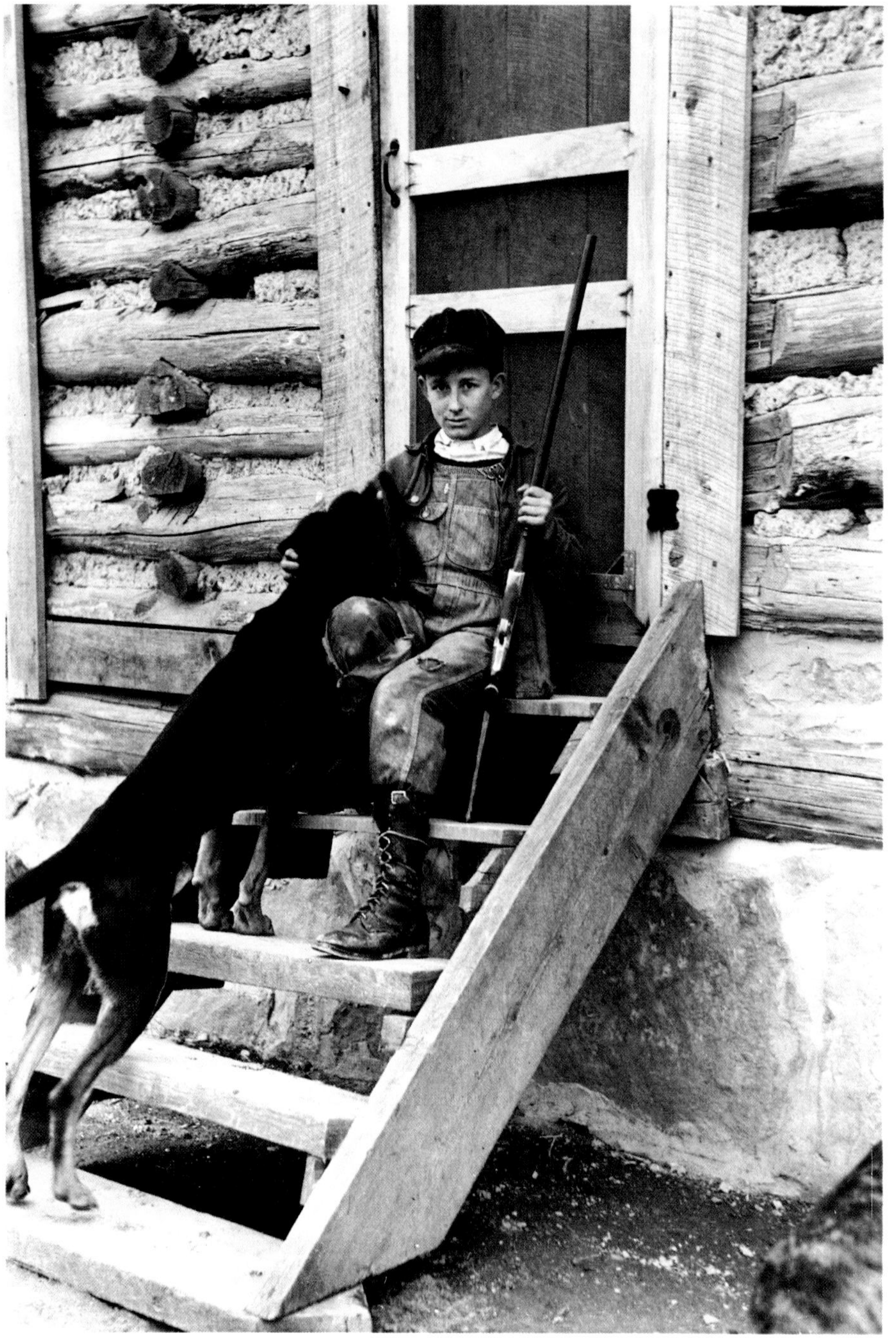

A farm boy and his dog, just returned from a hunting trip. Knox County, November 1940. Marion Post Wolcott.

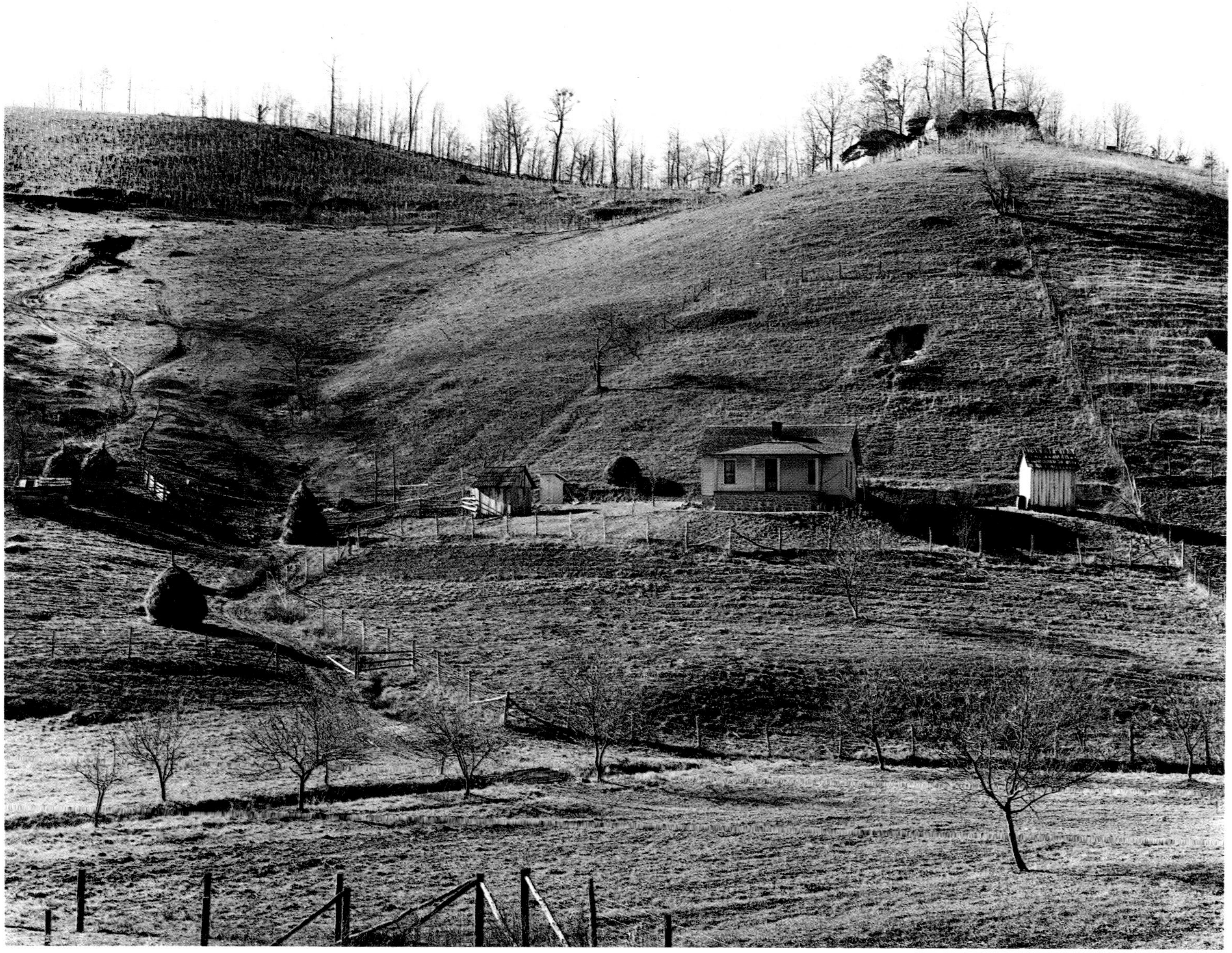

The farm of Mr. Jackson near Barbourville, November 1940. MARION POST WOLCOTT.

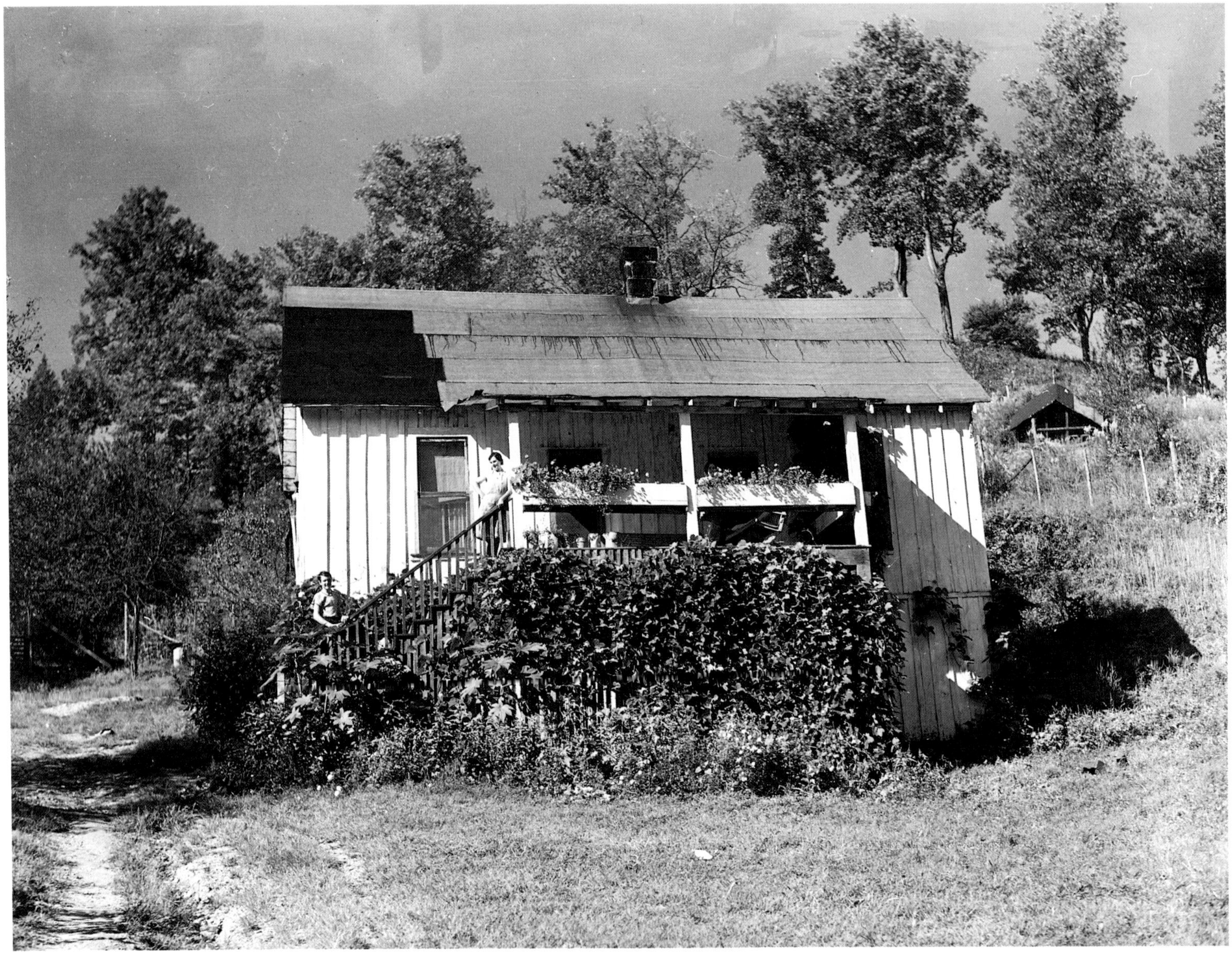

A mountain family and their saddlebag style house near Buckhorn, July 1940. MARION POST WOLCOTT.

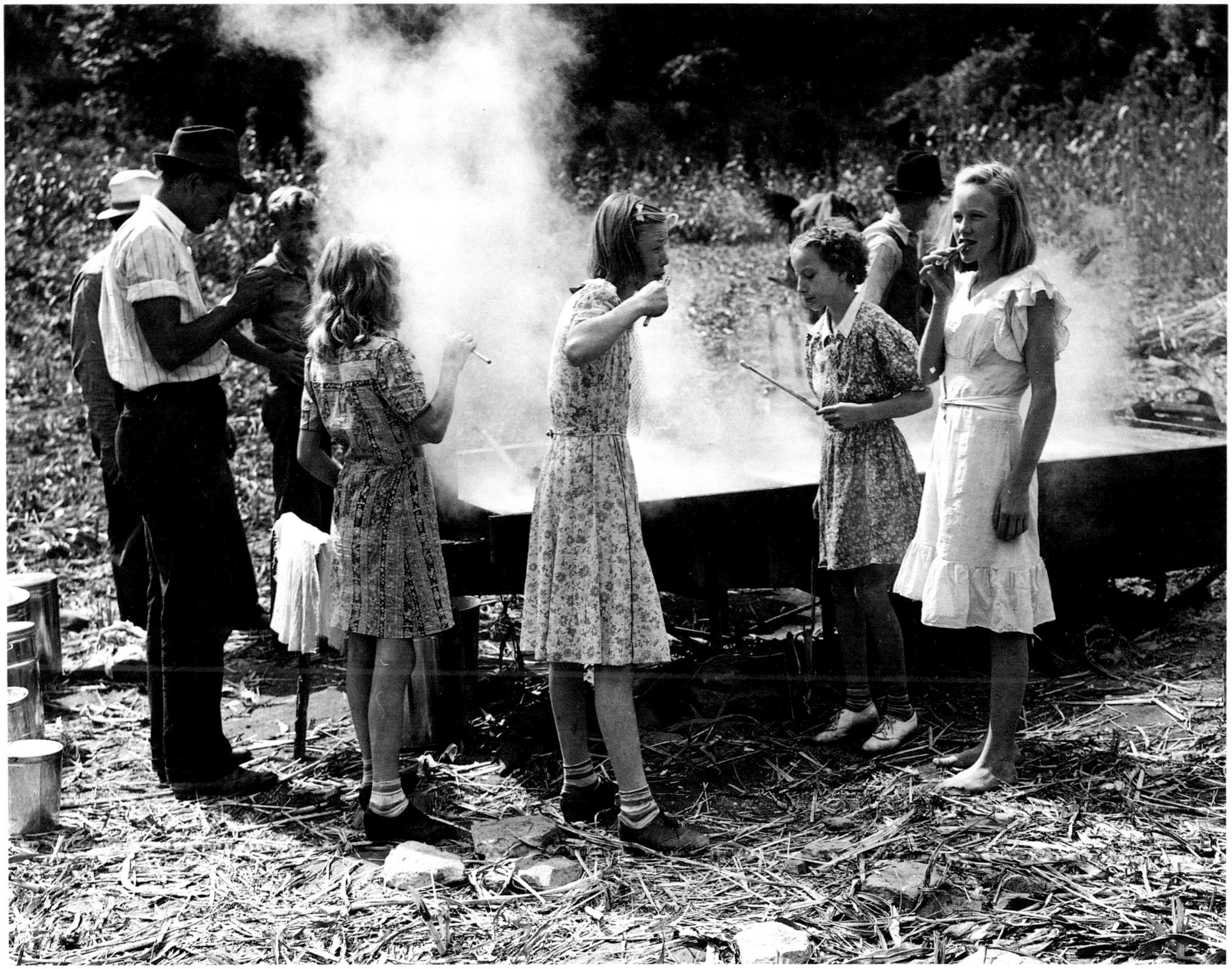

“Syruping off” at a sorghum mill near Jackson, September 1940. Many children stay away from school to enjoy this annual fall event. One man in the neighborhood does the work for others, taking a share of the syrup for his labor. MARION POST WOLCOTT.

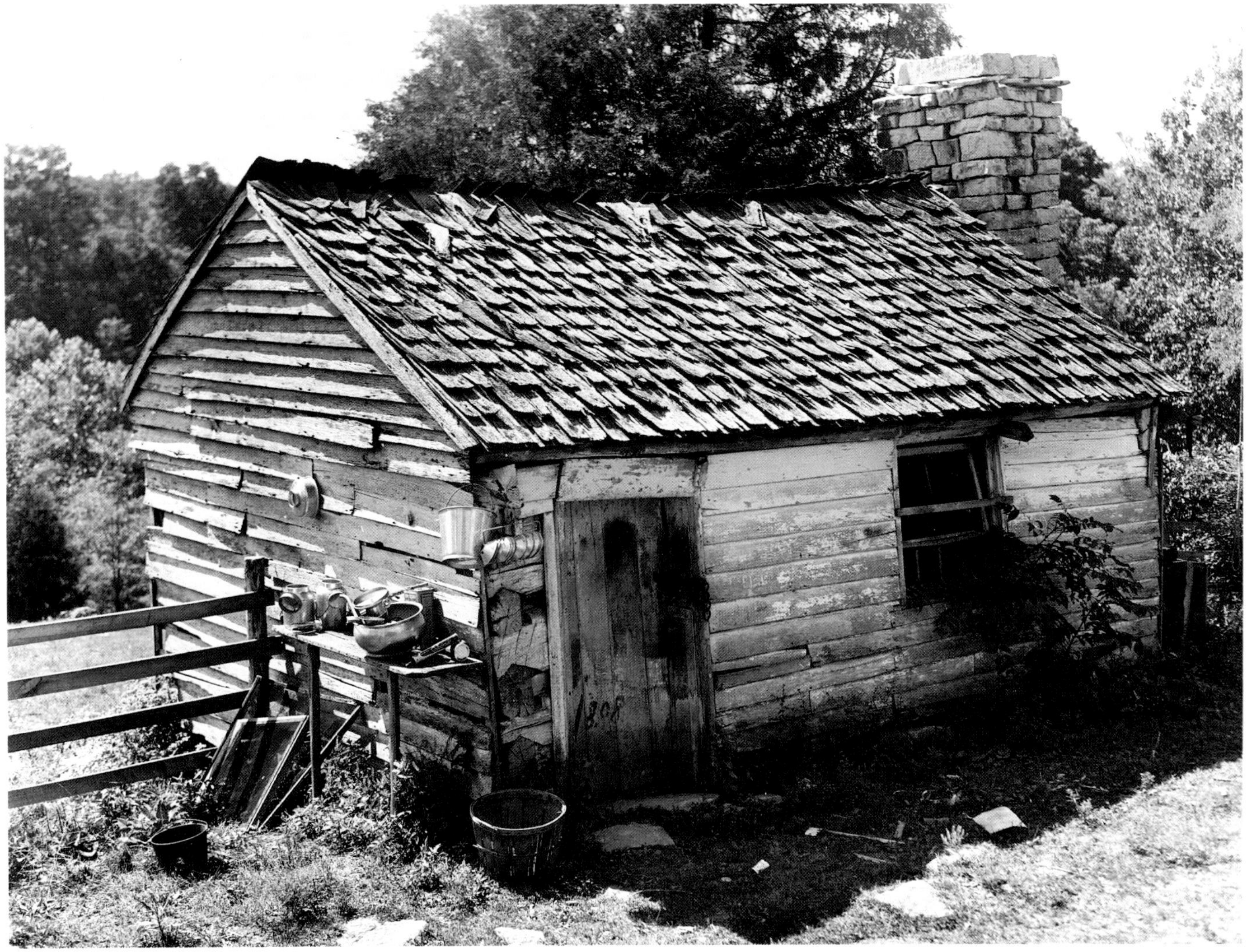

Former slave quarters near Bardstown, now used as a milk house. August 1940. Marion Post Wolcott.

Opposite: A mountain wife stands on the porch of her family's hand-hewn log house. Near Jackson, September 1940. The added room is probably used as the kitchen. Marion Post Wolcott.

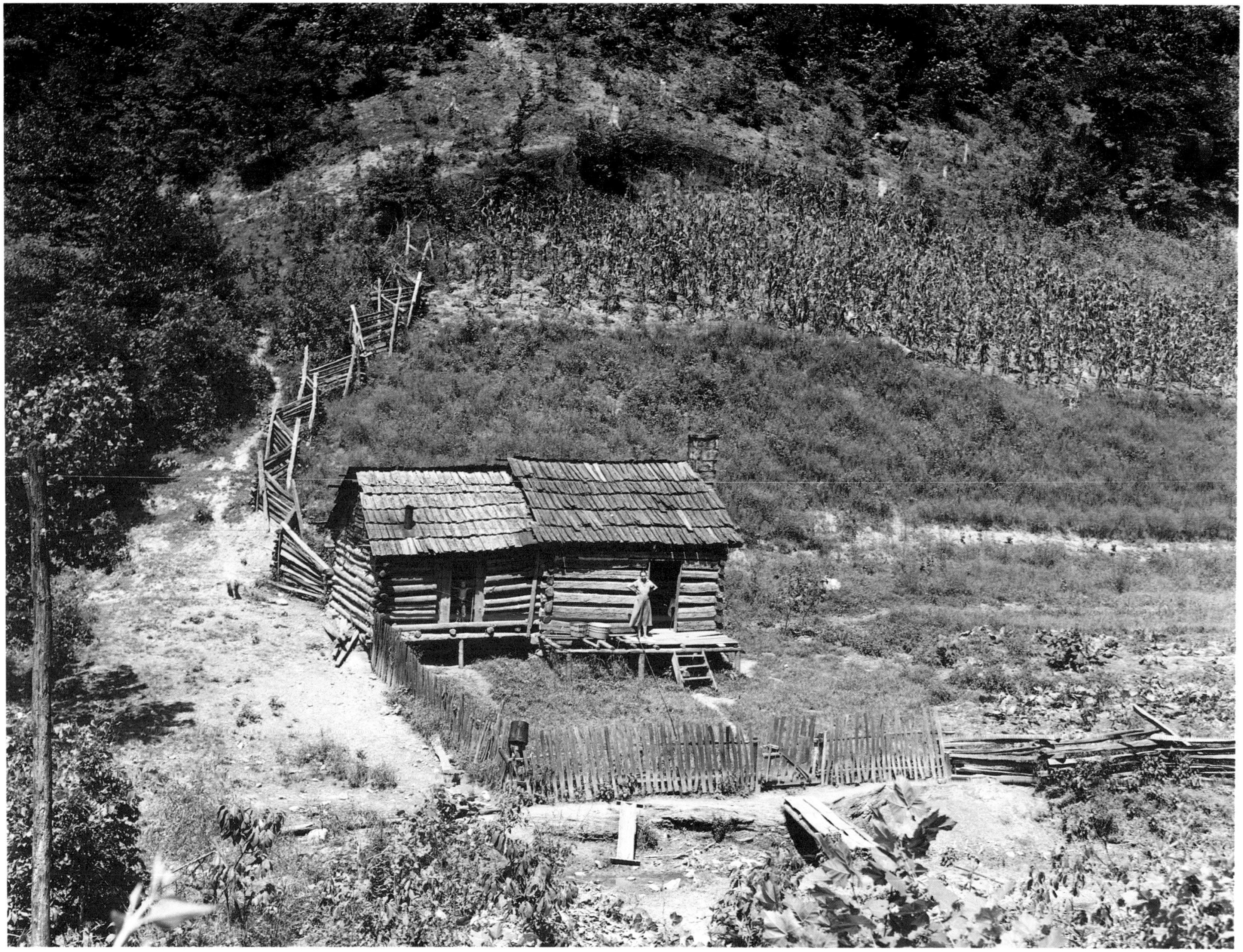

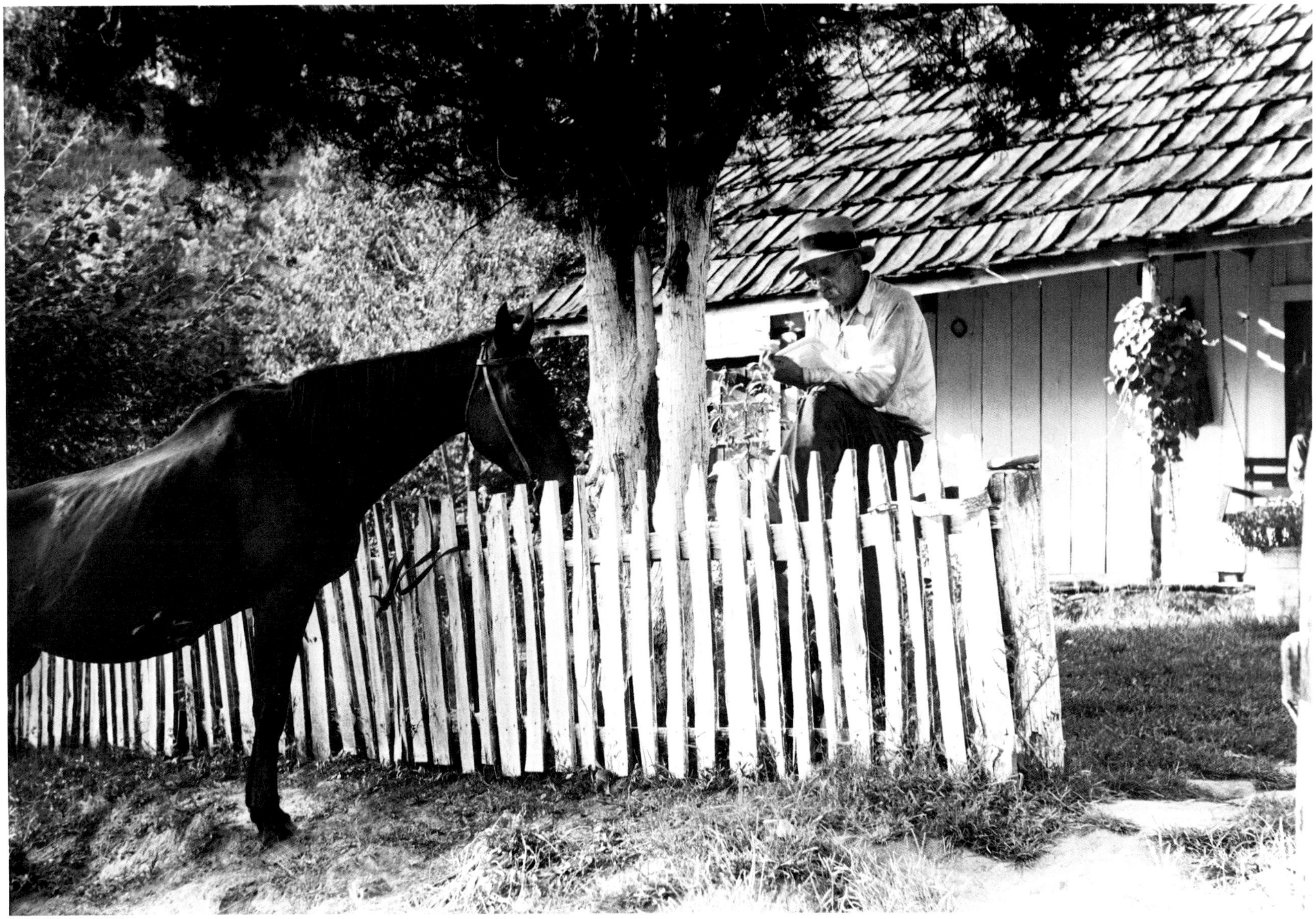

A mountain farmer reads his mail. Up Frozen Creek near Jackson, September 1940. Marion Post Wolcott.

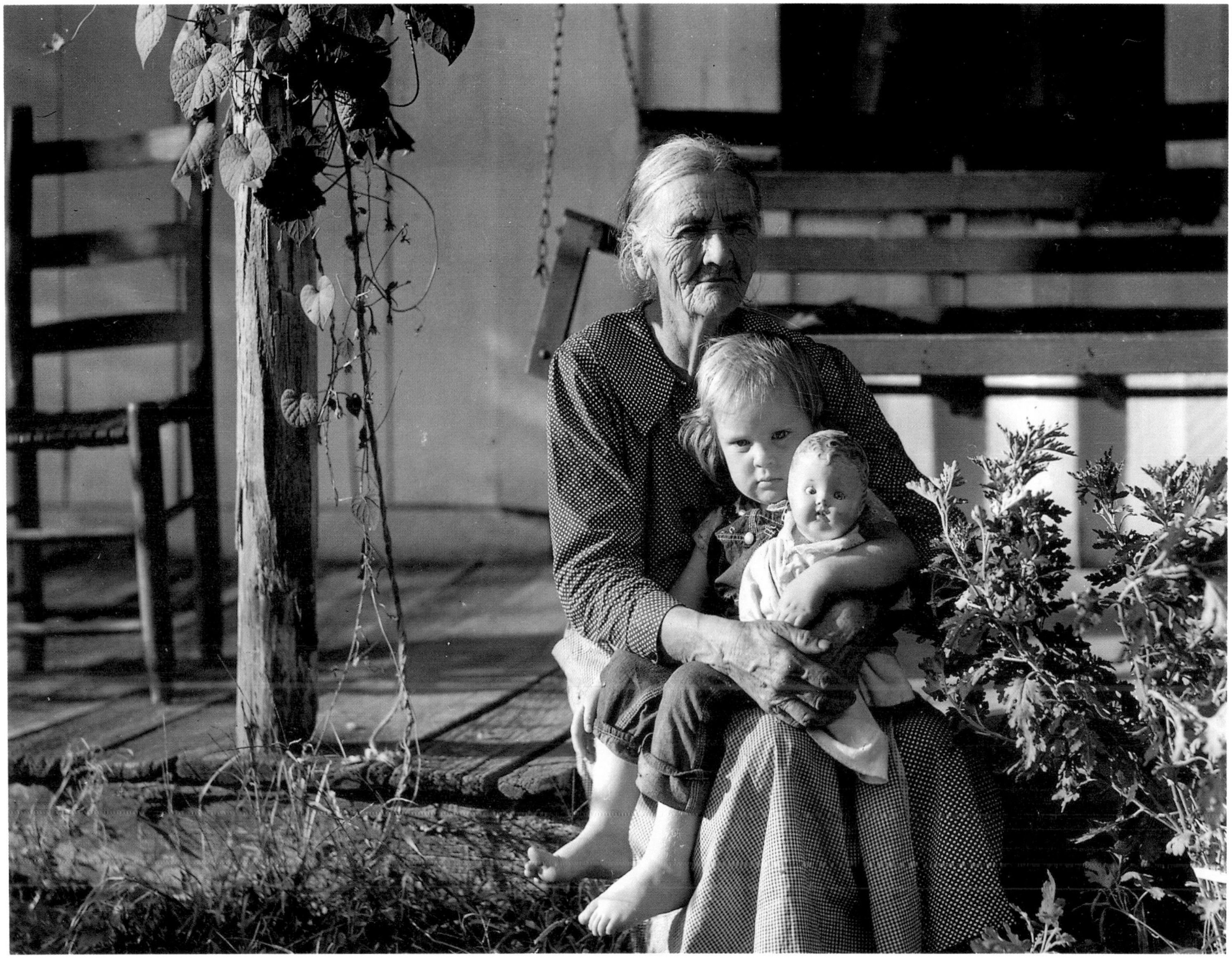

A woman and her grandchild on their porch. Up Frozen Creek, September 1940. Marion Post Wolcott.

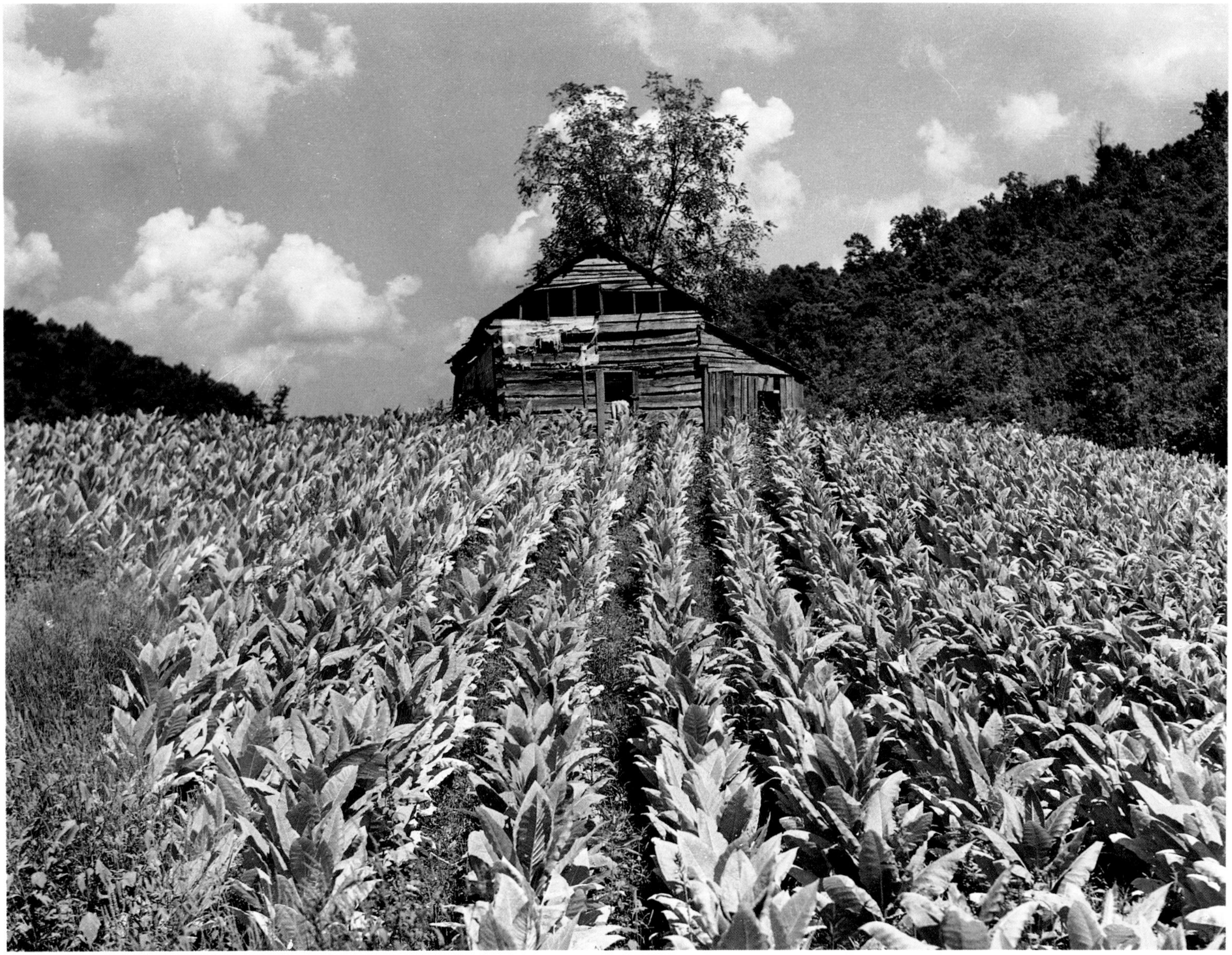

Burley tobacco, Kentucky's principal cash crop, grows on a small farm between Jackson and Campton. September 1940. MARION POST WOLCOTT.

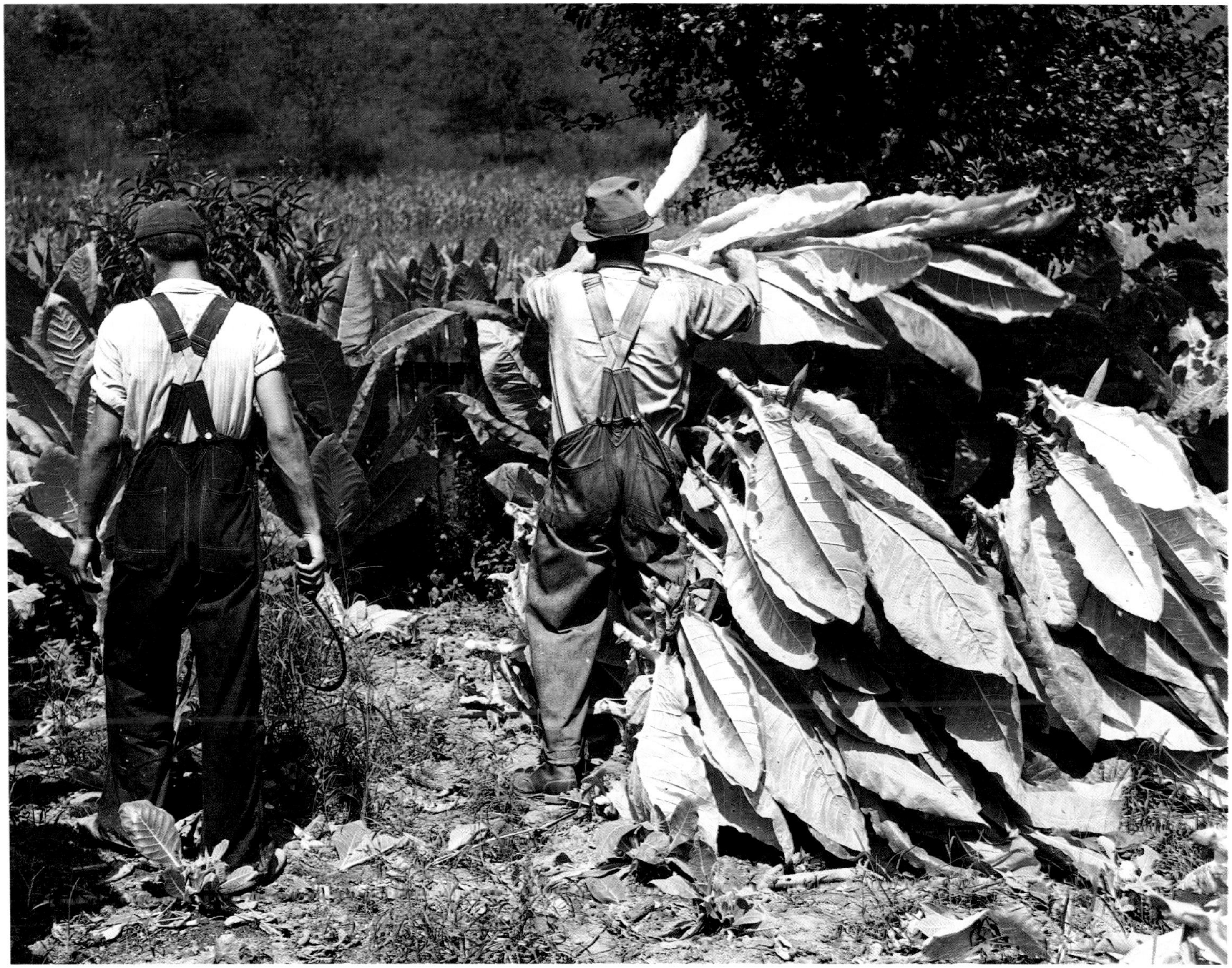

Tobacco is cut and put on stakes to wilt in the sun, the first stage in preparing it for market. Near Jackson, September 1940. Marion Post Wolcott.

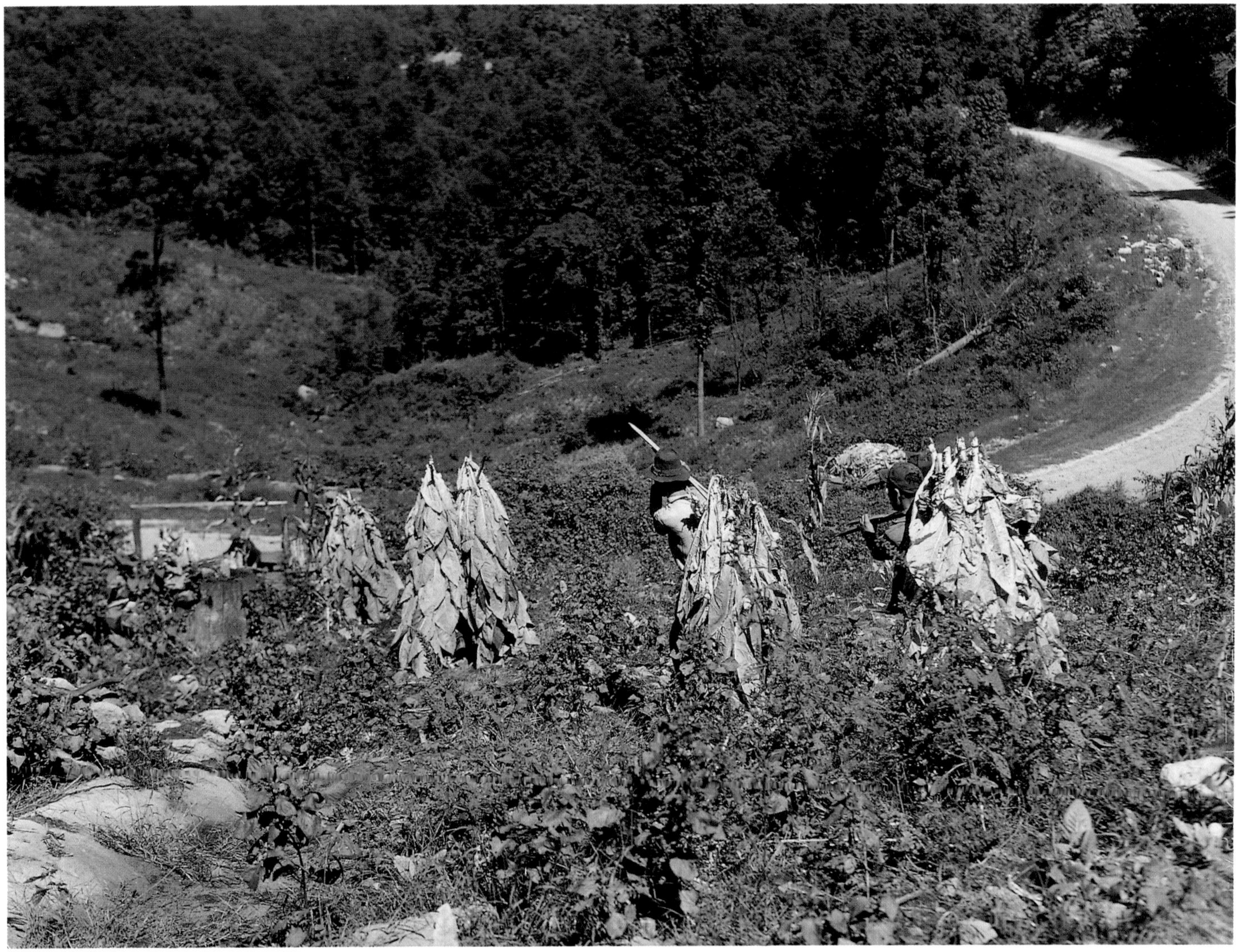

Sticks of cut burley tobacco are carried down a steep hillside to a waiting truck. Perry County, September 1940. Marion Post Wolcott.

Opposite: Wagons deliver tobacco to a barn on the farm of Russell Spears. Near Lexington, September 1940. Marion Post Wolcott.

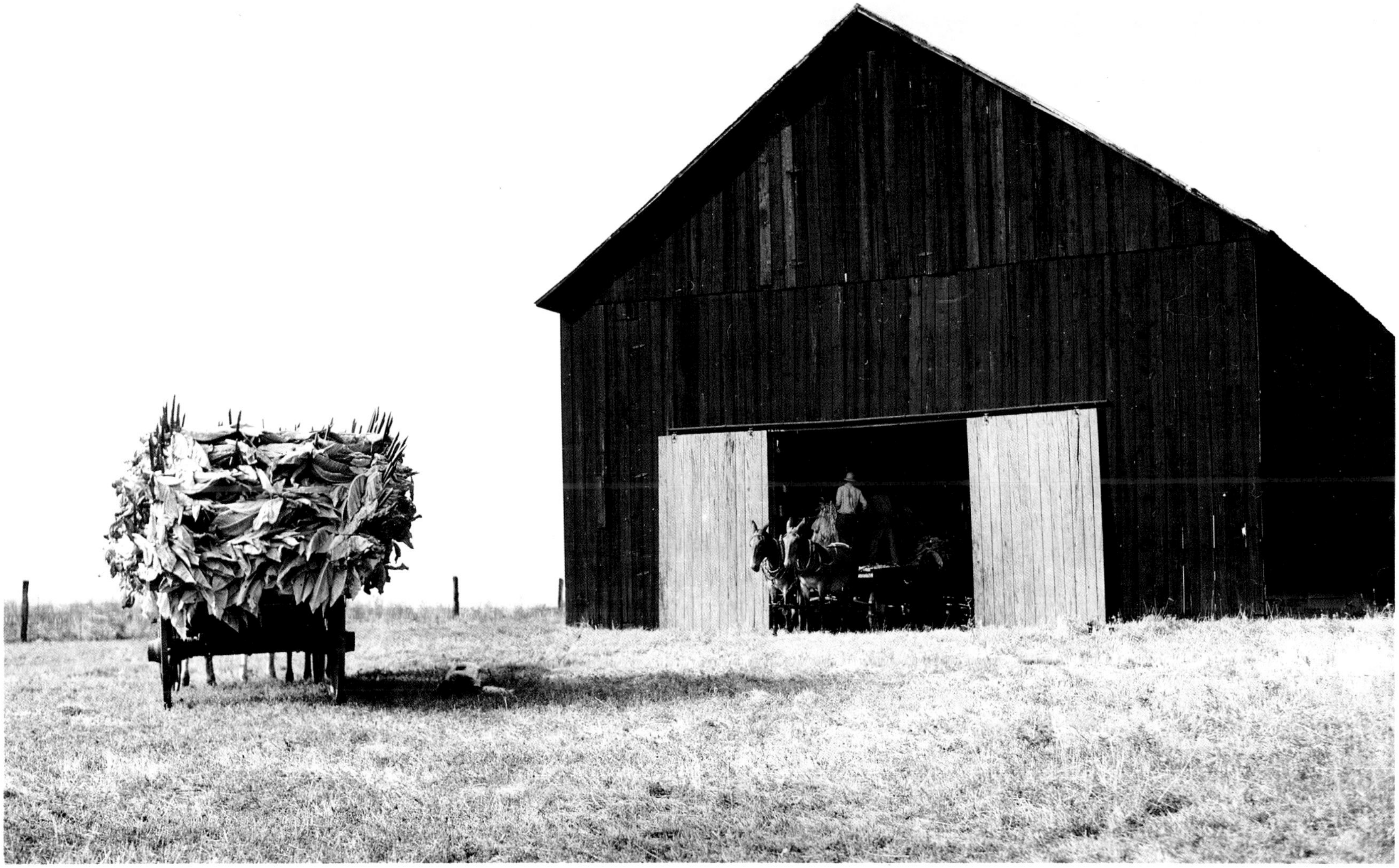

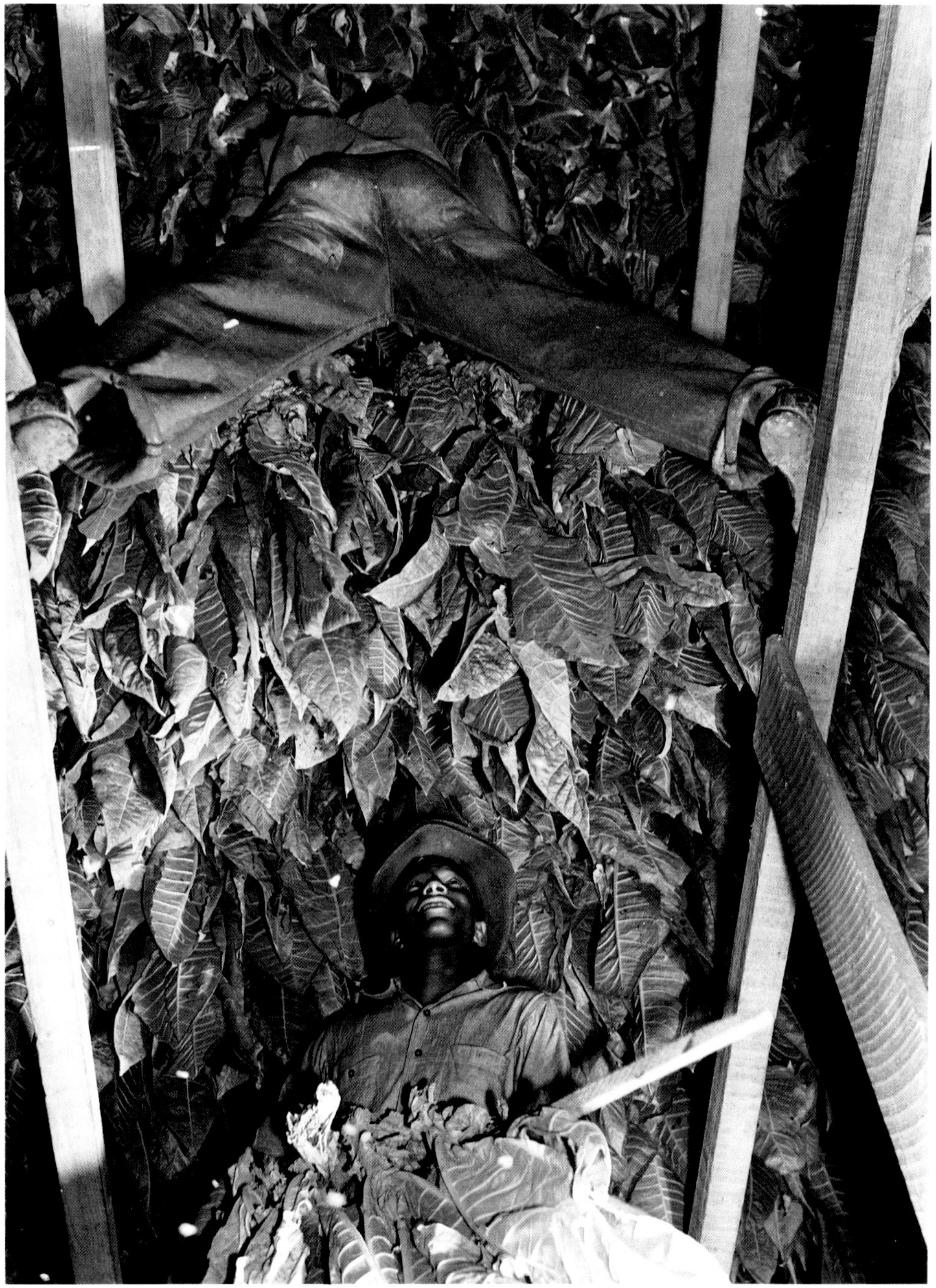

The tobacco is hung in the Spears barn for further drying and curing. MARION POST WOLCOTT.

Opposite: The ventilators of the Spears tobacco barn are opened during hot weather to speed drying. MARION POST WOLCOTT.

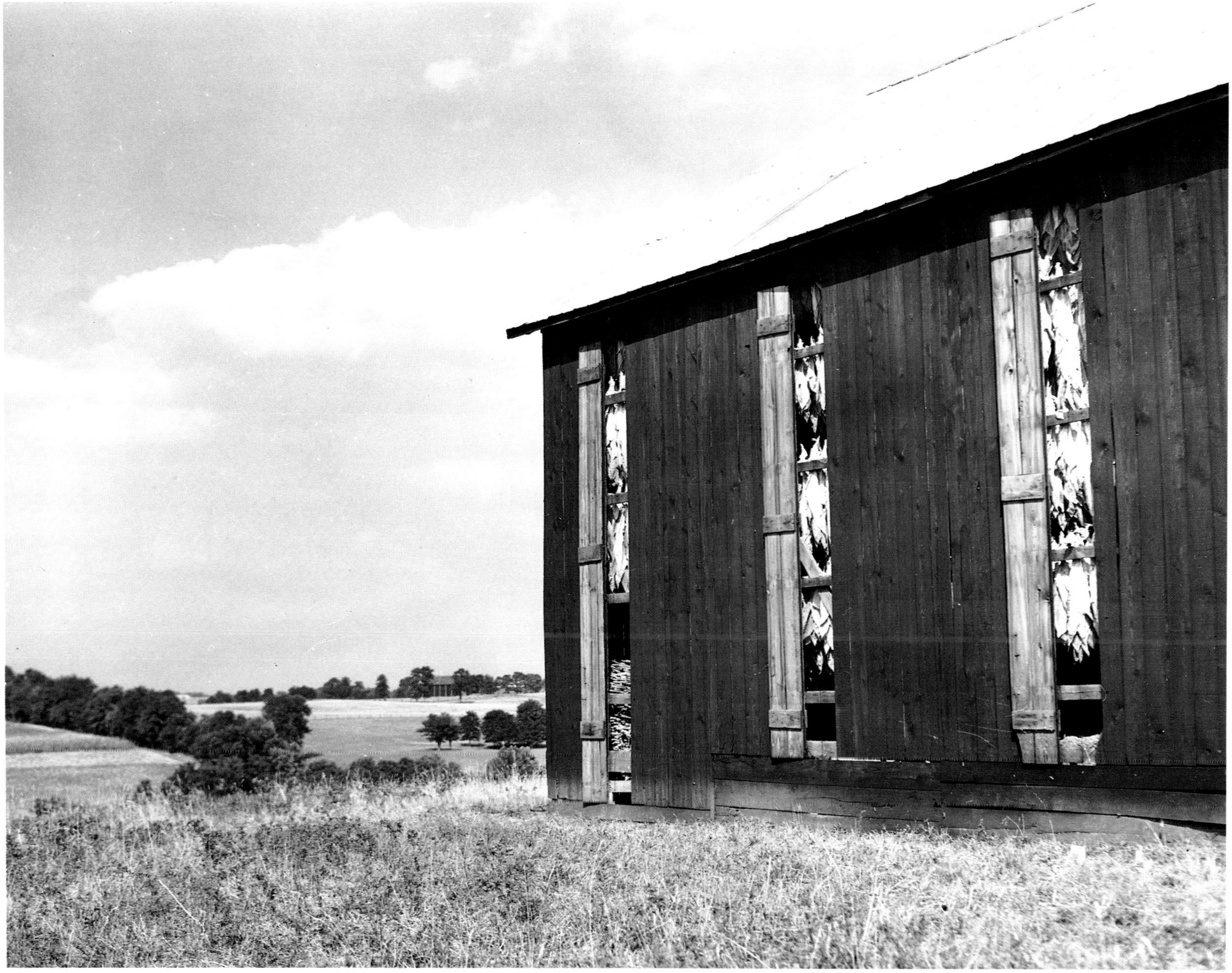

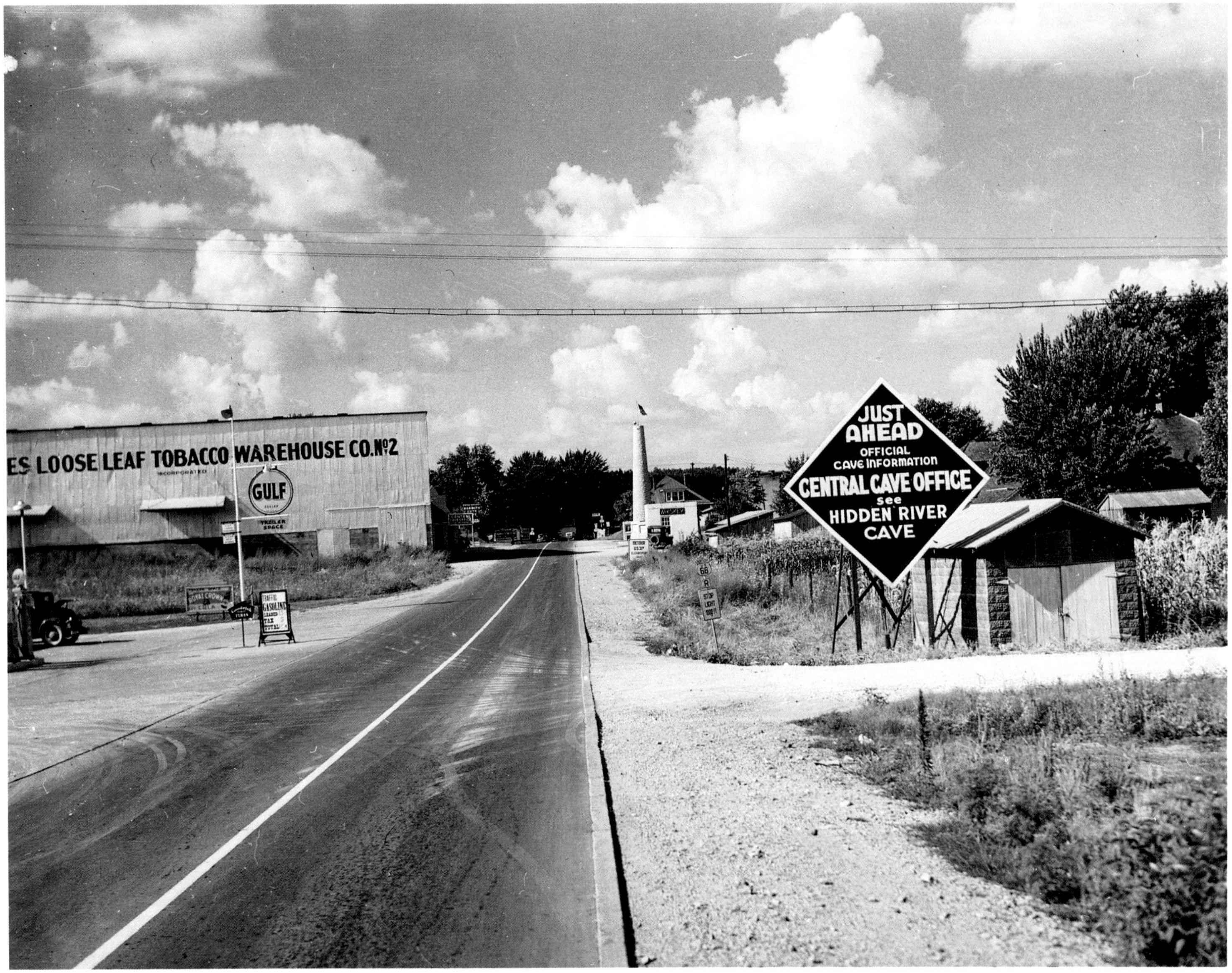

The final destination for part of the burley crop—a tobacco warehouse on the road into Cave City. July 1940. Marion Post Wolcott.

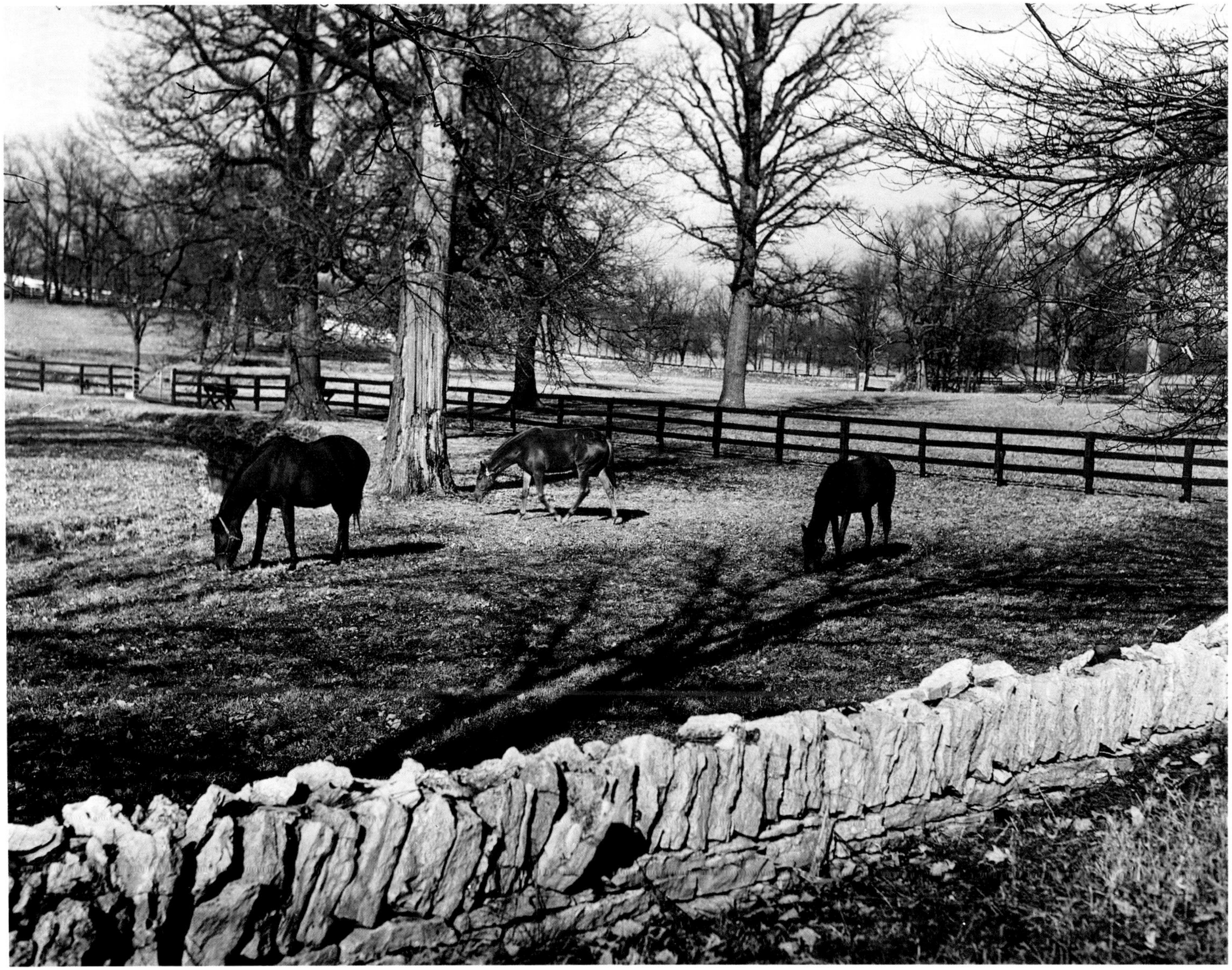

Horses graze on lush bluegrass on one of the horse farms for which the Bluegrass region of central Kentucky has long been famous. Fayette County, November 1940. JOHN VACHON.

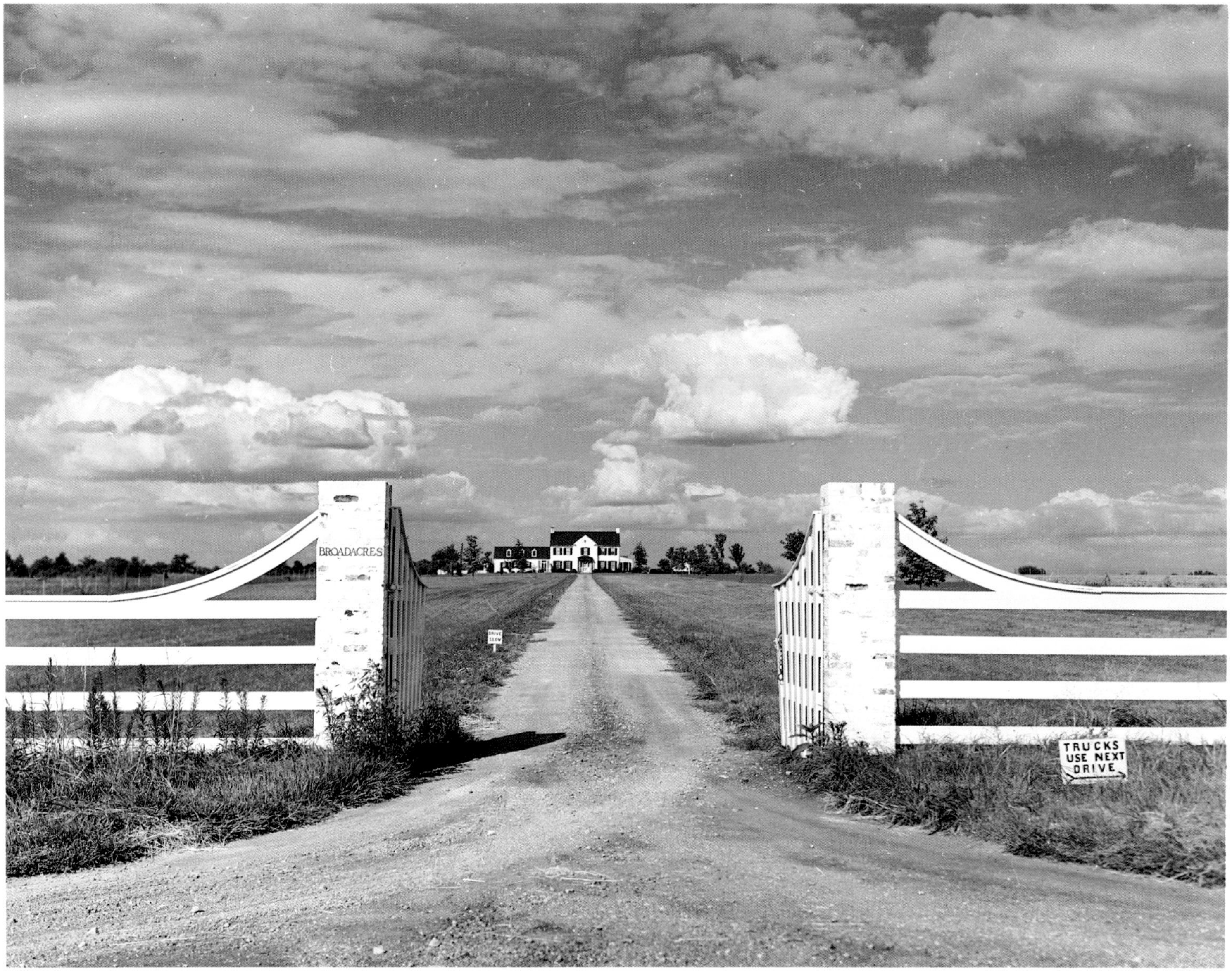

The entrance to Broadacres, Jefferson County, August 1940. MARION POST WOLCOTT.

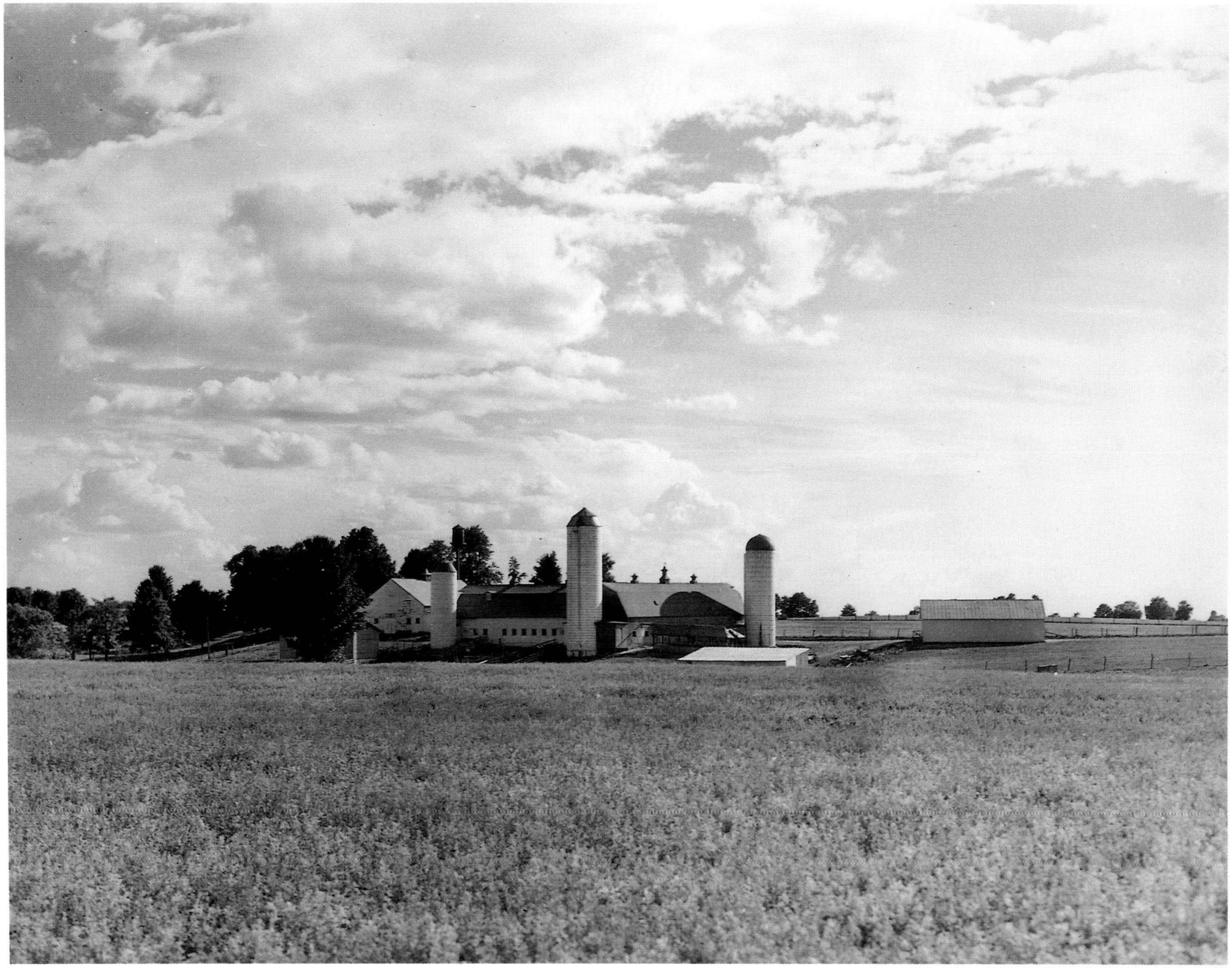

A large and prosperous dairy farm. Jefferson County, July 1940. Marion Post Wolcott.

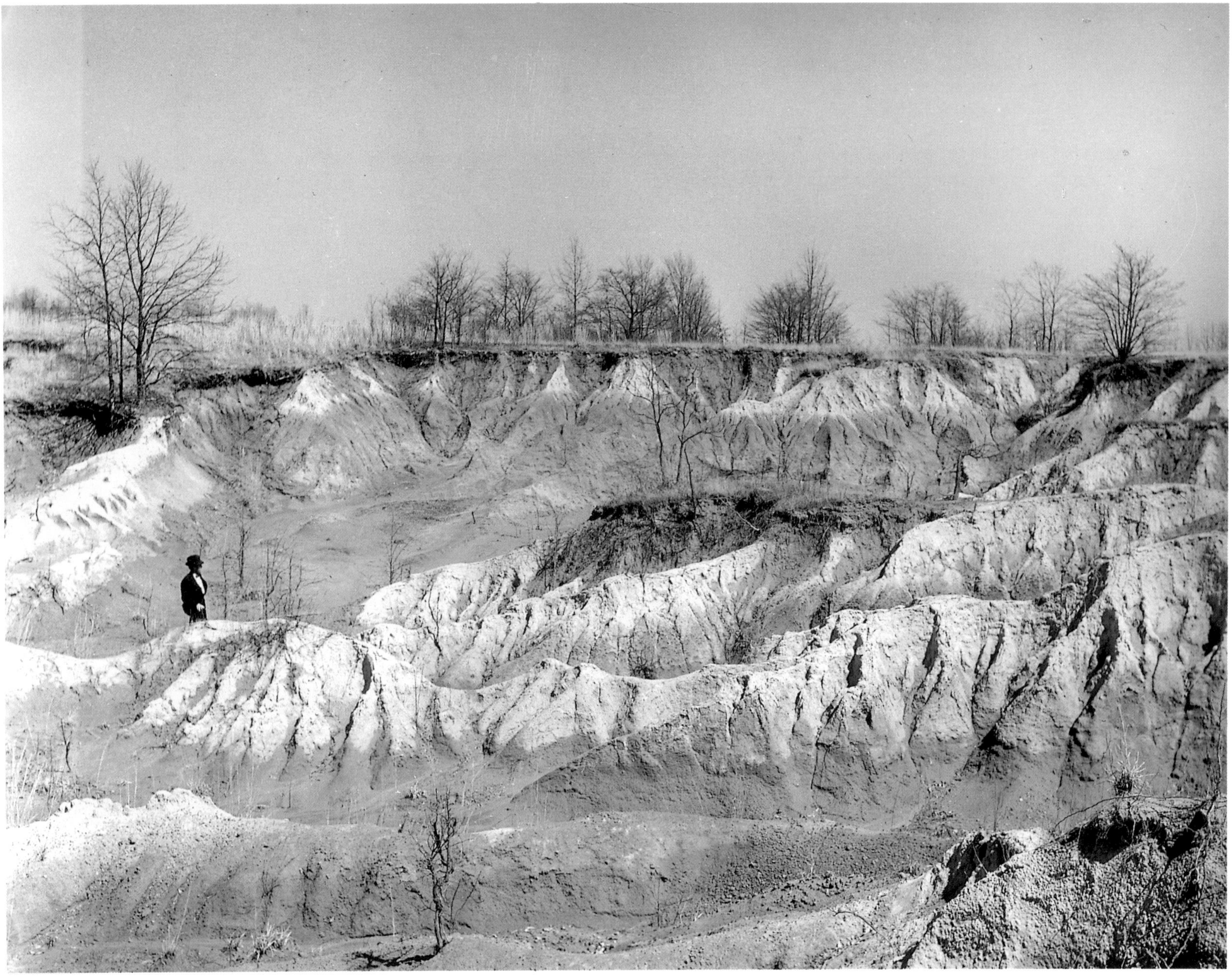

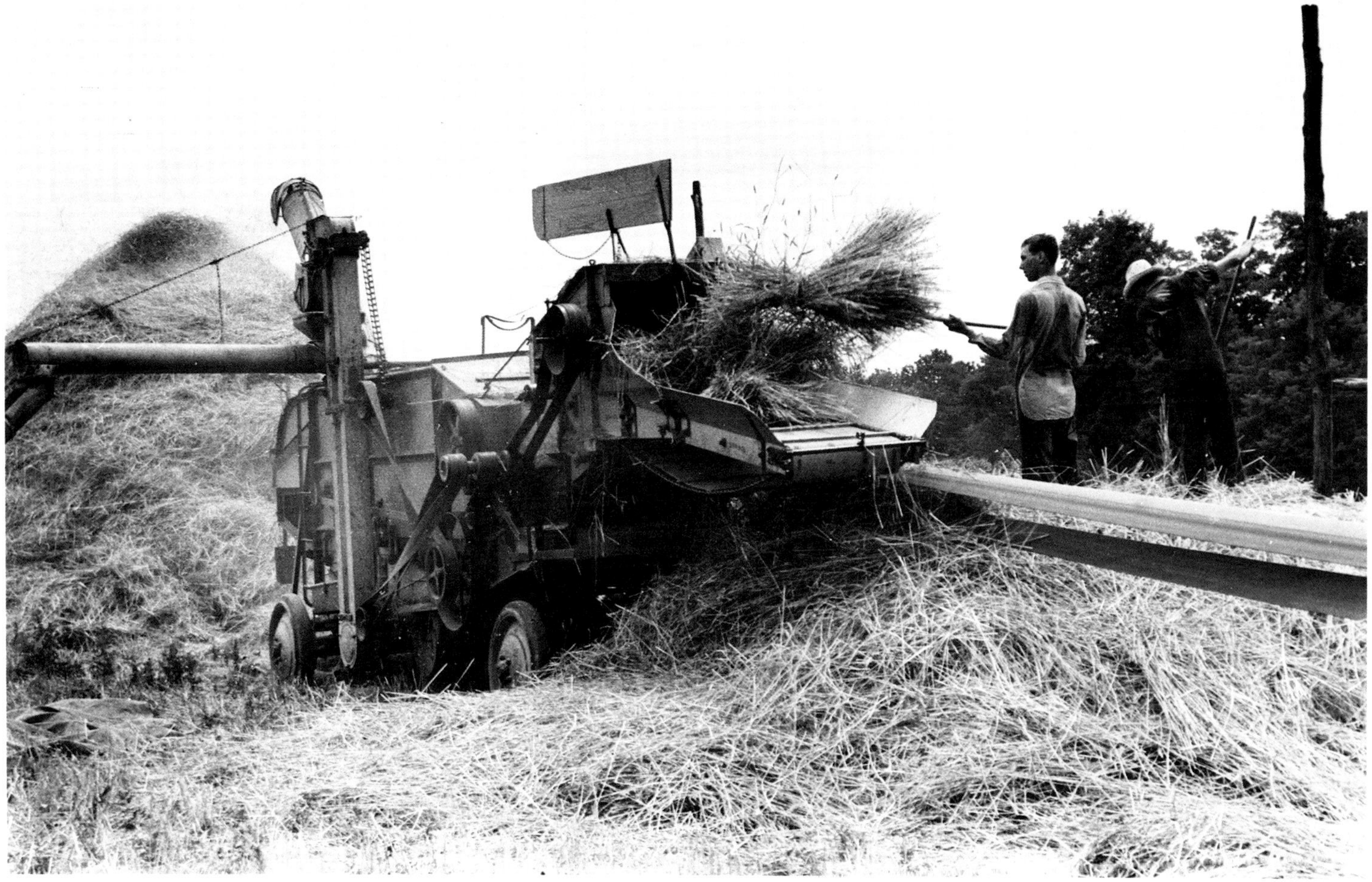

A farmer feeds his wheat into a modern threshing machine, a sign of the increasing mechanization of agriculture. Oldham County, July 1940. MARION POST WOLCOTT.

Opposite: An erosion gully in the Coalins Forest between the Tennessee and Cumberland rivers near Princeton. This forest reservation was part of an FSA reforestation and soil erosion control project. March 1936. CARL MYDANS.

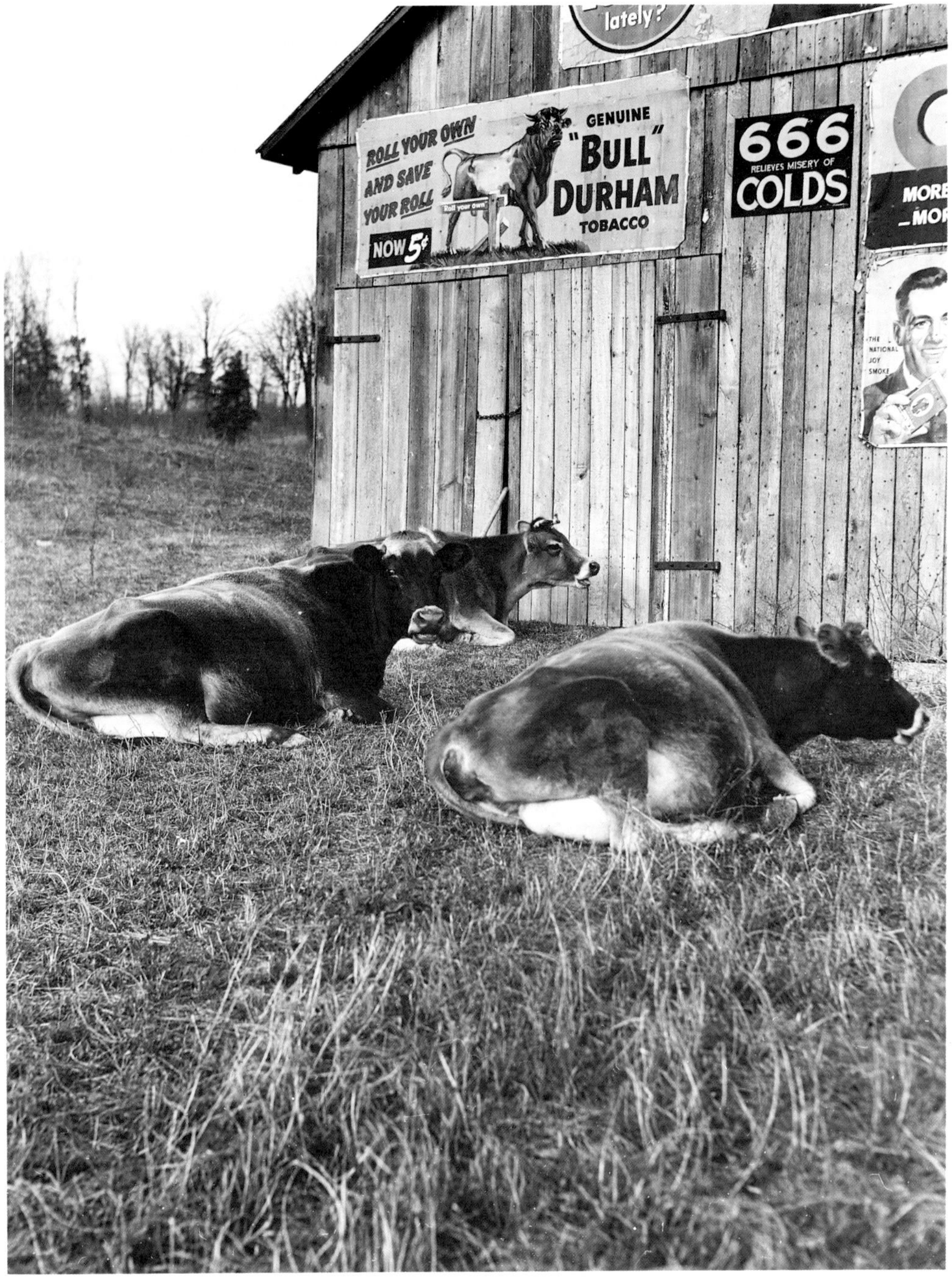

Cows take their ease beneath signs of the times. Nicholas County, November 1940. JOHN VACHON.

Opposite: A stone fence and barns, familiar sights in the Bluegrass region. The fence is constructed of limestone without mortar. Near Frankfort, August 1940. MARION POST WOLCOTT.

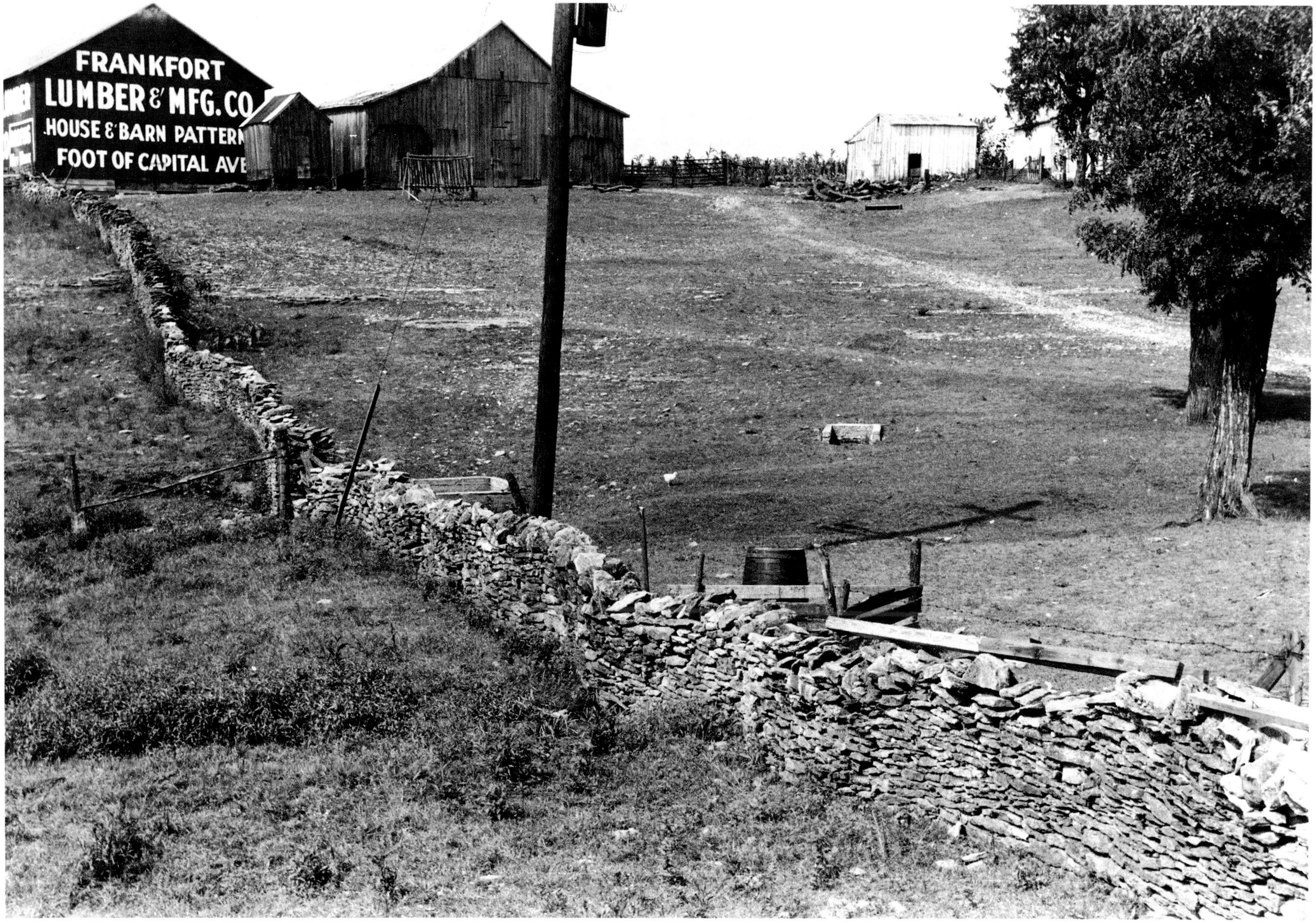
FRANKFORT
LUMBER & MFG. CO
HOUSE & BARN PATTERN
FOOT OF CAPITAL AVE

A preacher speaks at a memorial service.
Up Frozen Creek near Jackson, August 1940.
MARION POST WOLCOTT.

Religious Customs

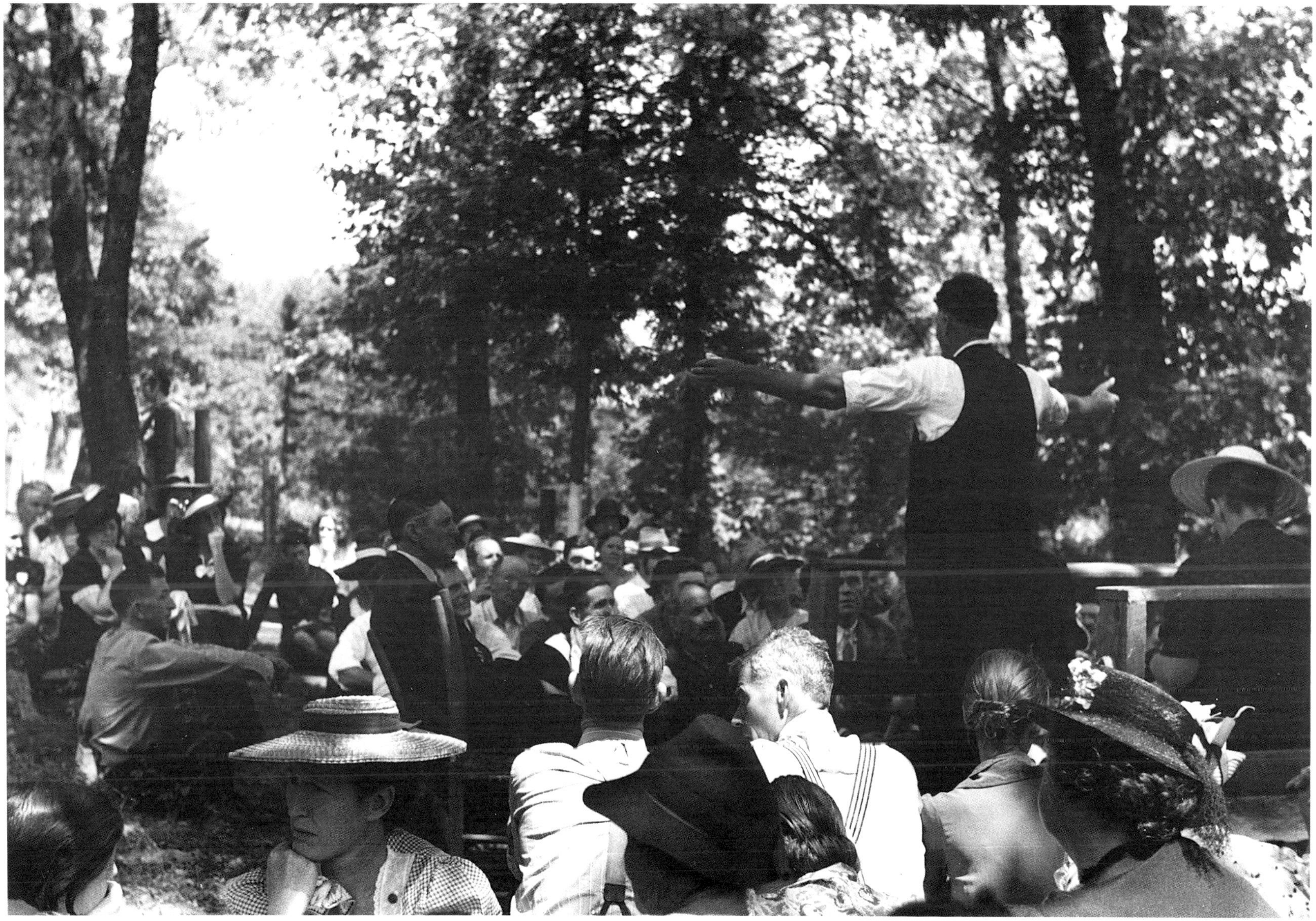

RELIGION has played a vital role in the life of Kentuckians from the state's earliest settlement. During her visits to Kentucky, Marion Post Wolcott frequently focused her camera on church functions, both religious and social. Wolcott's religious background is not known, but she was respectful of her subjects' beliefs, keeping a discrete, nonintrusive distance, as befitted an outsider. In one letter to Roy Stryker, she indicated that she had not photographed a footwashing service inside a church because the parishioners had asked her not to. She did, however, maintain her earthy sense of humor about this aspect of her work. Writing to Stryker after photographing at an outdoor memorial service in August 1940, she commented about herself: "The chiggers nearly ate out her belly button, among other delicate spots on her anatomy, after sitting on old wooden benches & climbing around in dry grass & weeds at the church picnic supper."

Wolcott's pictures show a variety of sites for worship, ranging from a high-style urban church to an outdoor baptismal service. Those pictures from Eastern Kentucky show the widest range of activity: itinerant lay preachers who felt called to the gospel by God rather than being ordained by man, and congregations gathered at the creek for a baptism by immersion, or socializing outside church after a service, or gathering outdoors in summer for memorial services delayed by winter road conditions.

Opposite: The car of an itinerant preacher in Campton for court day. September 1940. Marion Post Wolcott.

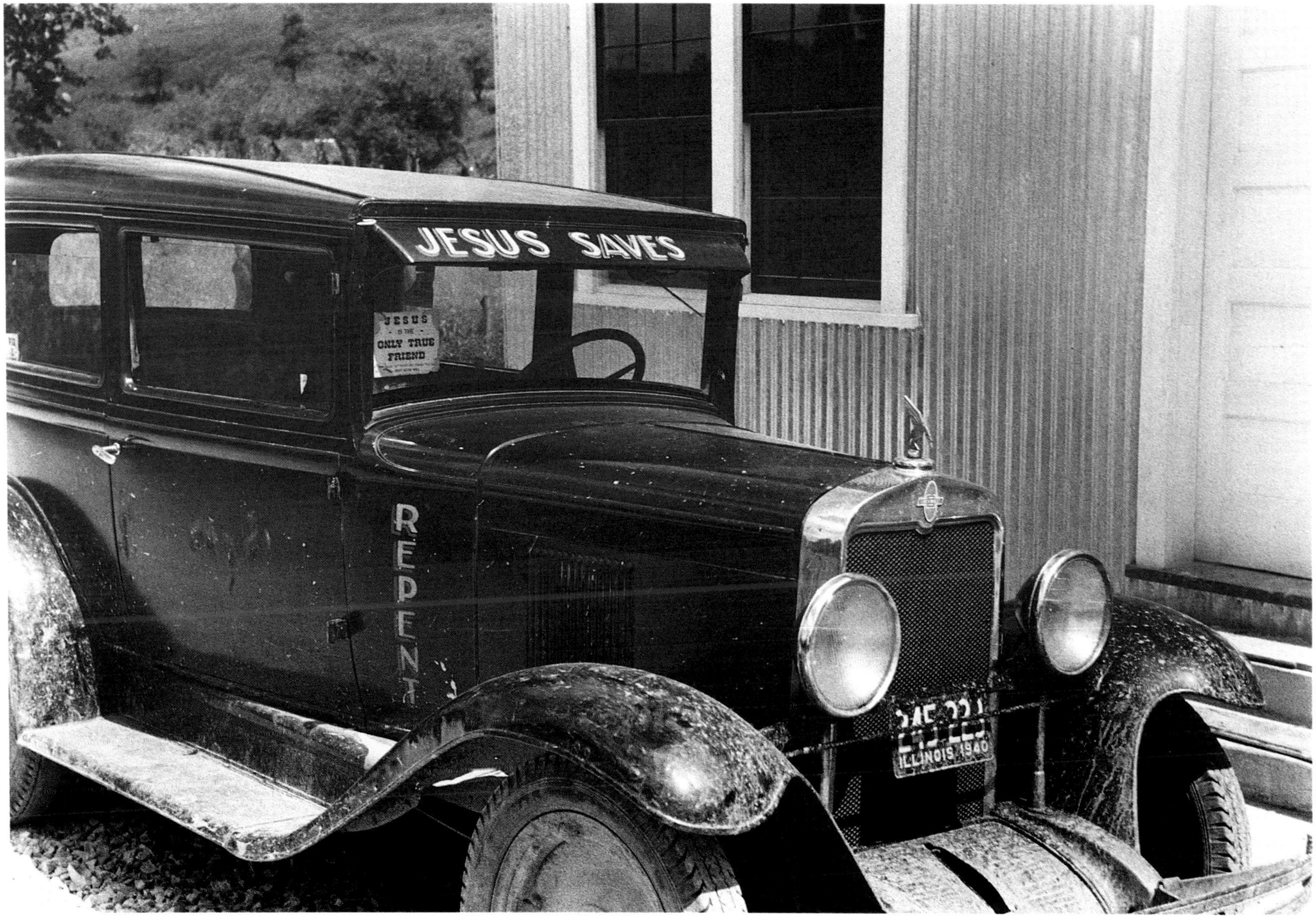
JESUS SAVES
JESUS IS THE ONLY TRUE FRIEND
REPENT
ILLINOIS 1940

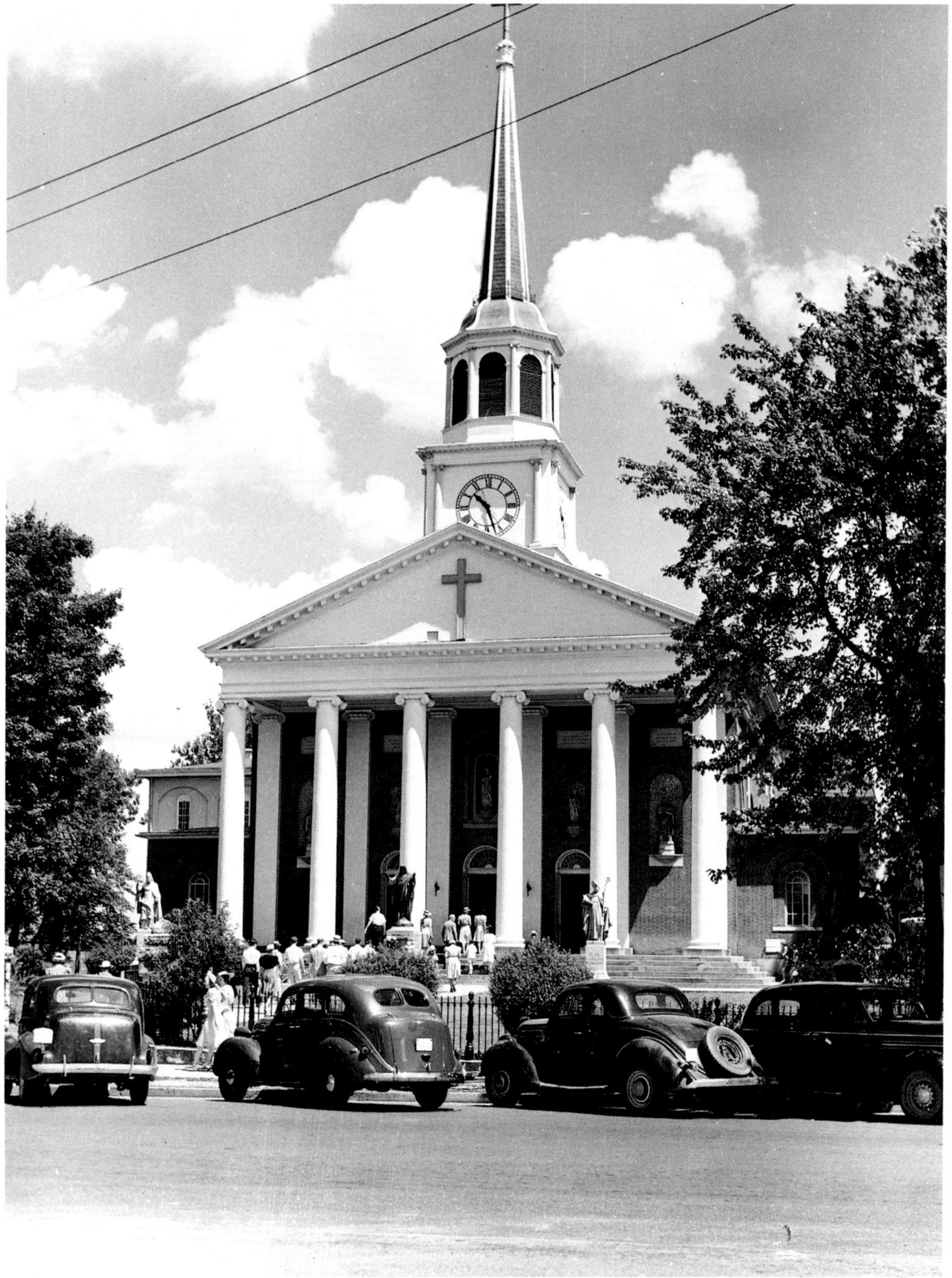

Parishioners enter St. Joseph's Cathedral, Bardstown. August 1940. Marion Post Wolcott.

Opposite: The congregation visit after Sunday service in Linwood. July 1940. Marion Post Wolcott.

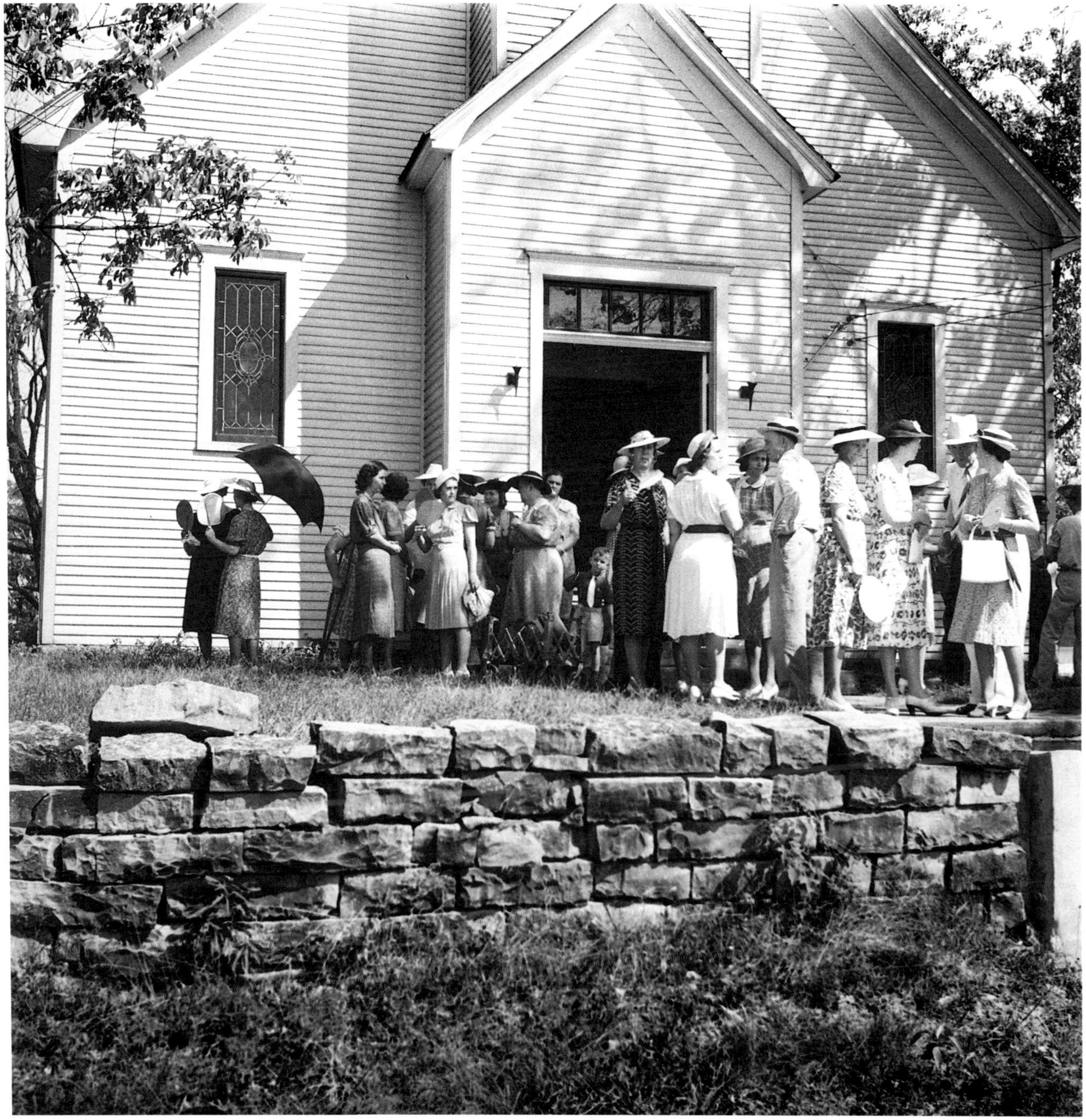

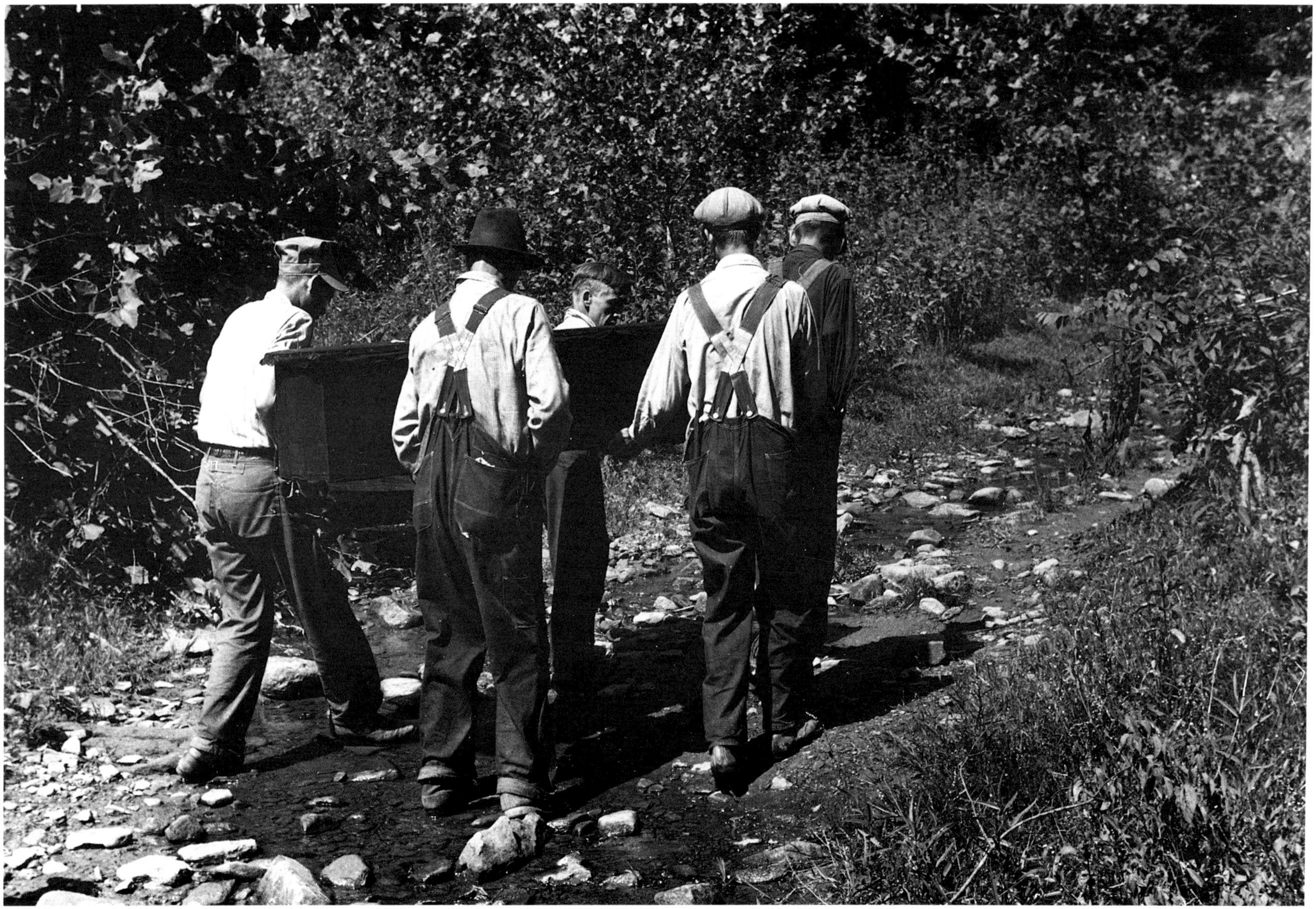

A homemade coffin is carried up the South Fork of the Kentucky River to the family plot for burial. Near Jackson, August 1940. MARION POST WOLCOTT.

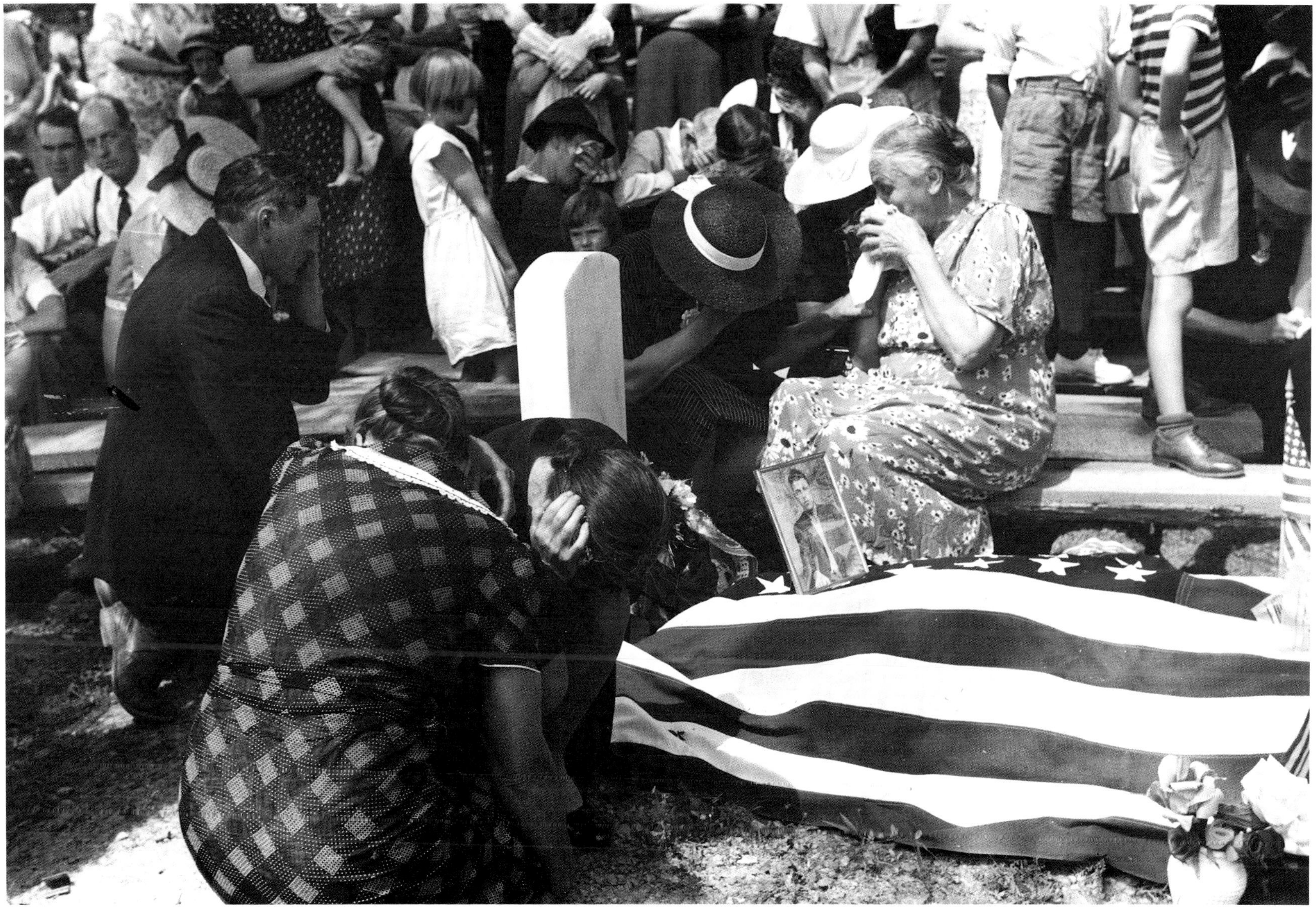

Relatives of the deceased weep at the grave. MARION POST WOLCOTT.

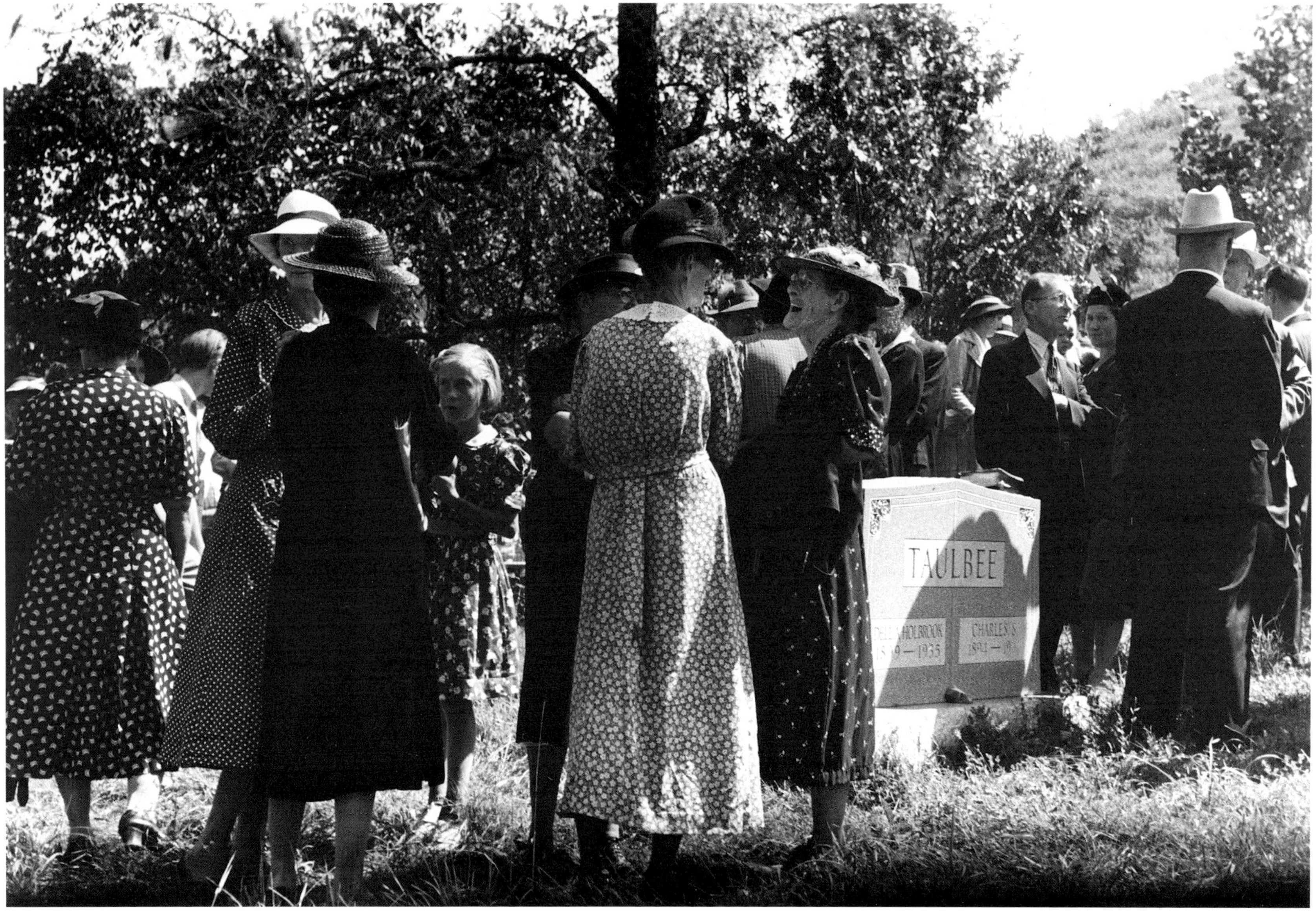

Visiting after the memorial service. MARION POST WOLCOTT.

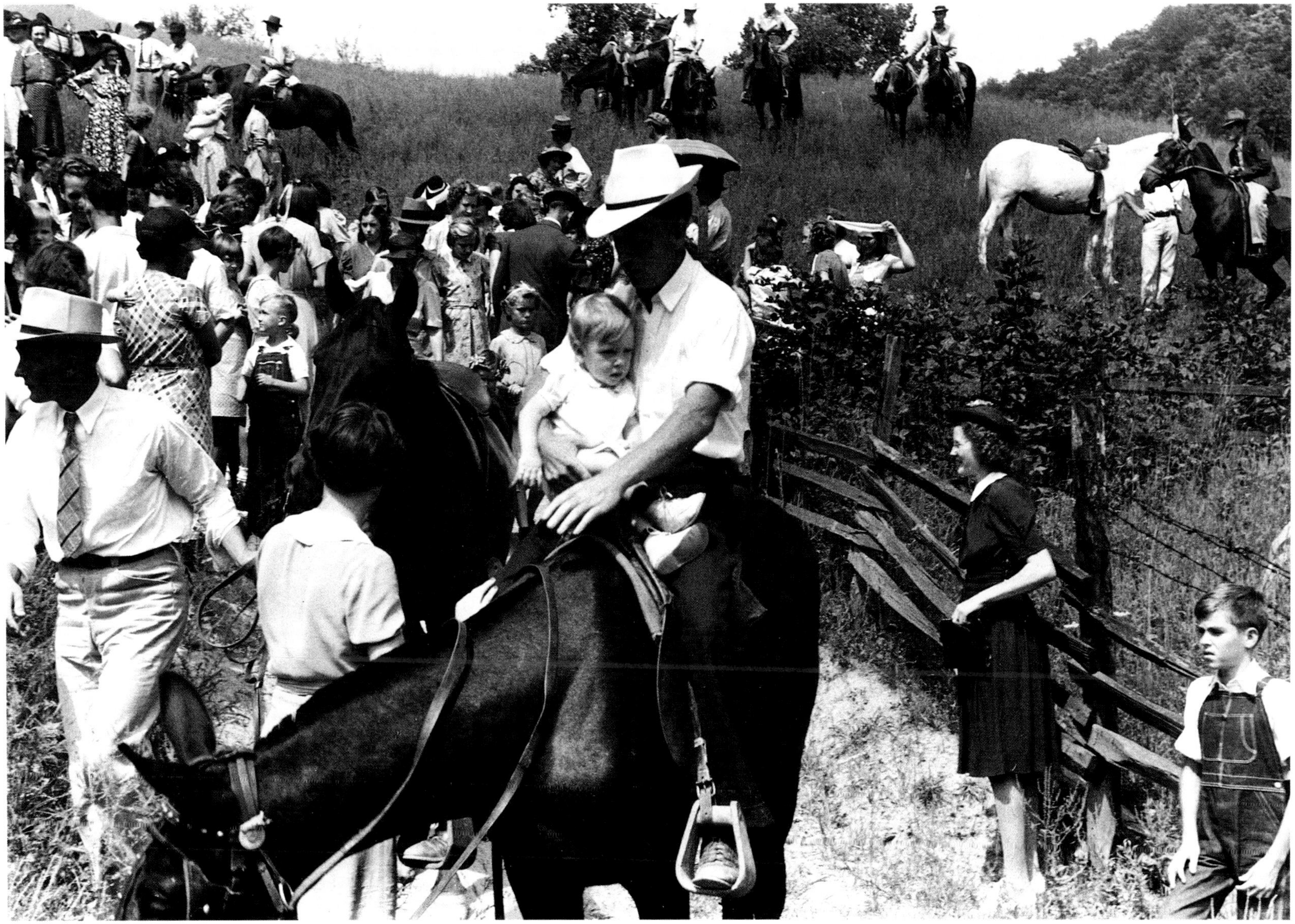

Relatives and friends leave after the memorial service. MARION POST WOLCOTT.

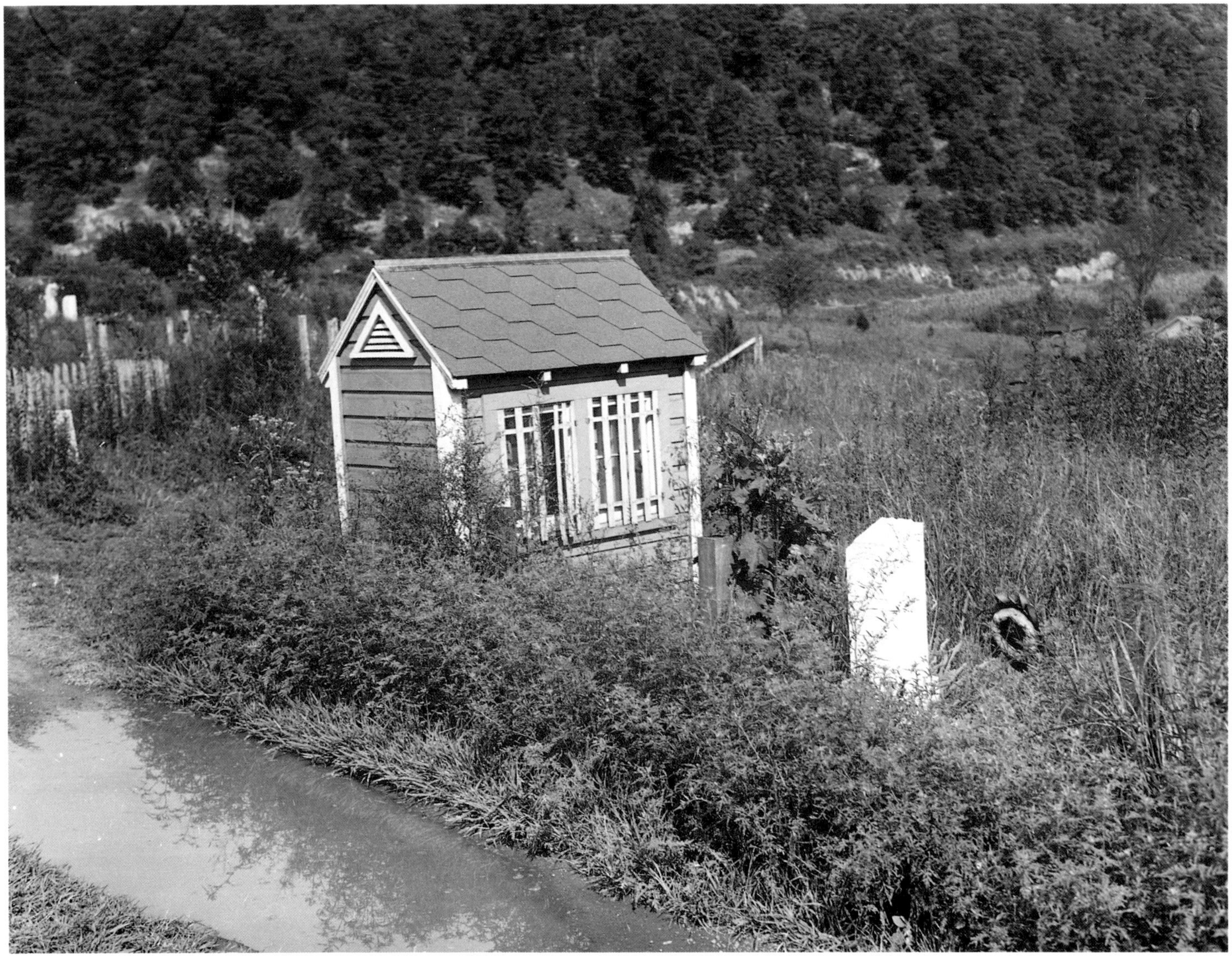

A gravehouse intended to provide a place of rest for the soul as well as to keep animals away from the remains. Such structures, which are found throughout the upland South, combine American Indian, African, and European traditions. Near Hazard, September 1940. MARION POST WOLCOTT.

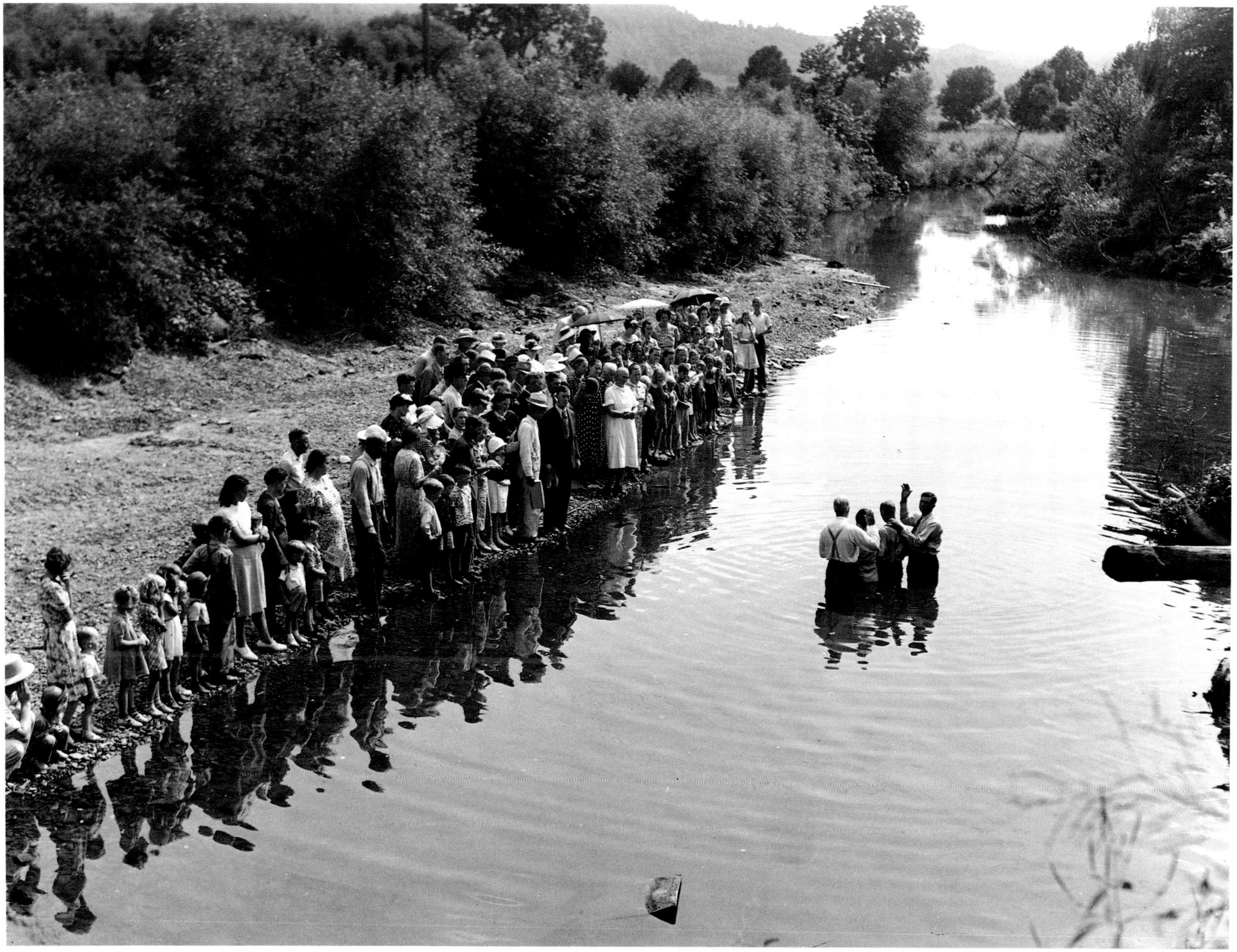

Members of the Primitive Baptist Church of Morehead attend a baptism by immersion in a creek. August 1940. MARION POST WOLCOTT.

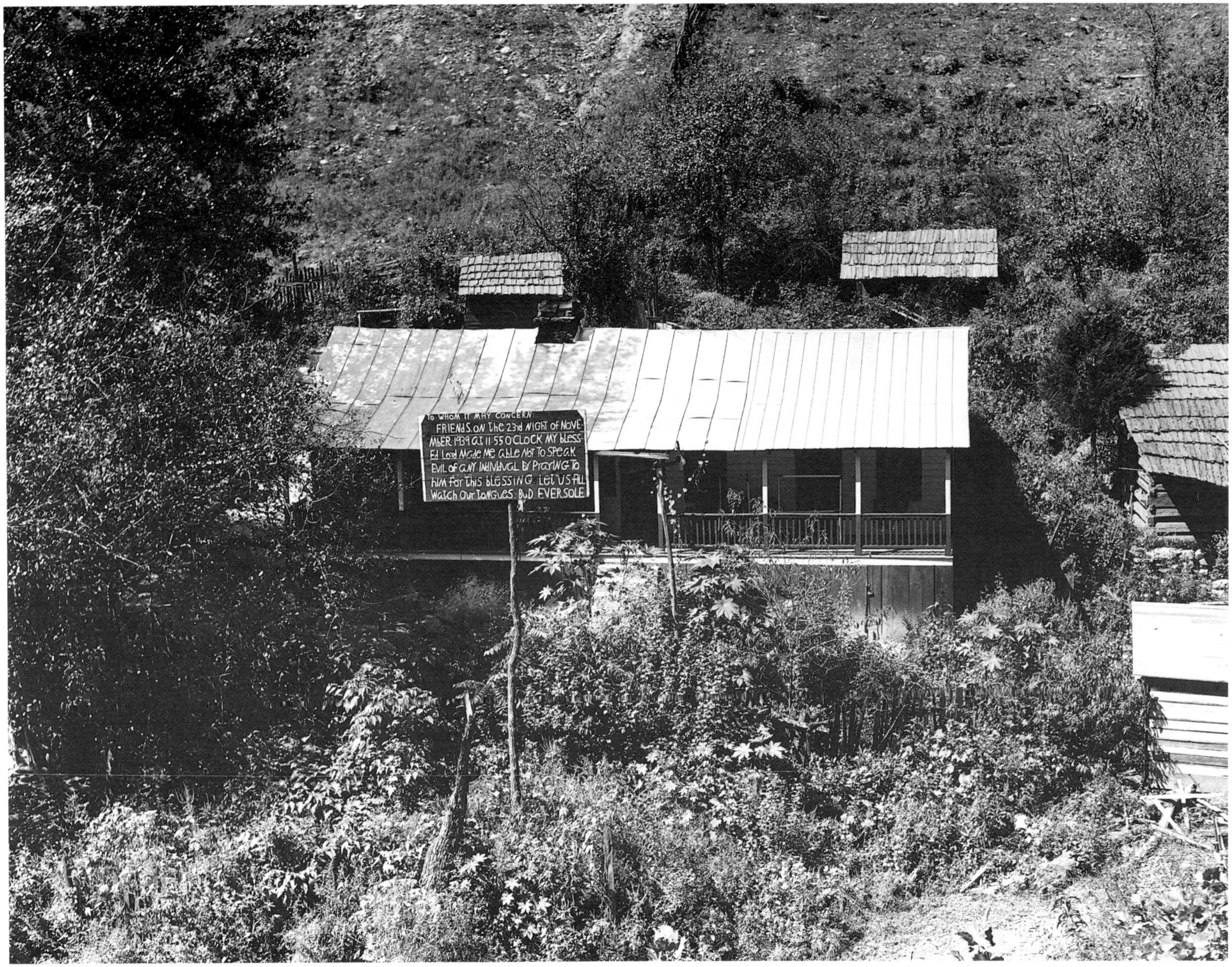

A sign in front of a mountaineer's home announces the end of a feud with one of his neighbors. Up Squabble Creek near Buckhorn, September 1940. MARION POST WOLCOTT.

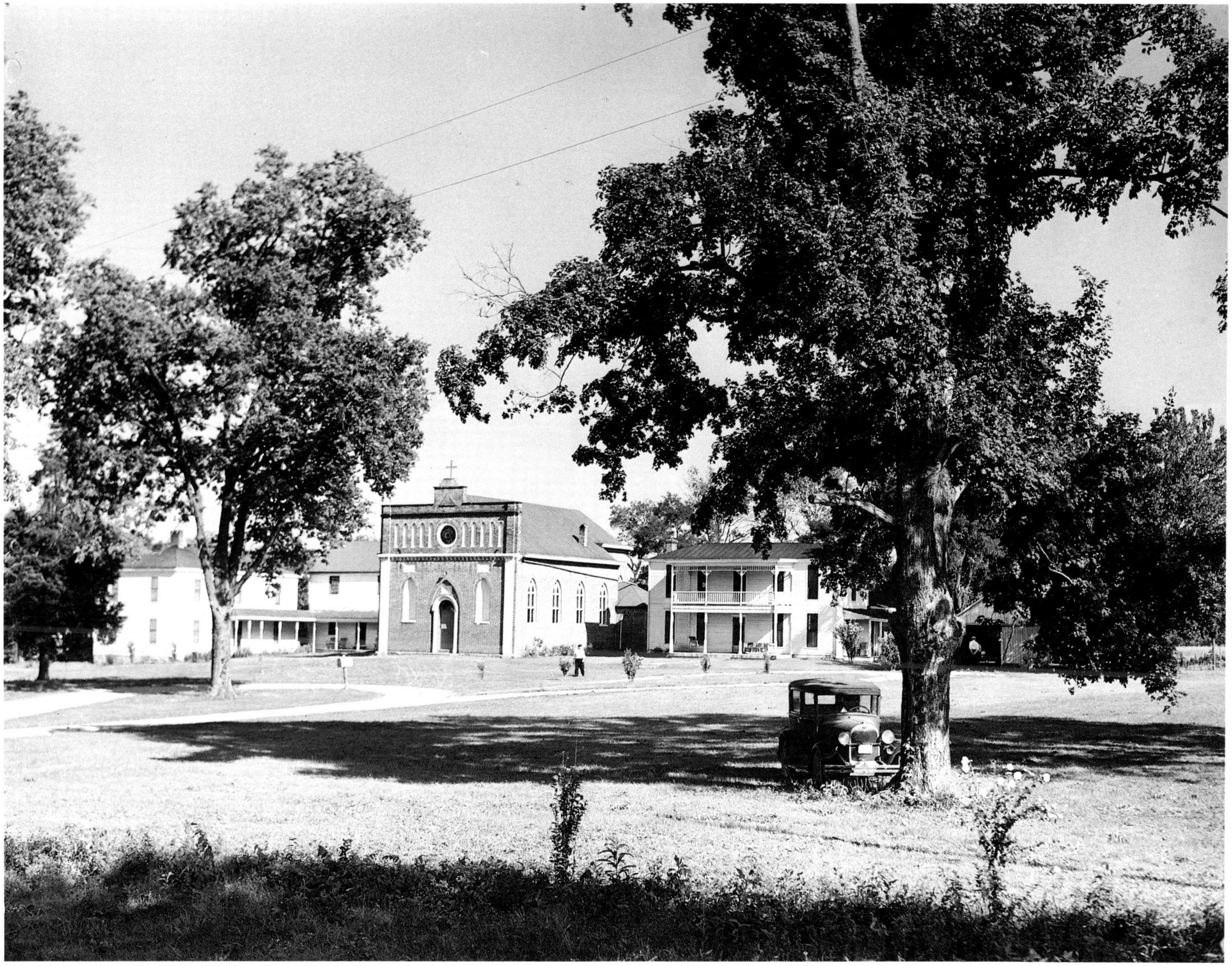

The grounds of St. Thomas Church in Bardstown. August 1940. Marion Post Wolcott.

Lessons in the Fugate School.
Breathitt County, September 1940.
Marion Post Wolcott.

Education

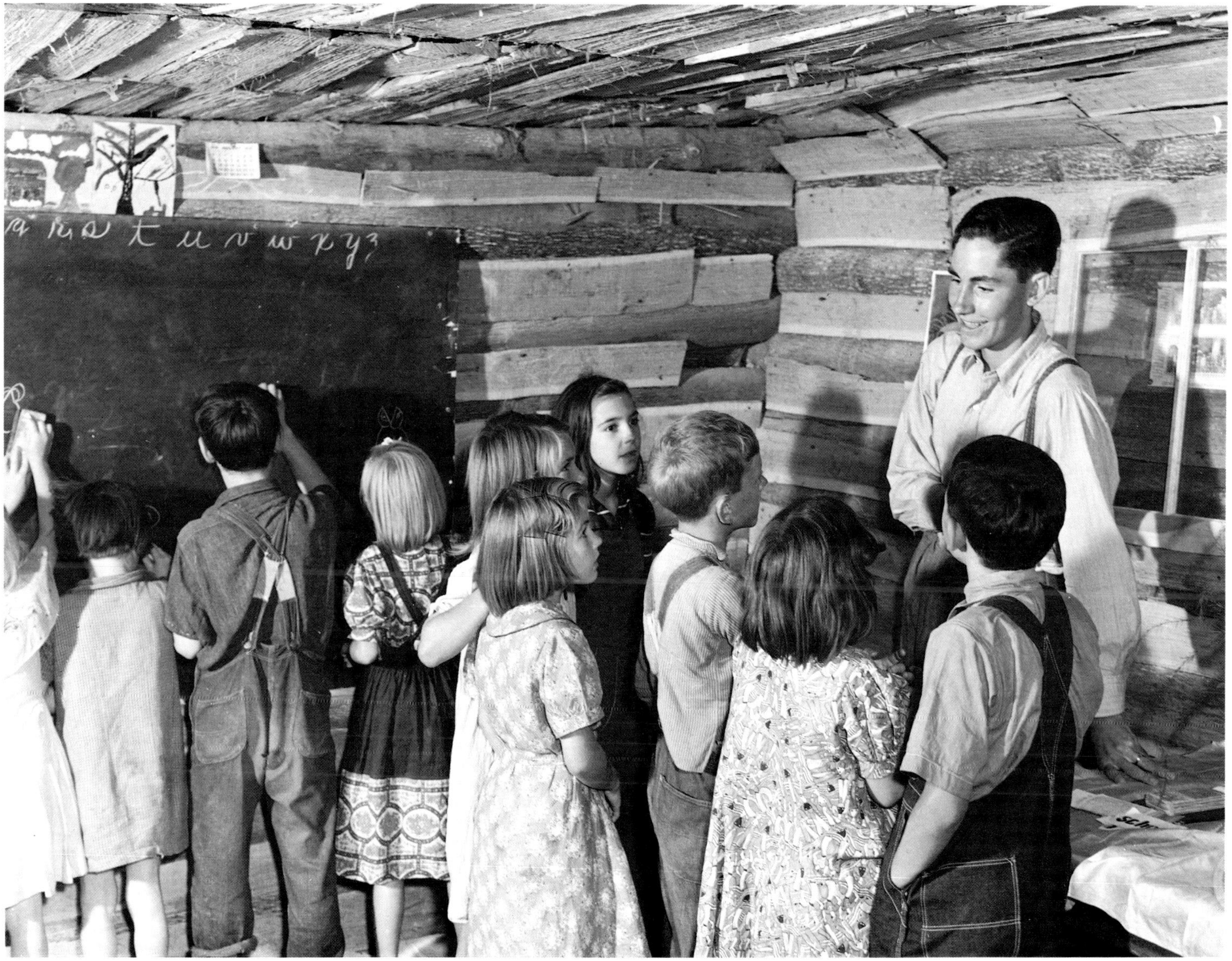

IMPROVED EDUCATIONAL resources were one of the New Deal's most lasting legacies to the nation. This was especially important in Kentucky, where in some areas resistance still existed to the principle of tax-supported public education. An example of the reluctance to commit public funds to general education was the lack of textbooks, which meant that students had to purchase their own or do without. Not until 1934 did Kentucky students begin to receive free textbooks, but by 1940 all grade school pupils in the state had a complete set bought with public funds.

The one-room schoolhouse was still the norm in many areas of Kentucky in the 1930s, but with financing from the Public Works and Works Progress Administrations, the state moved toward consolidation of schools and construction of more adequate buildings. In 1935 more than 200,000 Kentucky students attended 5,367 single-teacher eight-grade schools. With partial federal funding, that number of buildings was reduced by 1,000 by 1939.

Improved transportation in rural areas also helped reduce the fragmentation of Kentucky's educational efforts. Marion Post Wolcott noted that in Breathitt County, where school children had to walk long distances over bad roads and up creek beds, the school year began in July and ended in January because few children had shoes or sufficient clothing to walk to school in winter. Despite bare feet and ragged clothes, the children in these photographs look happy, learning their lessons, eating their lunches from the traditional lunch pails, and playing the games that Kentucky children have always played.

Because most of the education pictures taken in Kentucky were designed to show the need for improvement in the public schools, especially overcrowded conditions, only a few of the better schools and institutions of higher learning were photographed.

Opposite: Walking home from school. Breathitt County, September 1940. Marion Post Wolcott.

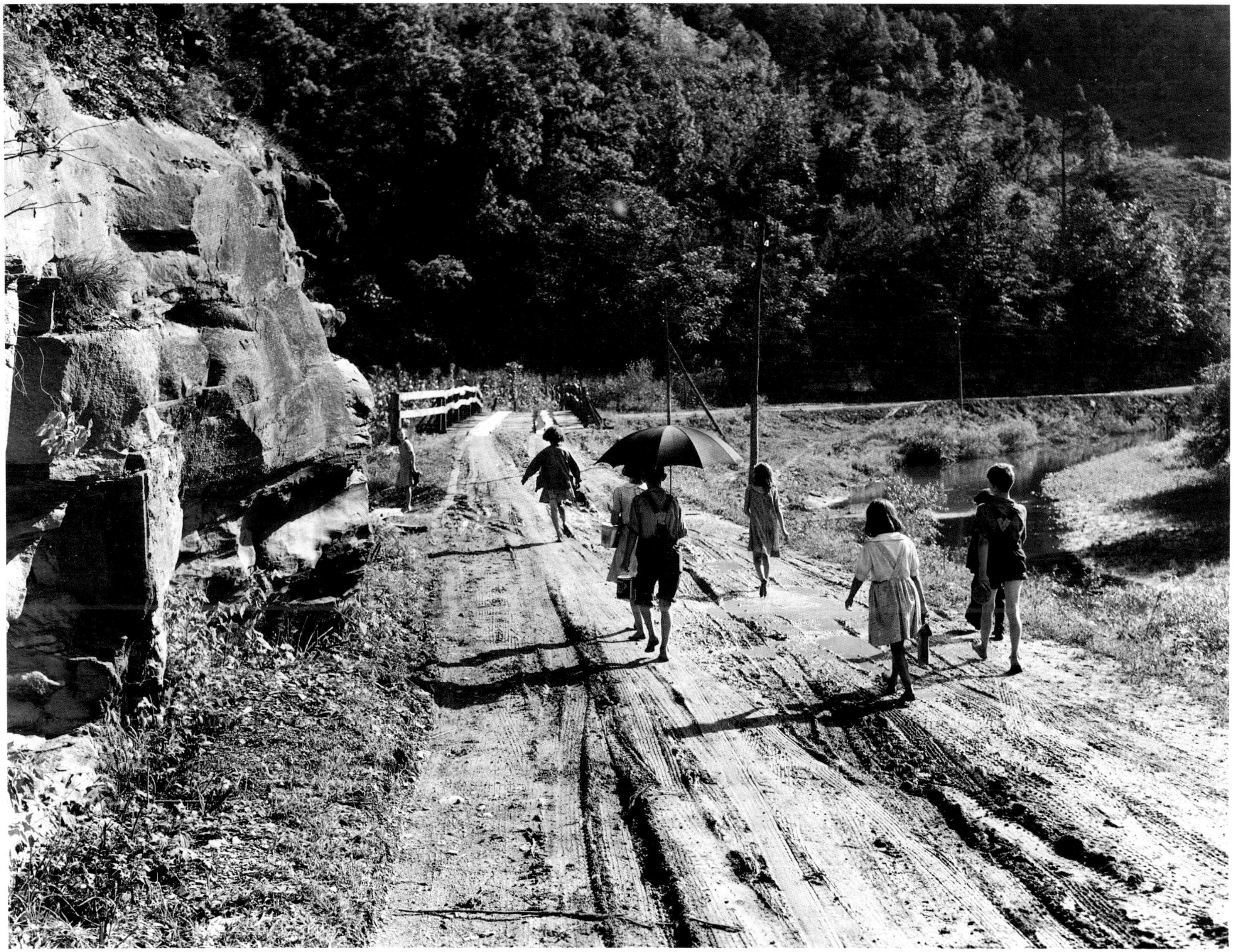

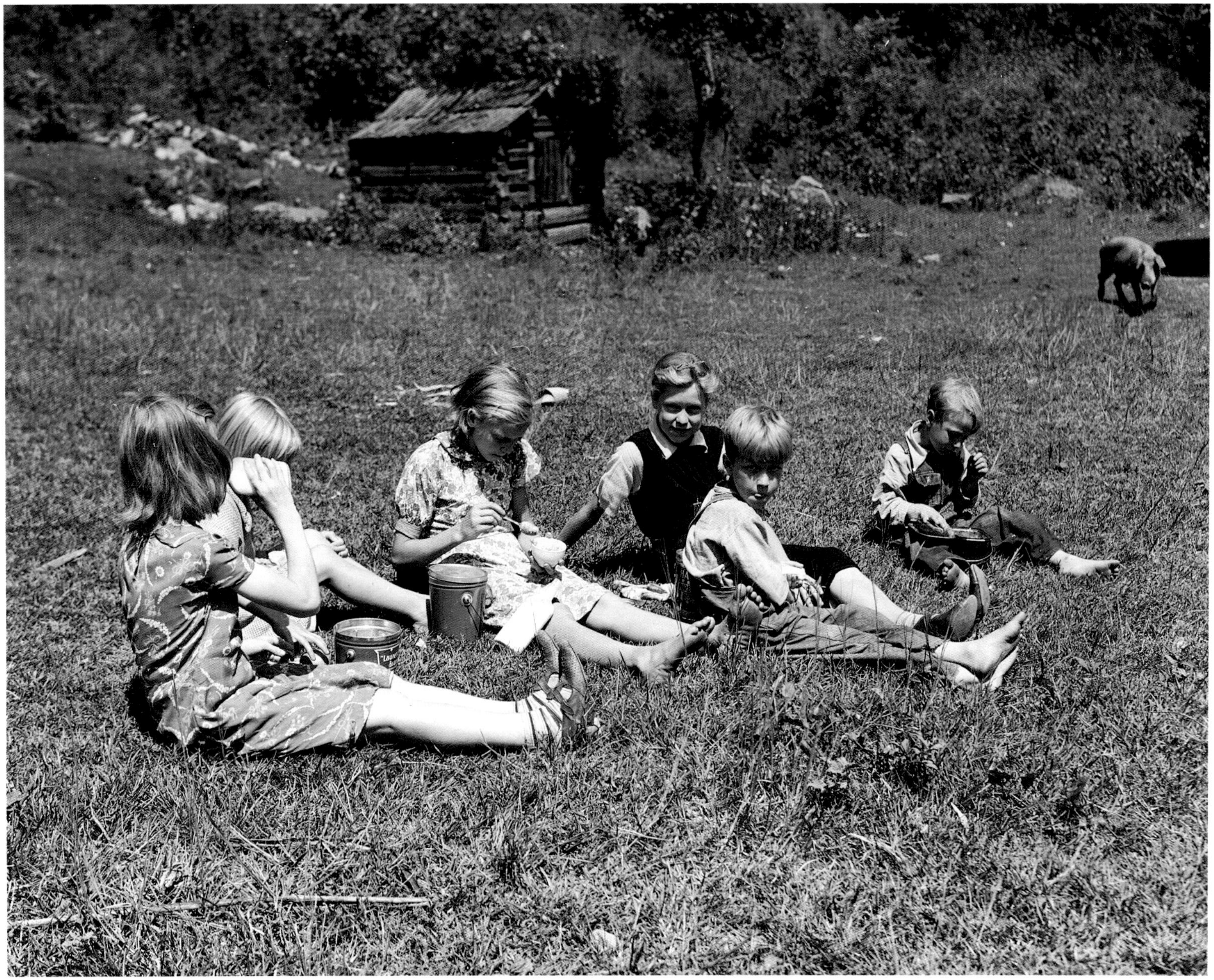

Lunch time at school. Breathitt County, September 1940. MARION POST WOLCOTT.

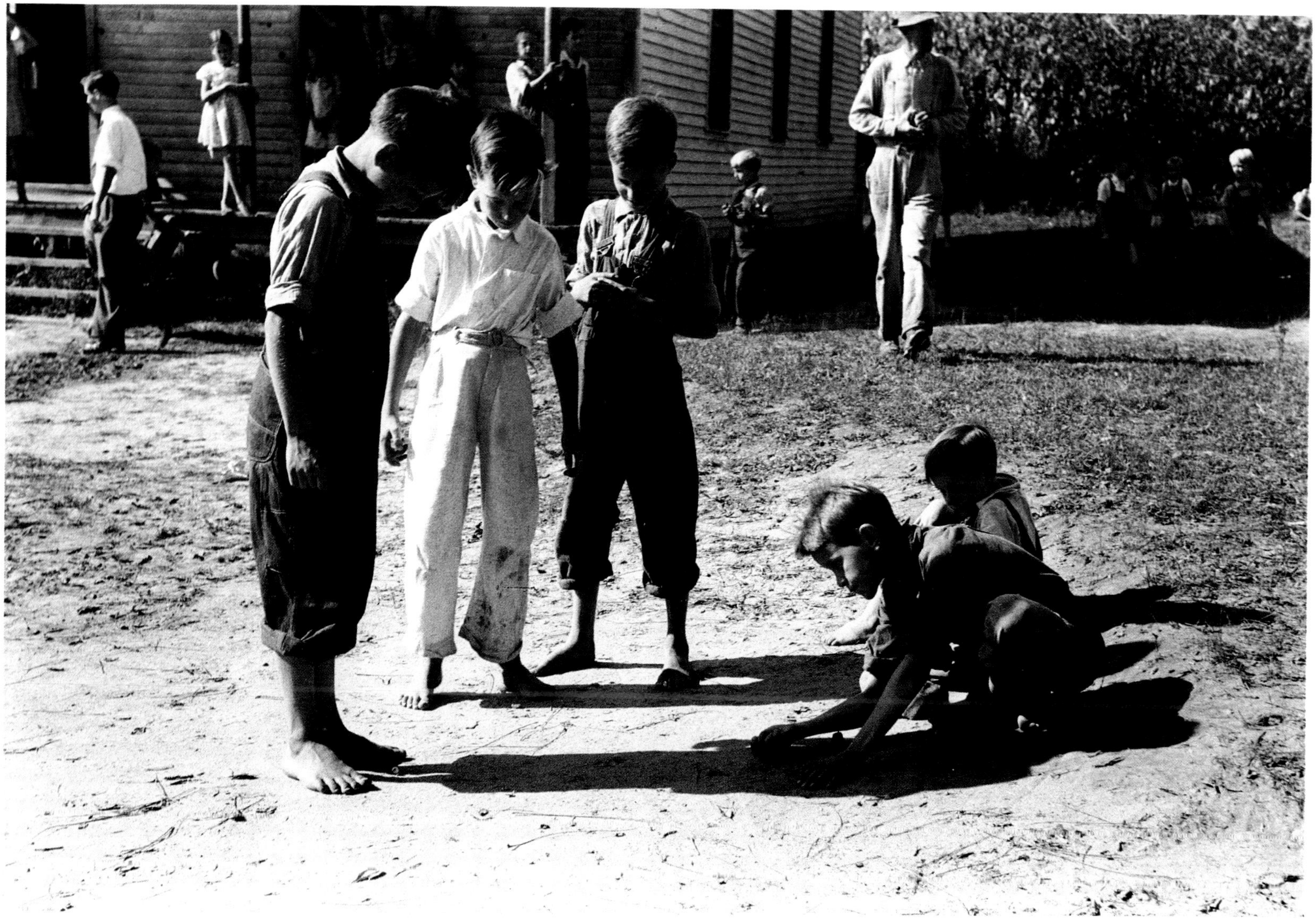

Playing marbles after school. Breathitt County, September 1940. MARION POST WOLCOTT.

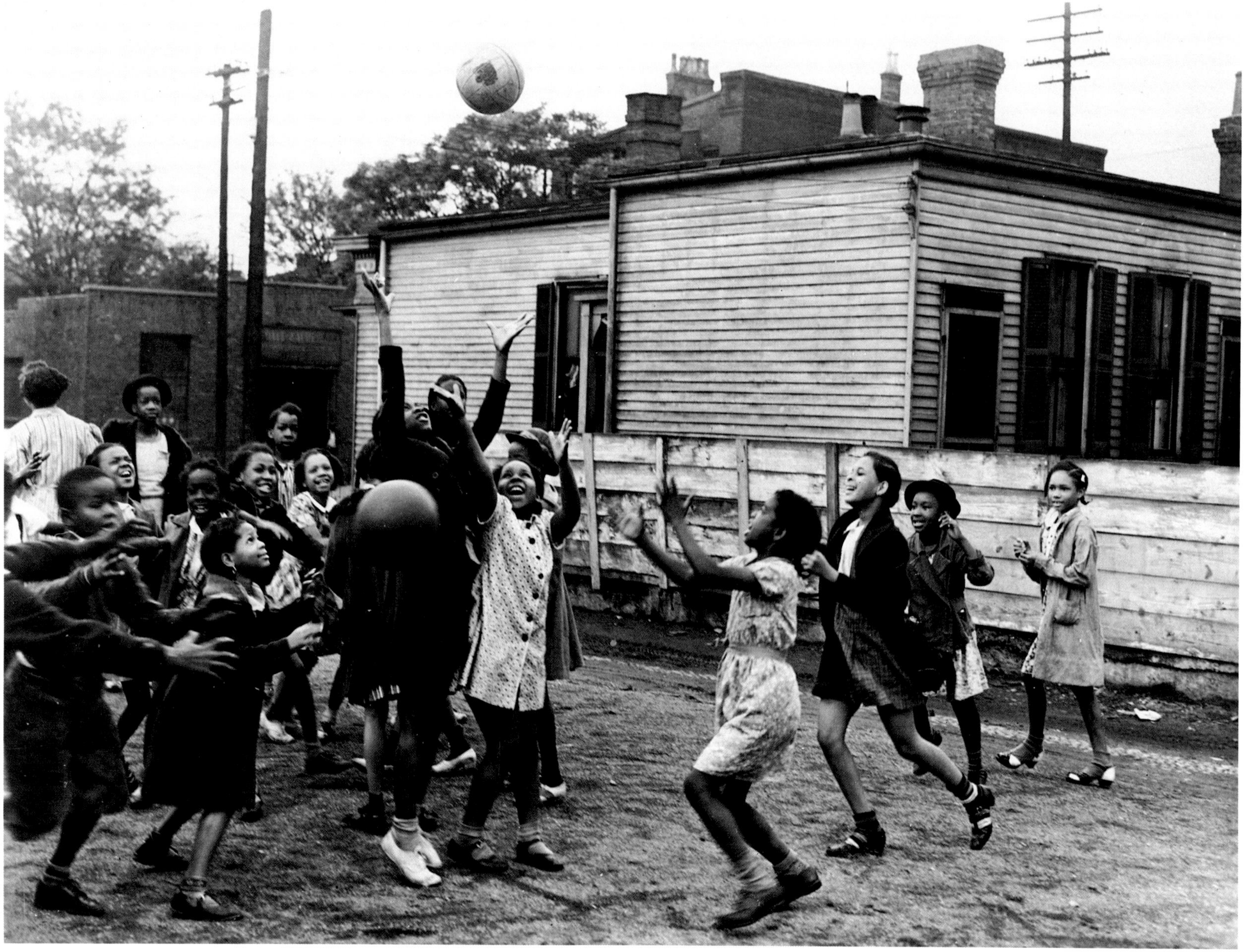

Playing ball at Booker T. Washington School, Louisville. 1940-1943. Taken for the Public Health Service, probably by Marion Post Wolcott.

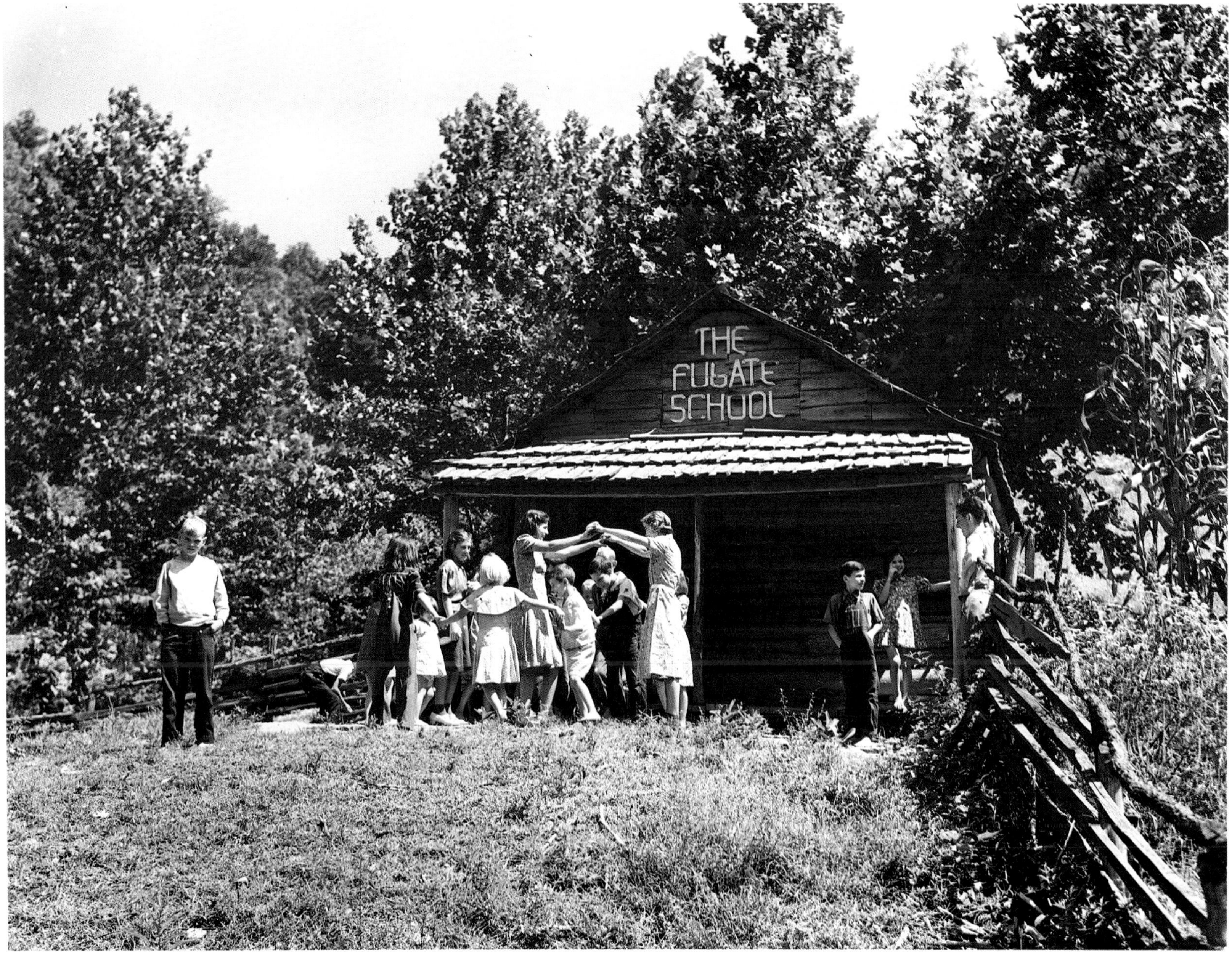

A game of London Bridge at Fugate School. Breathitt County, September 1940. MARION POST WOLCOTT.

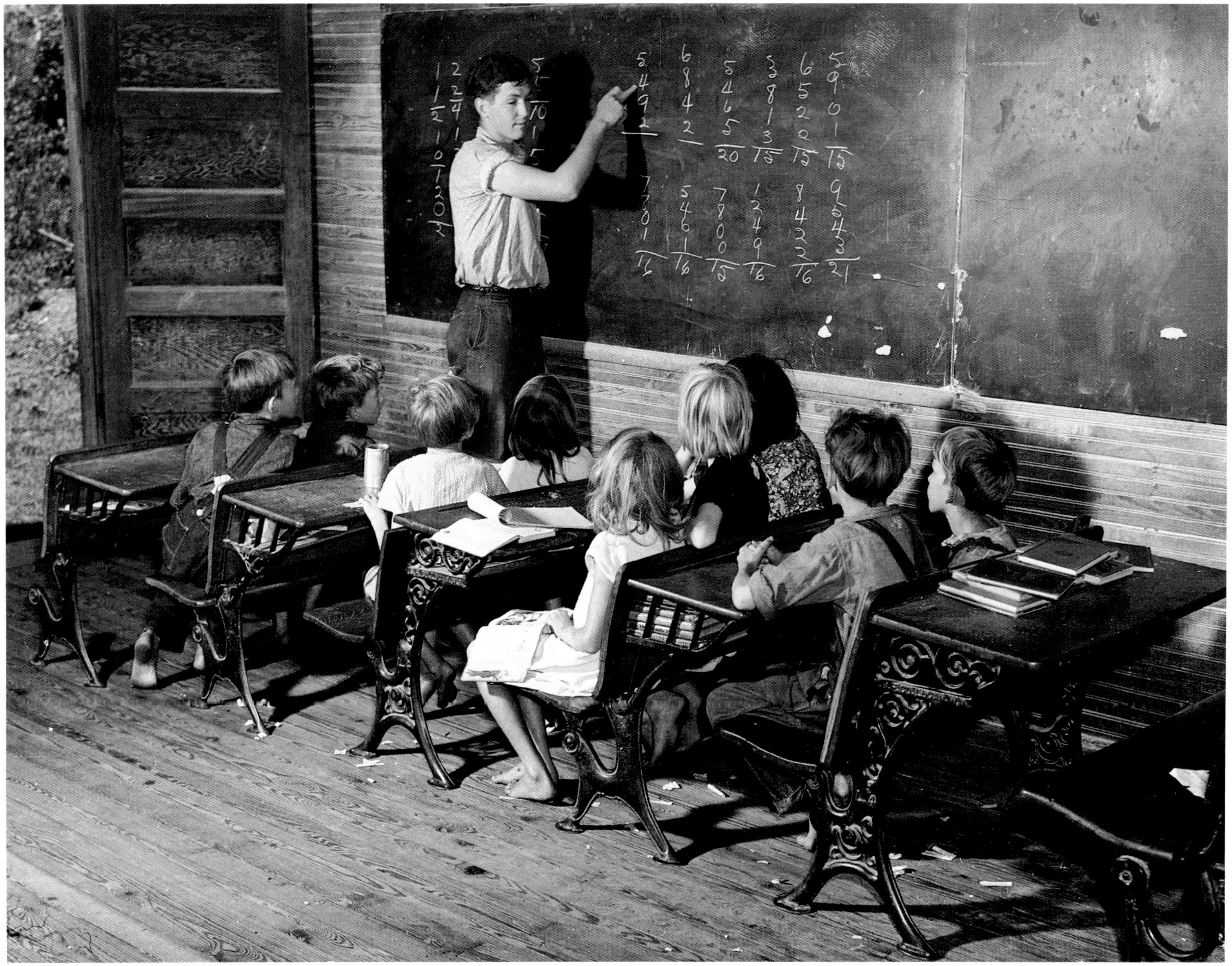

An arithmetic lesson in a one-room school. Breathitt County, September 1940. MARION POST WOLCOTT.

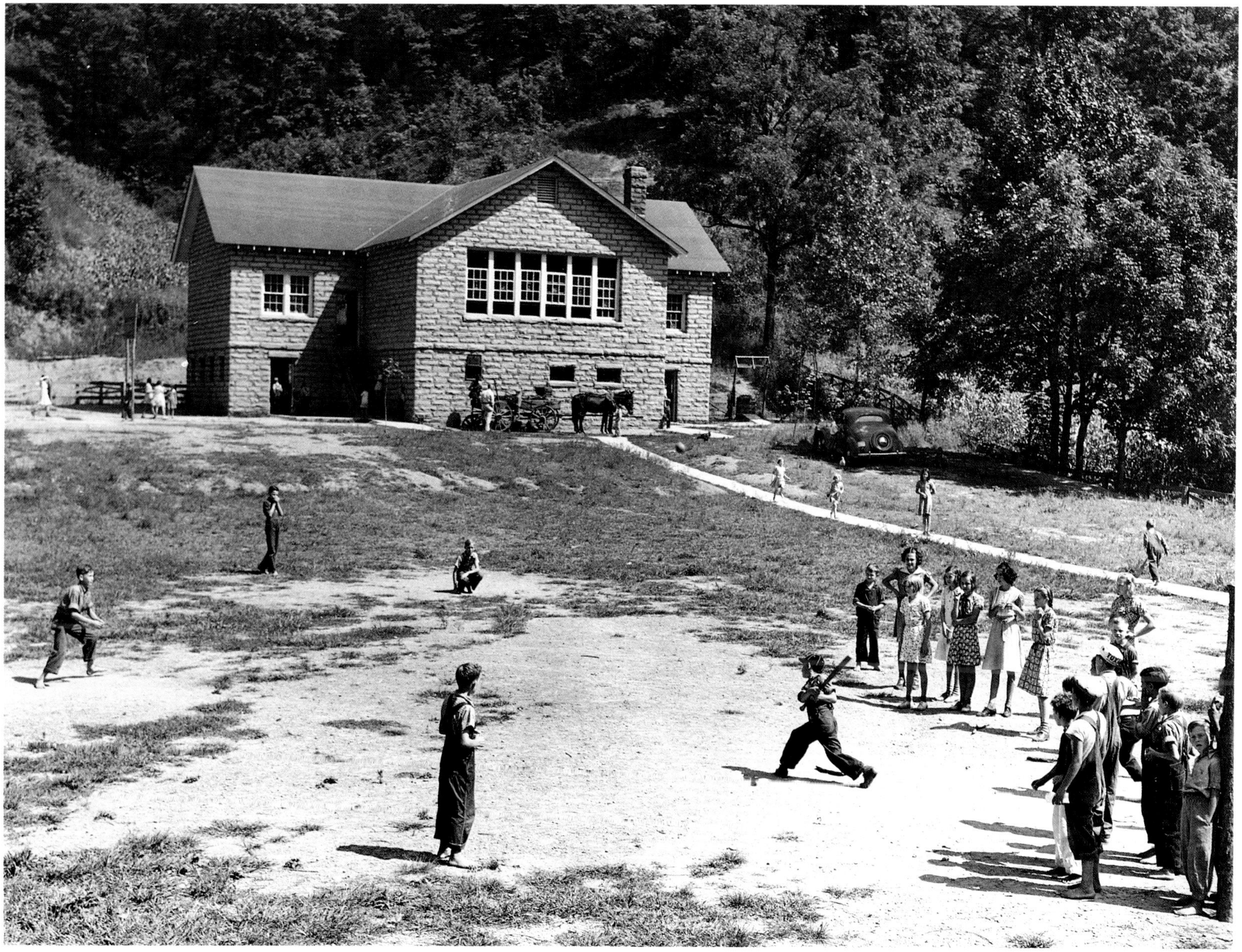

Softball near Big Rock school, one of the new consolidated schools being constructed with federal assistance. Superintendent Marie Turner wanted them built of stone because so many wooden schools had burned. Breathitt County, September 1940. MARION POST WOLCOTT.

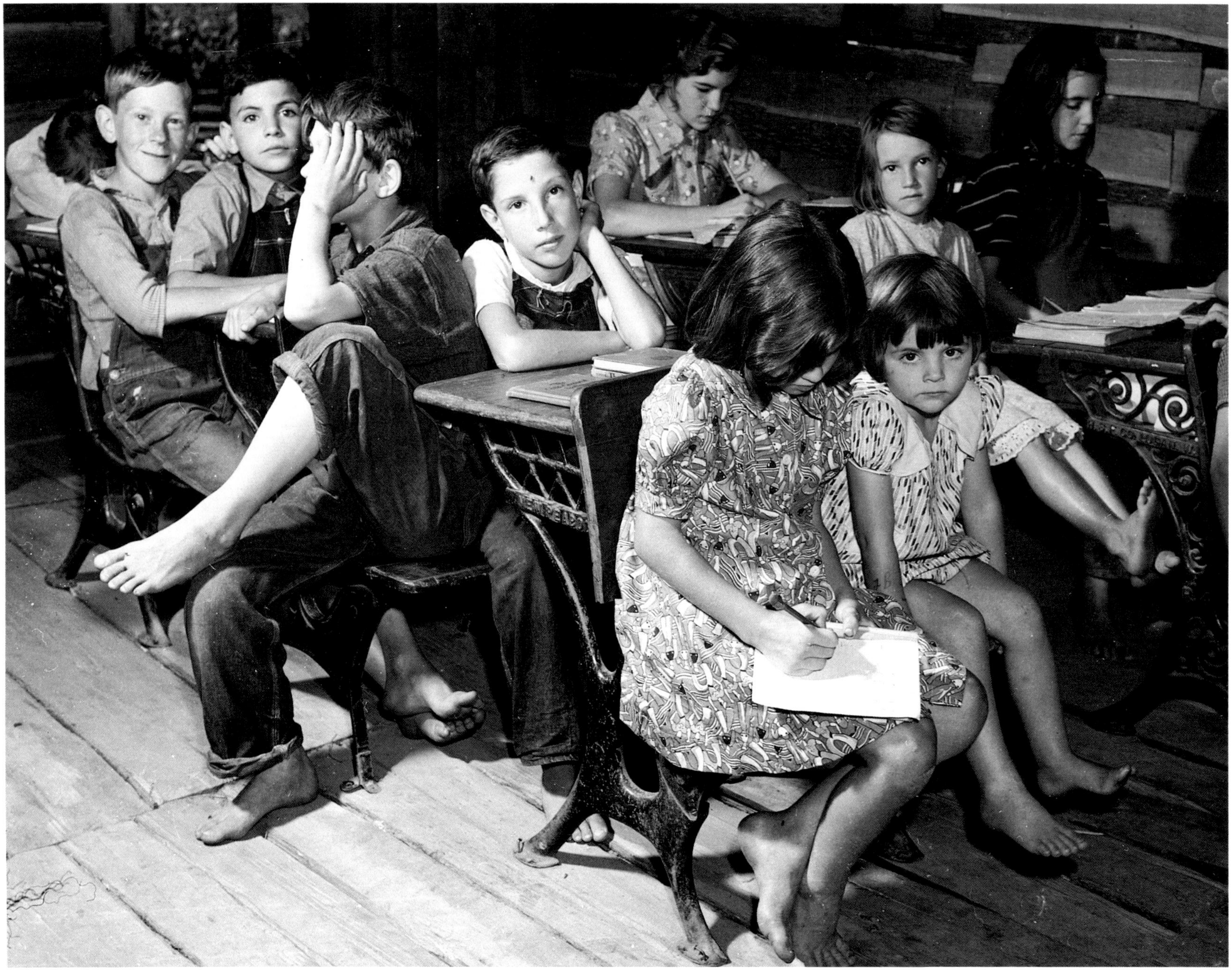

Sharing desks. Breathitt County, September 1940. MARION POST WOLCOTT.

Both the cooks and the winning bidders enjoy the pie and box supper, which will raise money for repairs and supplies for Quicksand School. Breathitt County, September 1940. MARION POST WOLCOTT.

Social Gatherings

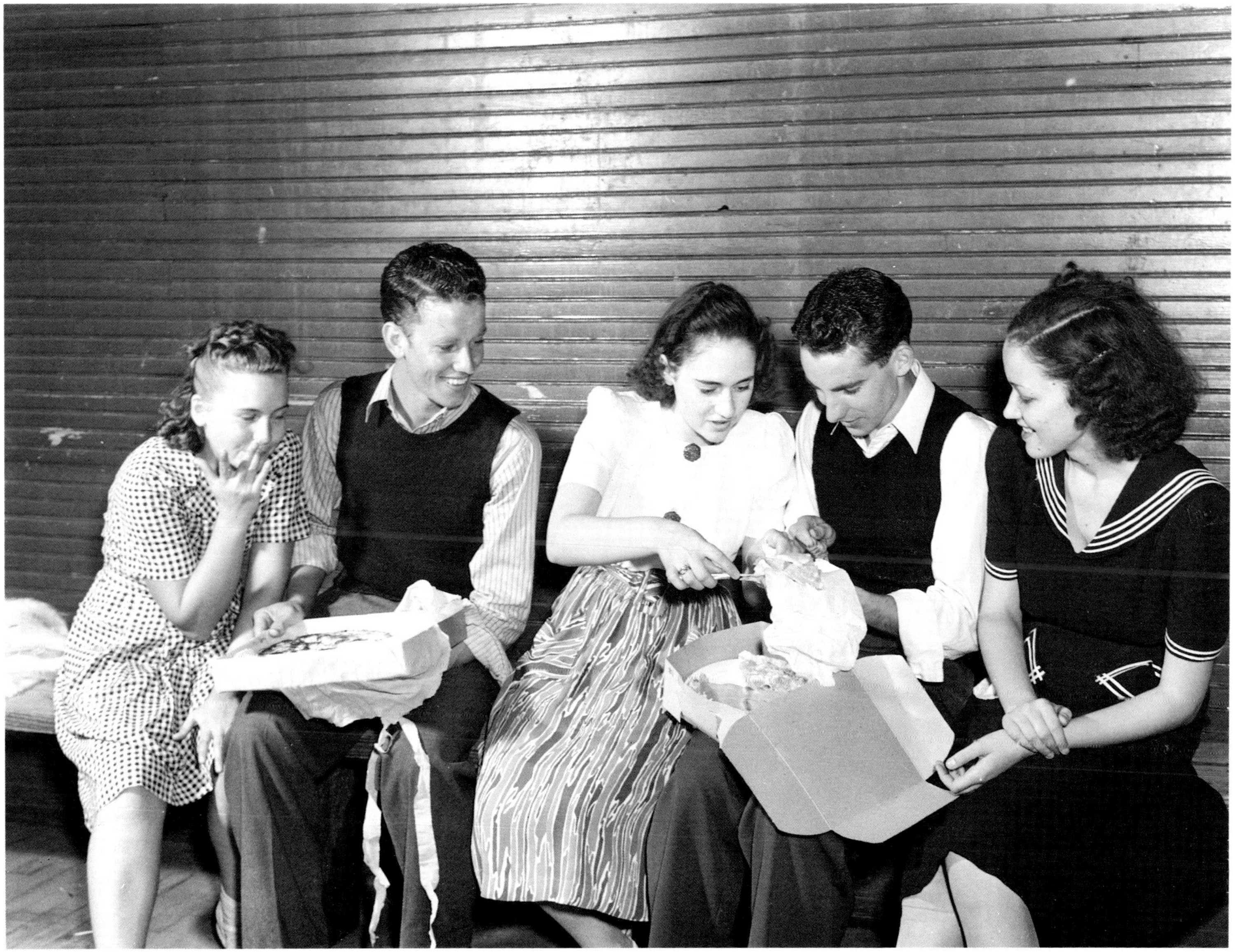

PHOTOGRAPHER Marion Post Wolcott set out with a very clear agenda to document social events in Kentucky. On May 30, 1940, soon after her arrival in the state, she wrote to Roy Stryker, "I'm going to try to get the exclusively & typically Southern stuff first—crops, and big church benefit picnics, farm auctions, revival meetings, etc. now." Later that summer, on August 16, she reported to Stryker's secretary, Clara Dean "Toots" Wakeham:

> I've done county fairs & horse shows, church supper, American Legion fish fry . . . & chased around trying to find a good big all day with dinner served on the grounds farm auction. They're an event. All the auction companies all over the state think I'm buying a huge place, so I may be forced to bid. I've got a good one lined up, if it doesn't rain. . . .
>
> I've made arrangements to photograph a "pie supper"—for the benefit of the rural school. The girl who made the pie auctions it off to the highest bidder who is usually her boyfriend, or hopeful. It's their best way of raising money.

Another typically southern event Wolcott photographed was Court Day. Court Day originated when the itinerant court met at the county seat and county residents gathered to serve on the jury, to hear the local news, and to socialize with their neighbors. Churches served fundraising "dinners on the grounds" and merchants and vendors harangued customers. Jockey Day, or Third Monday, as it was commonly called, developed when local traders drove their herds of draft animals to the county seat to take advantage of the crowds present on Court Day. There they swapped their horses, mules, and donkeys, "jockeying" for the best trades or deals. This custom is sometimes carried on now in swap meets held on Third Monday.

County fairs too drew the FSA photographers. Some of Wolcott's liveliest pictures were taken at the Shelby County Horse Show and Fair. Here was an opportunity for horse breeders and trainers to display their prized specimens, for farmers to speculate on races, for women to socialize, and for children to gawk at carnival attractions.

Opposite: Watermelons for sale on court day. Jackson, September 1940. MARION POST WOLCOTT.

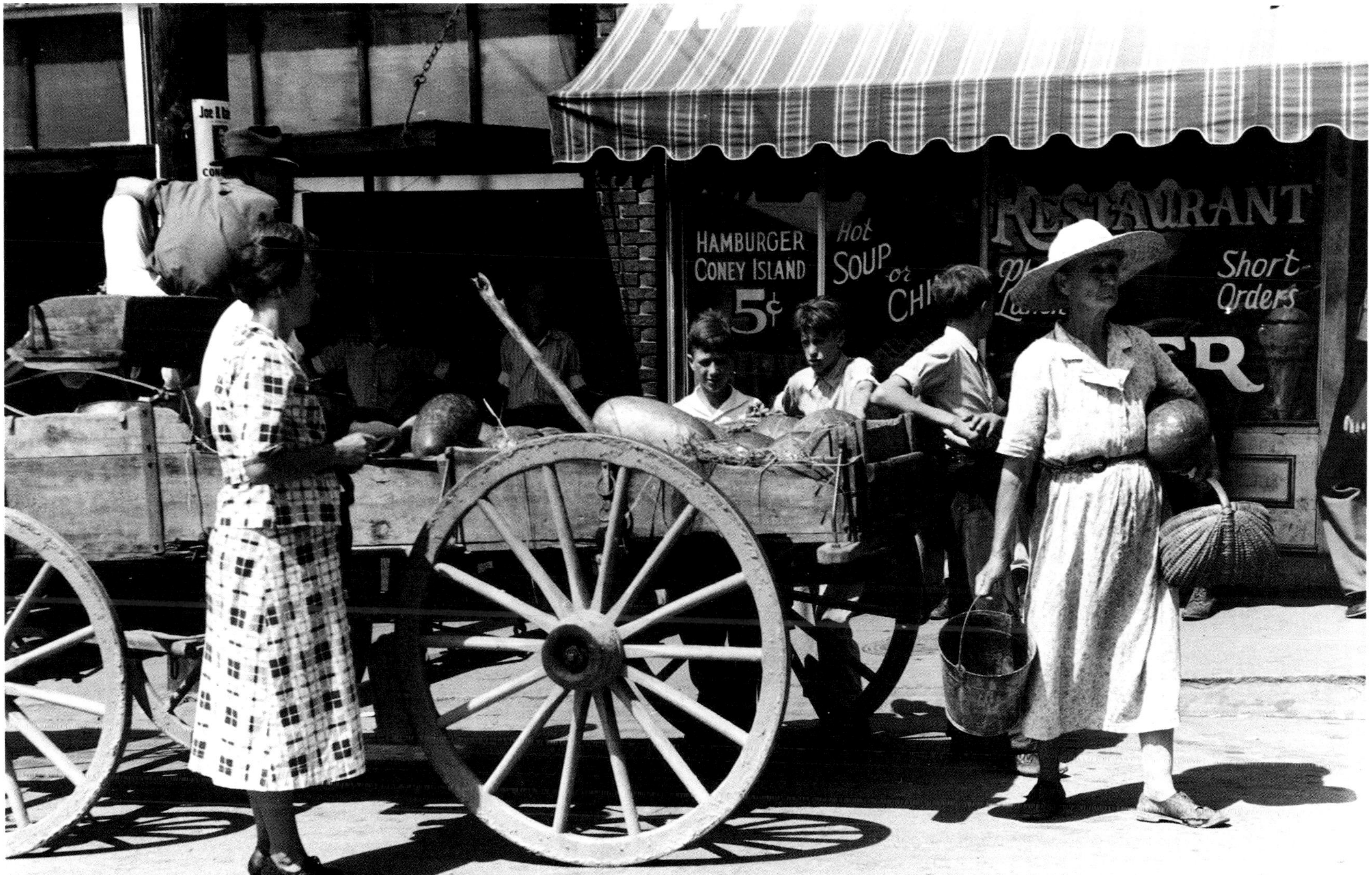
HAMBURGER
CONEY ISLAND
5¢
Hot
SOUP
Short
Orders

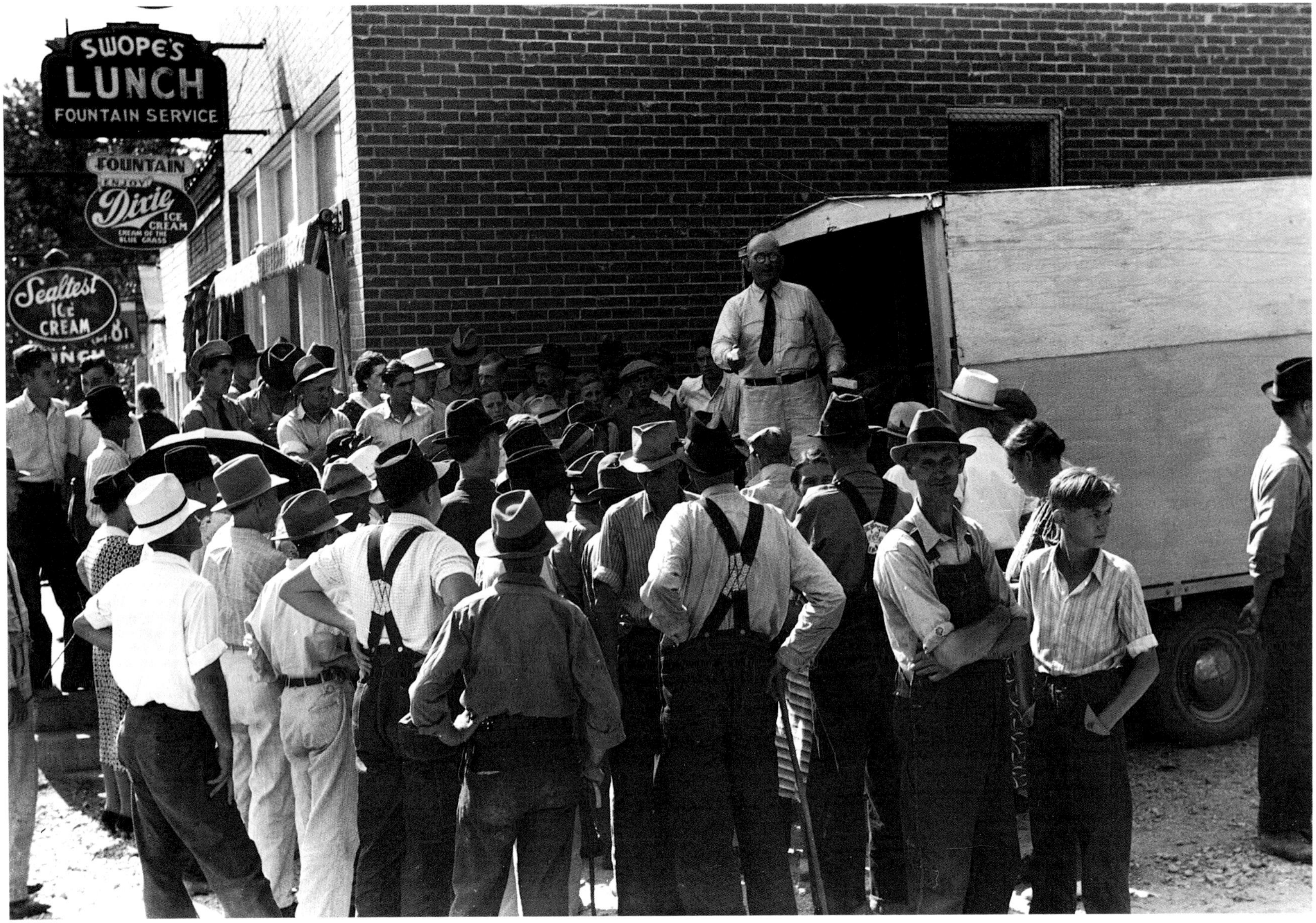

An itinerant salesman harangues farmers gathered in town on court day. Campton, September 1940. MARION POST WOLCOTT.

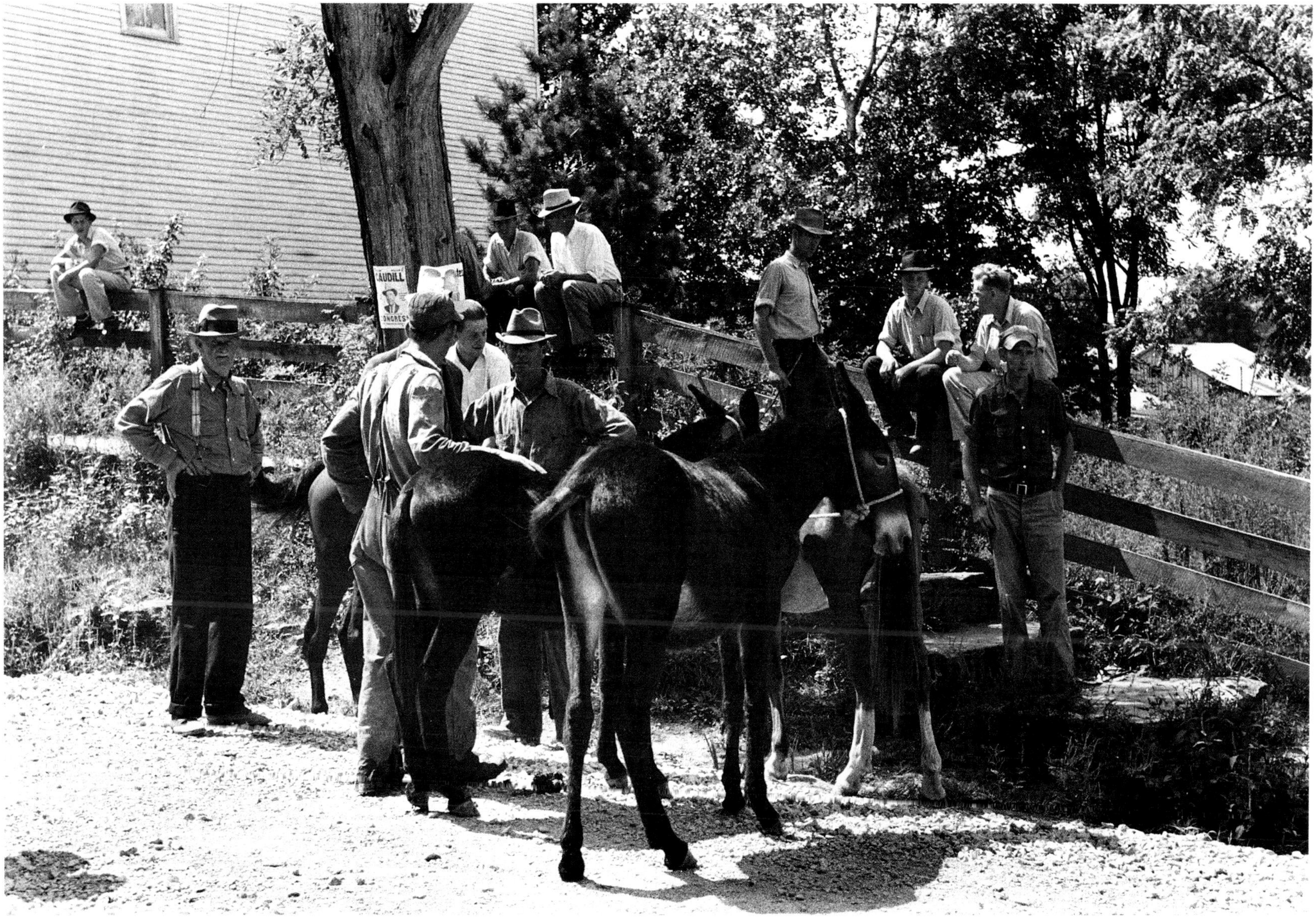

Mules and horses are traded on jockey day. Campton, September 1940. MARION POST WOLCOTT.

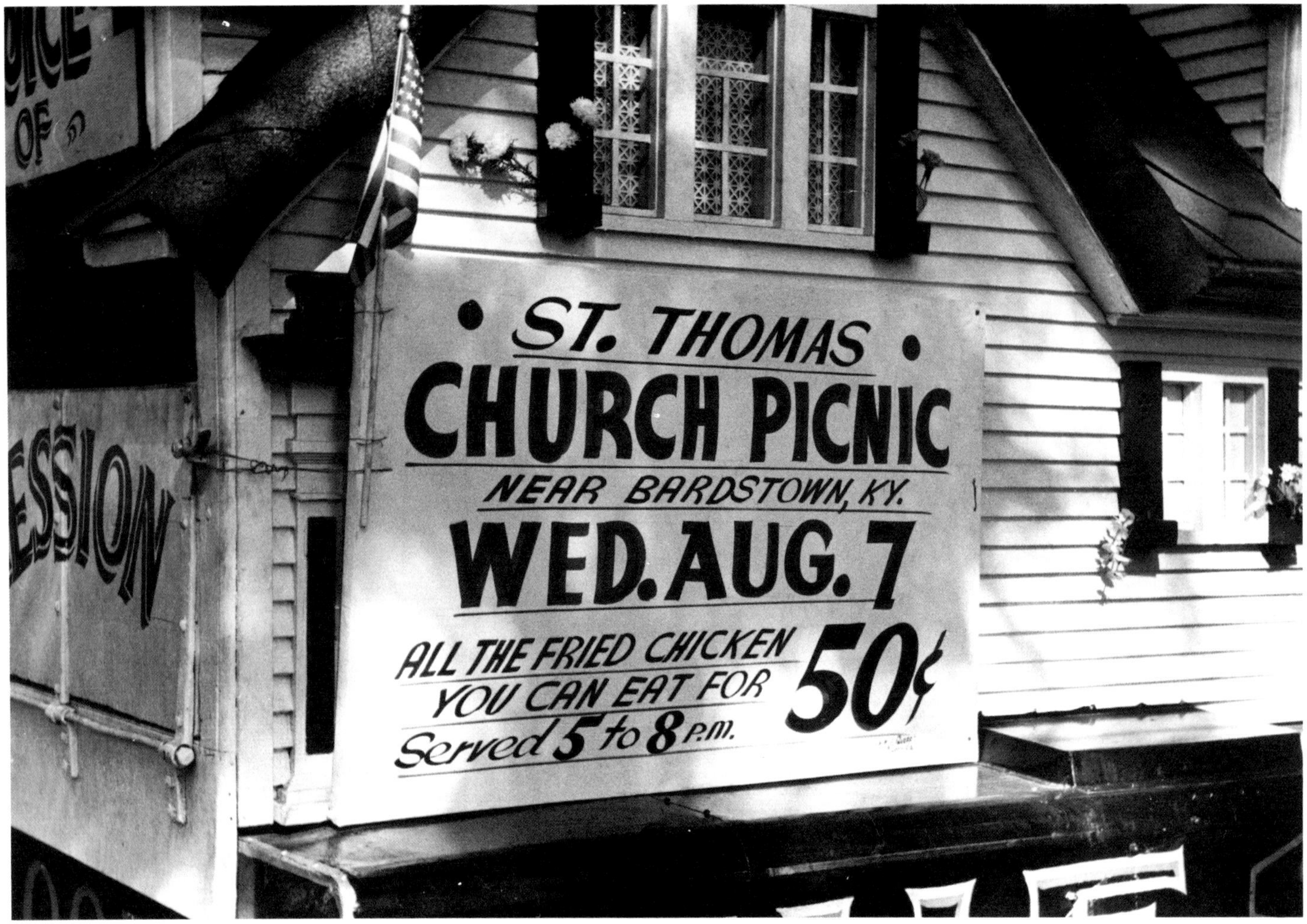

All you can eat. August 1940. MARION POST WOLCOTT.

Opposite: Peeling and slicing tomatoes for the church benefit supper. MARION POST WOLCOTT.

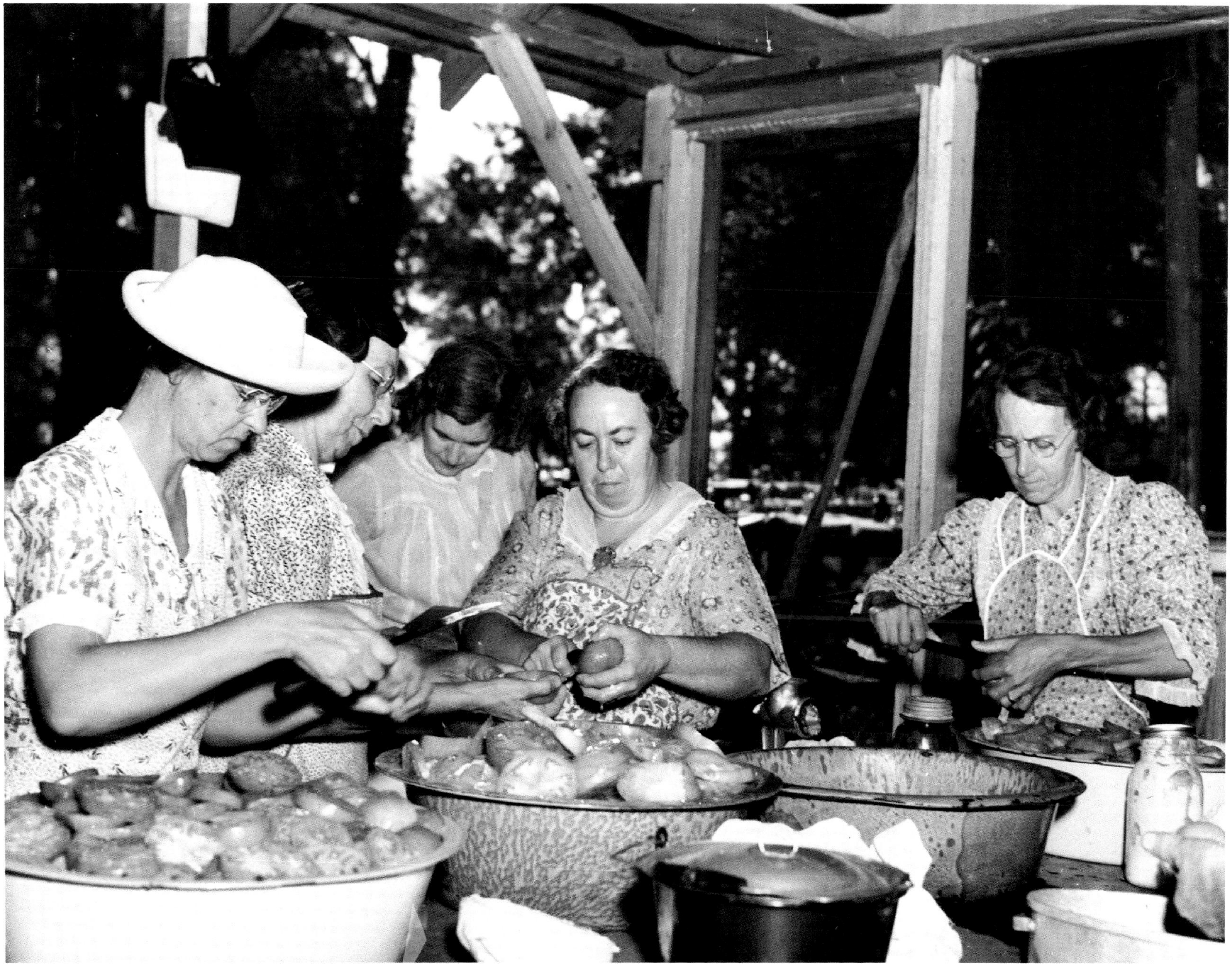

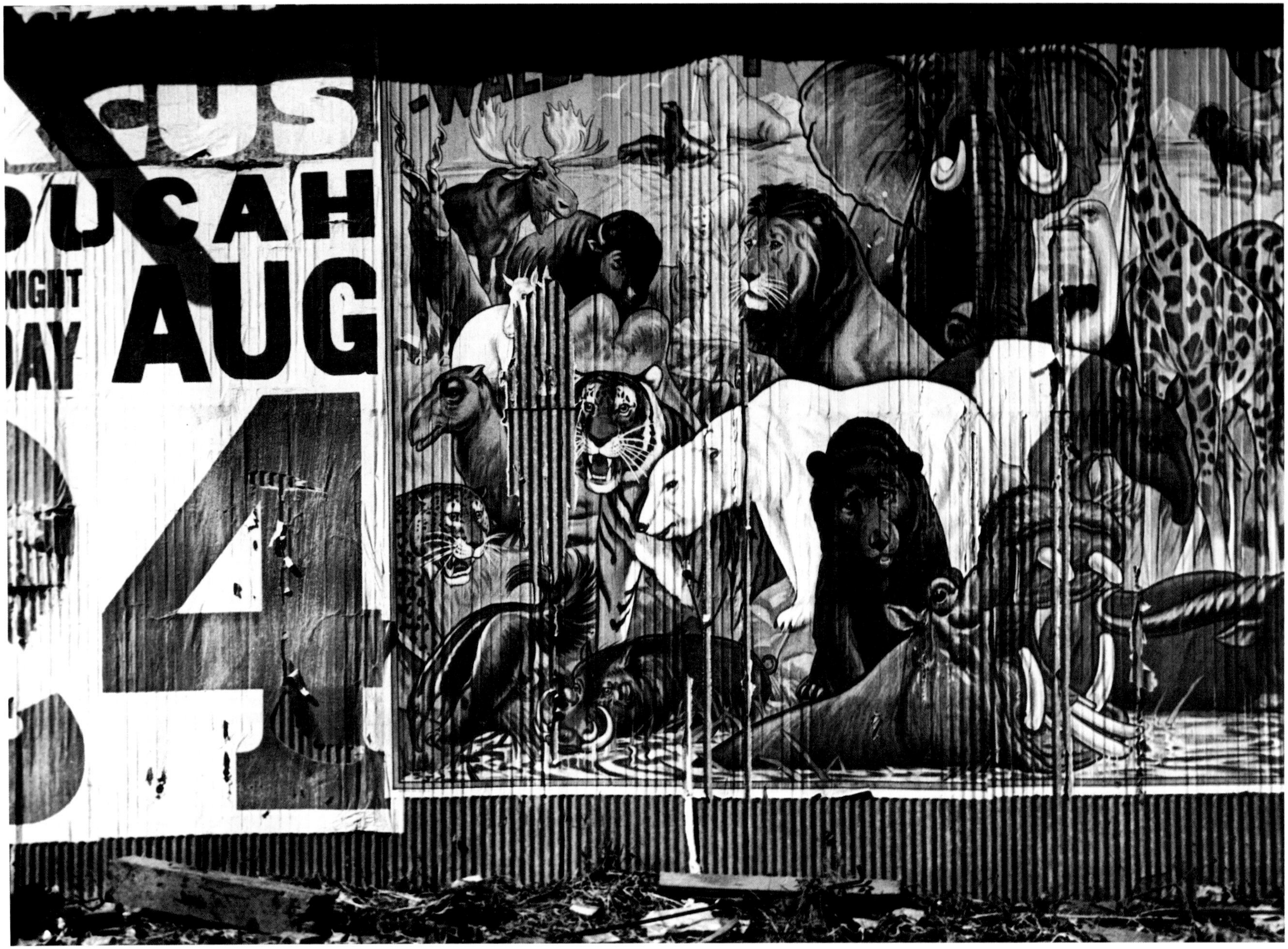
CUS
UCAH
NIGHT
AY
AUG
4

Opposite: Circus poster. Smithland, September 1935. BEN SHAHN.

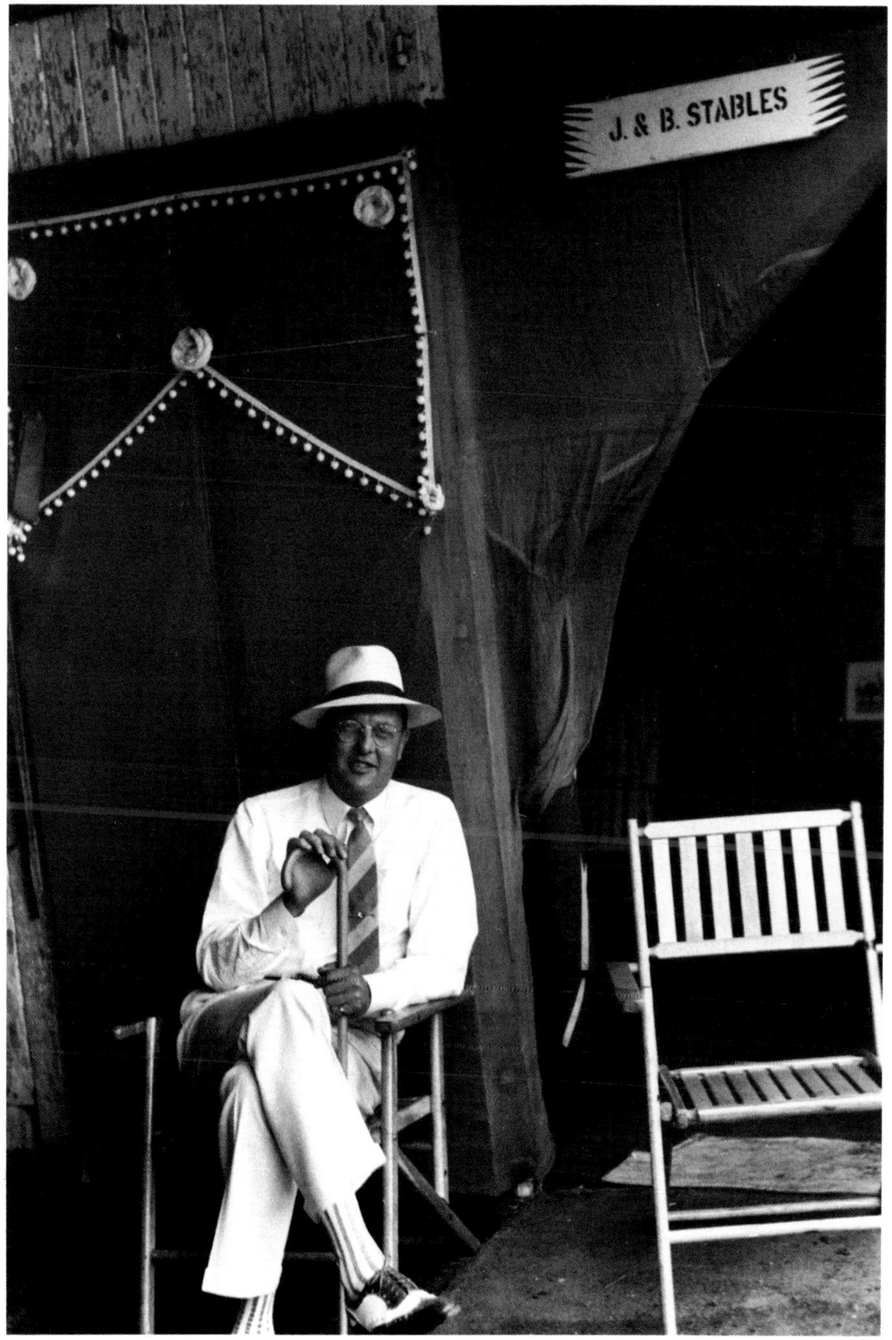

A horse owner from Louisville relaxes at the Shelby County Horse Show and Fair, Shelbyville, August 1940. MARION POST WOLCOTT.

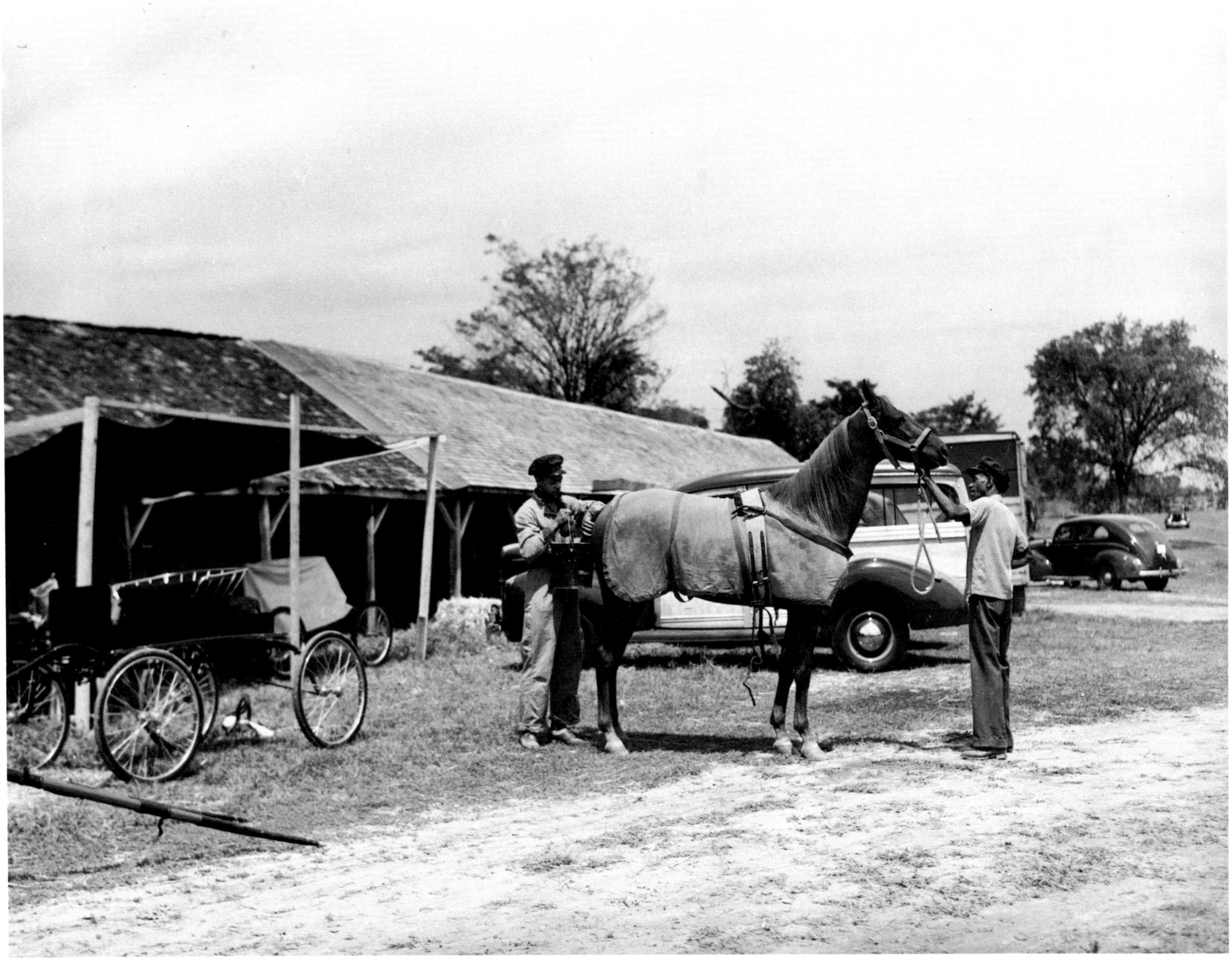

Grooming a horse for entry at the fair. Shelbyville, August 1940. MARION POST WOLCOTT.

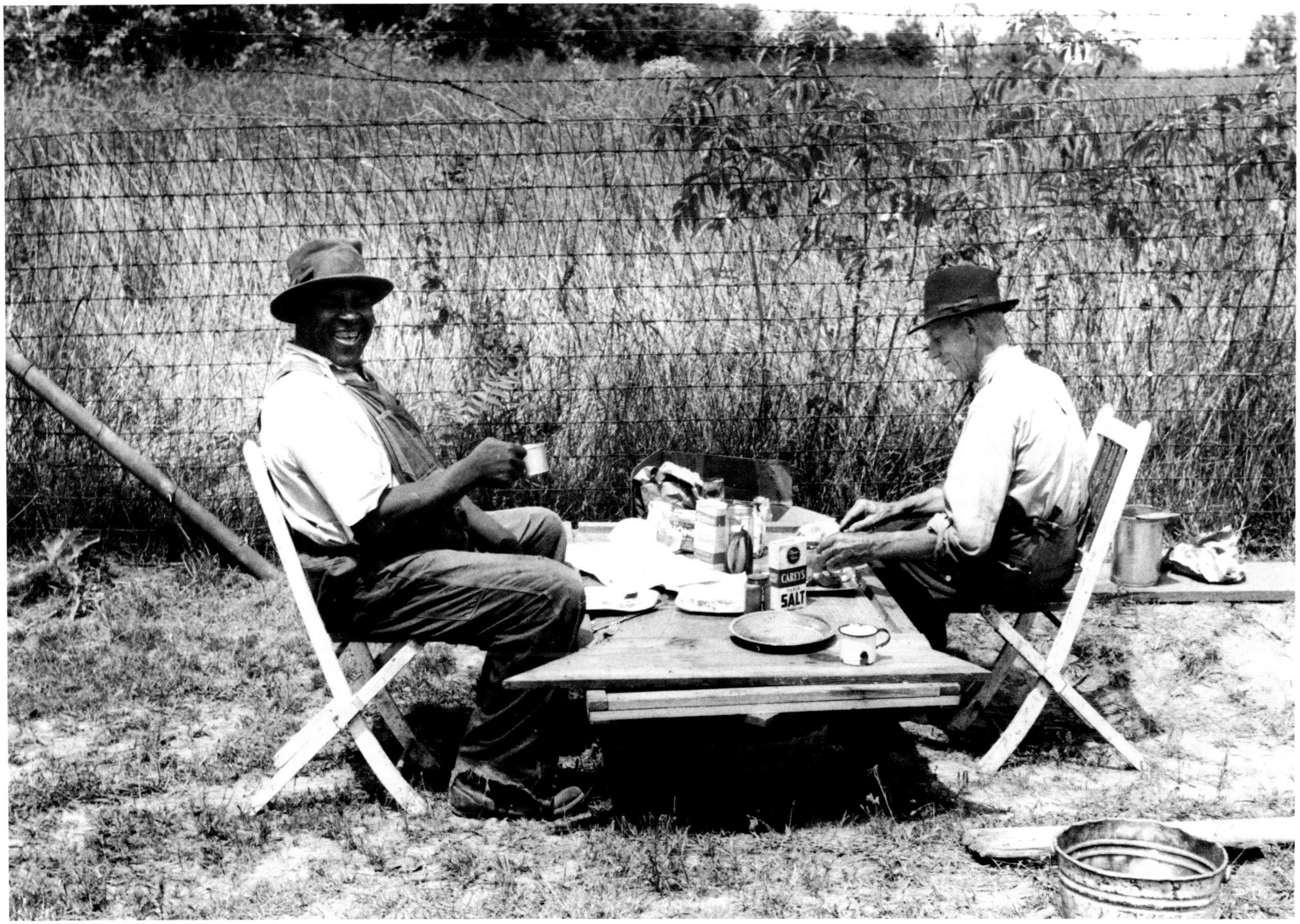

Luncheon on the fairgrounds for a trainer and a stable hand. Marion Post Wolcott.

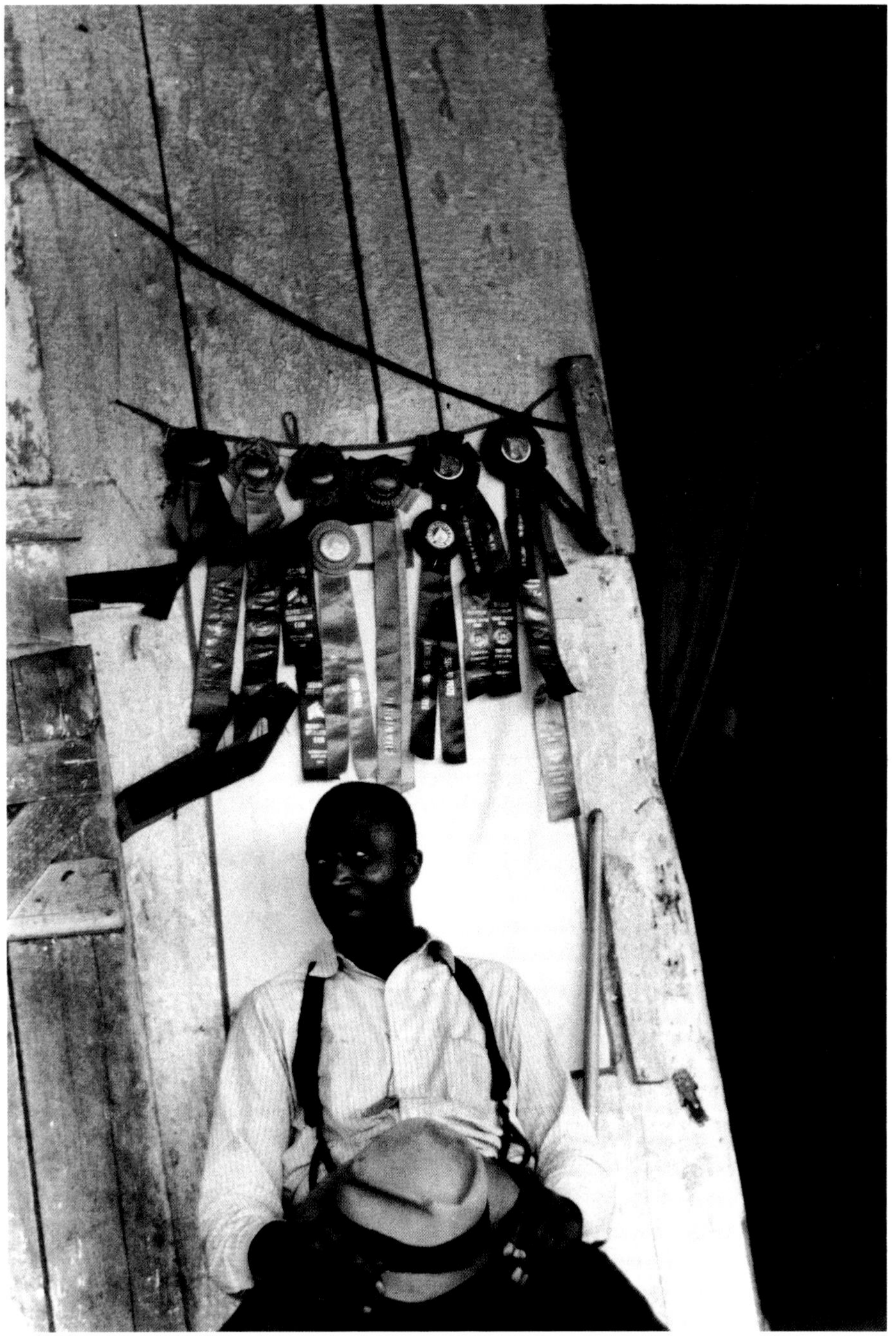

A trainer displays winning ribbons at the fair. MARION POST WOLCOTT.

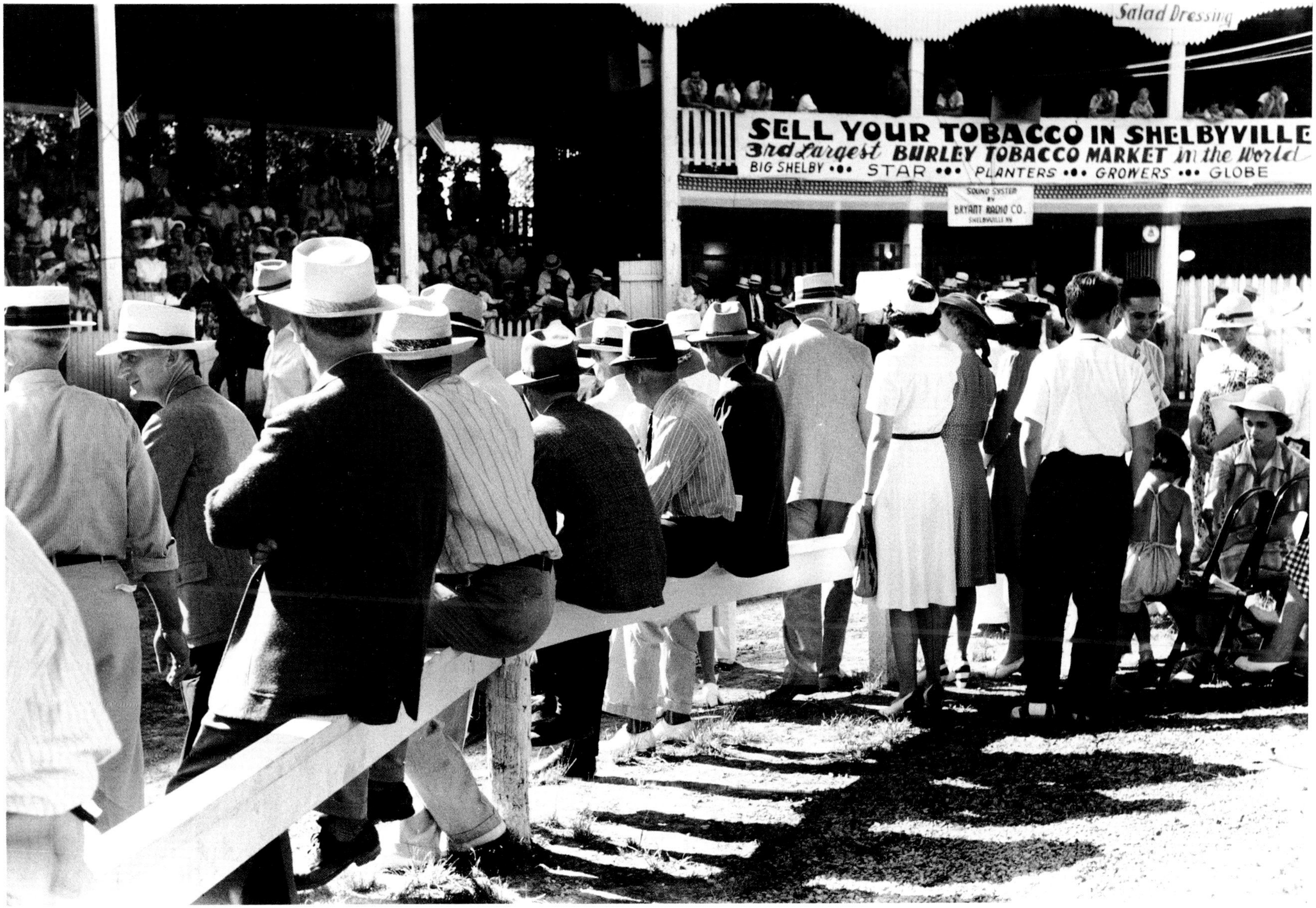

Watching the race from the inner circle. MARION POST WOLCOTT.

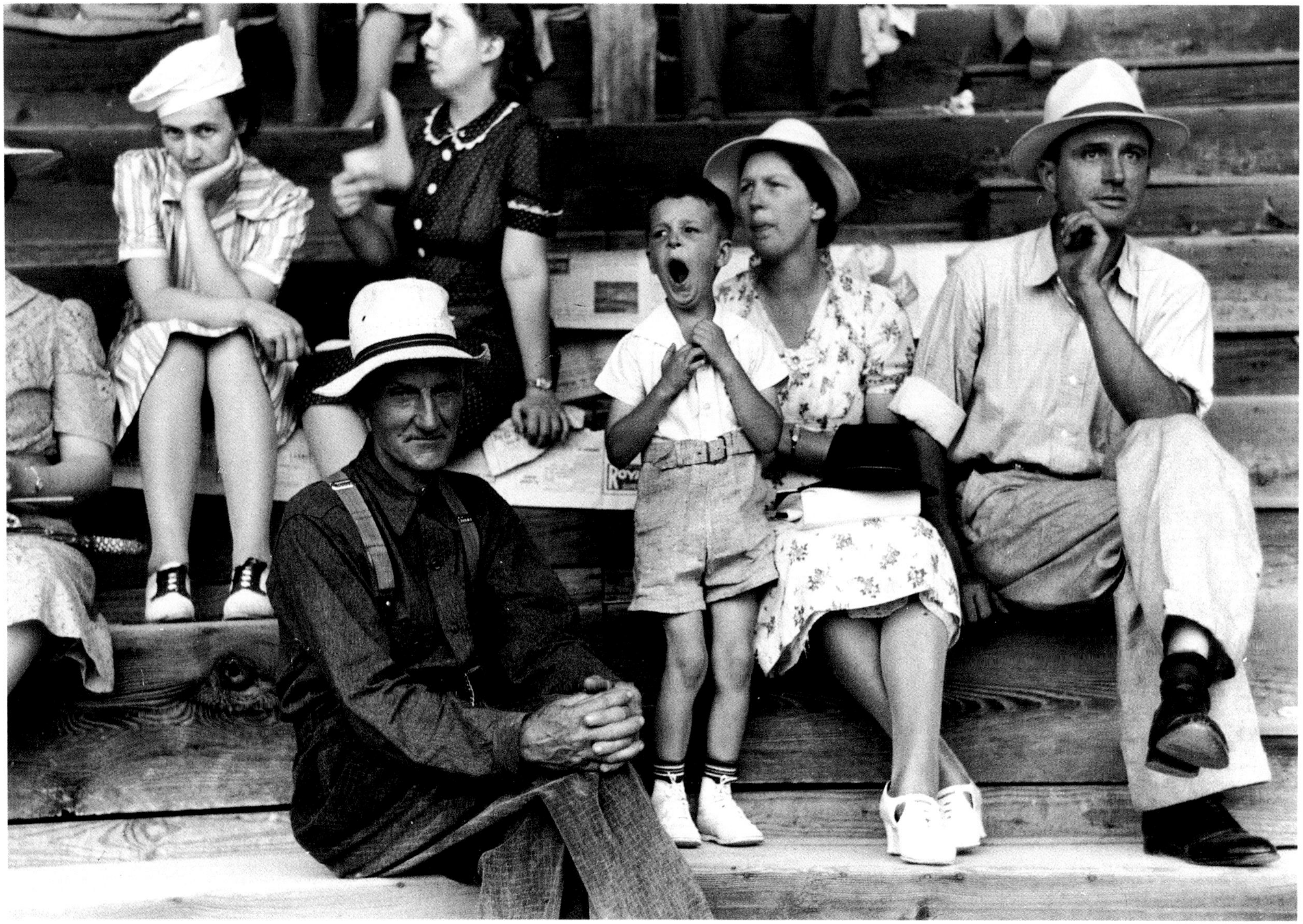

Spectators at the fair. Shelbyville, August 1940. Marion Post Wolcott.

Opposite: A sulky race, run clockwise. Mercer County, August 1940. Marion Post Wolcott.

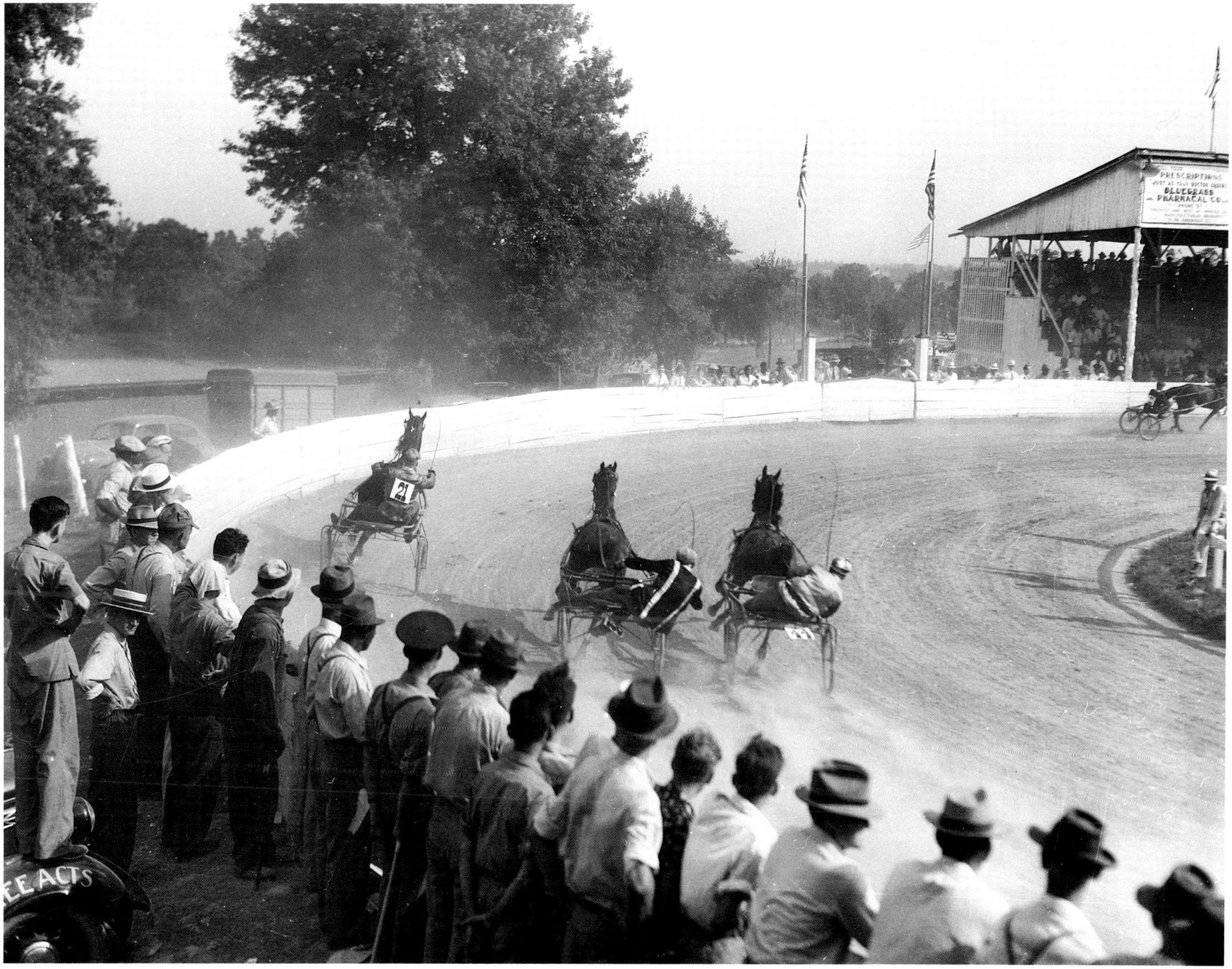
PRESCRIPTIONS
BLUEGRASS
PHARMACAL CO.
21

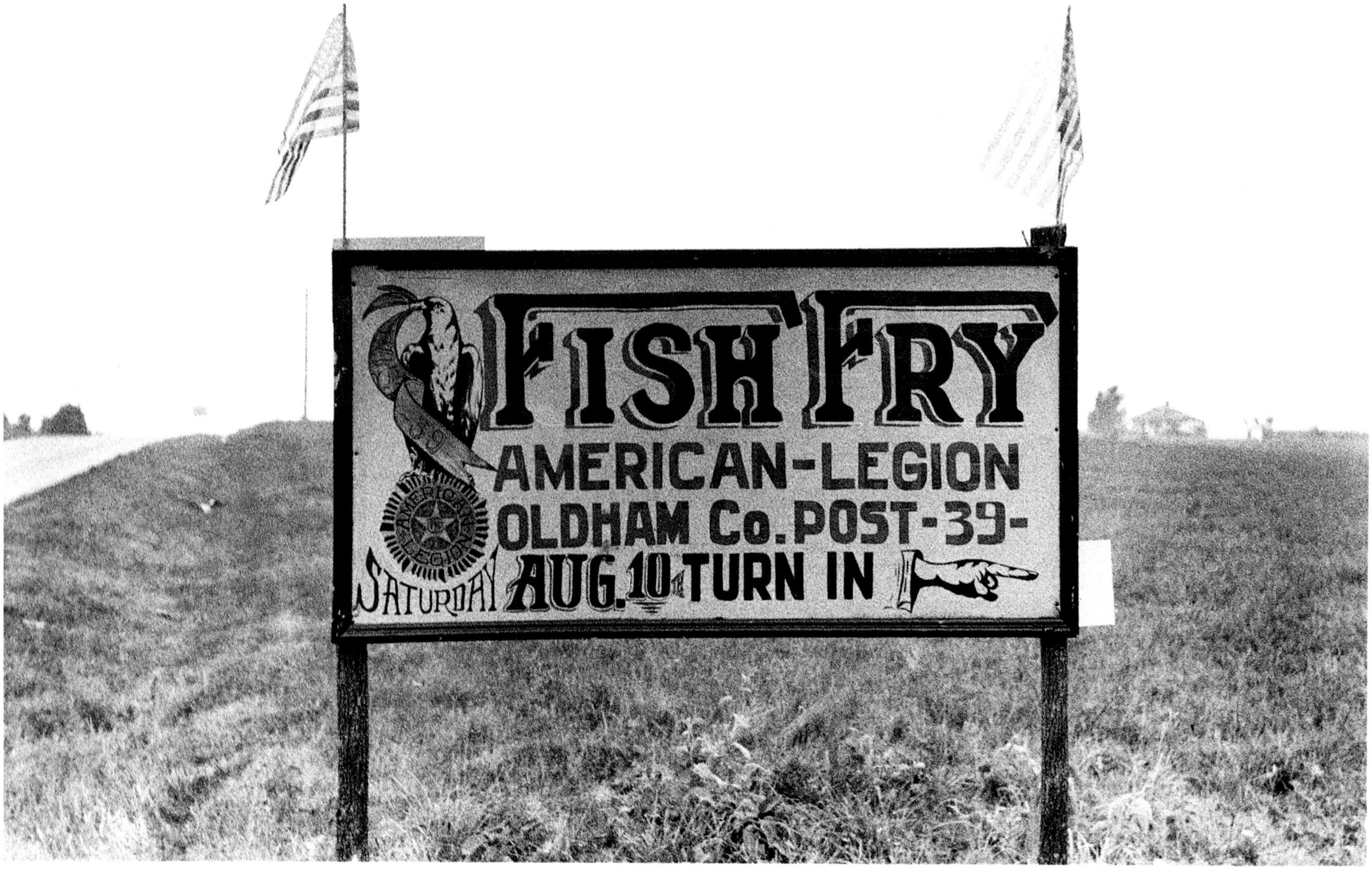

A sign directing the way to a fish fry. August 1940. MARION POST WOLCOTT.

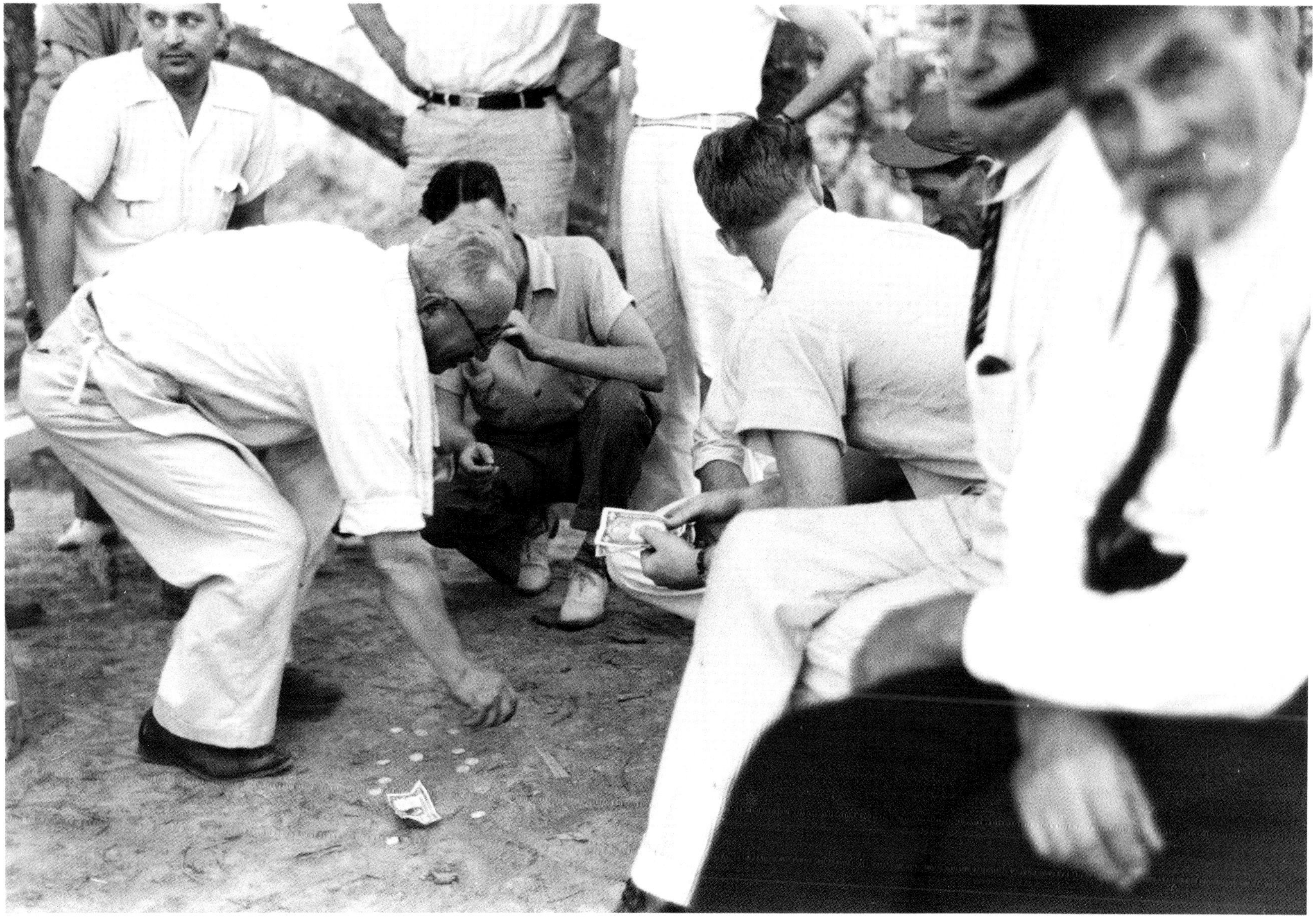

Shooting craps, a popular pastime at the American Legion fish fry. MARION POST WOLCOTT.

Loafing in front of the store.
Irvington, May 1938. RUSSELL LEE.

Cities and Towns

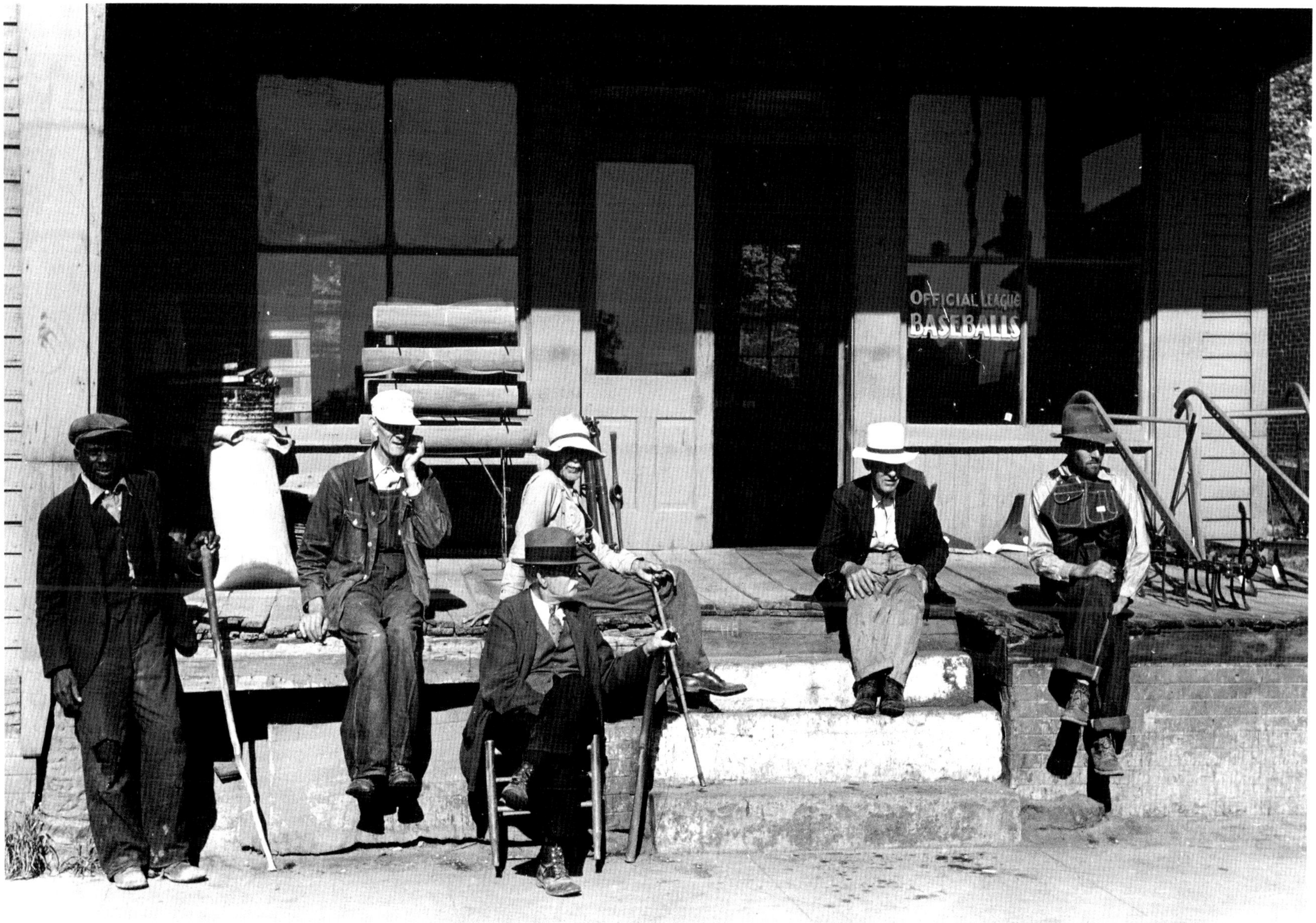

ONE OF Roy Stryker's primary interests in the FSA photographic survey was in documenting the American small town. He described the small town as "the cross-roads where the land meets the city, where the farm meets commerce and industry. It is the contact point where men of the land keep in touch with a civilization based on mass-produced, city-made gadgets, machines, canned movies and canned beef. Inevitably any attempted coverage of our Farm population must include the Farmers' place-of-exchange, an exchange of produce for cash, for manufactured goods, an exchange of gossip and ideas."

Because of the importance Stryker placed on this subject, every FSA photographer carried a permanent small-town "shooting script"—in mind, if not in the pocket. Stryker's shooting scripts included structures as diverse as ice cream parlors and funeral parlors and especially such "gathering places" as theaters, restaurants, and garages. Also on his list were such familar objects as fire hydrants, sprinkler wagons, signs, and menus. Human subjects were to include the people of the town going about their work or just loafing and visiting with neighbors over the back fence.

Stryker's hopes for a complete documentation of small-town America were never fully realized, but some of the most interesting FSA photographs of Kentucky were taken in the state's smaller cities and towns, often while the photographers were passing through en route to assignments elsewhere. Although their pictures may suggest tourist-type shots because of shortness of time and lack of contact with the residents, they give a hint of the character of these places.

The FSA photographers' trips to Kentucky's larger urban centers often came about because of work they were doing for other government agencies, such as the Public Health Service. Few of the urban photographs show signs of the dramatic economic and social paralysis that was part of the Great Depression and that caused such deep changes in both urban and rural areas. Nor do they reveal the massive rural-to-urban shift in population taking place during the 1930s and early 1940s. What they show is people going about their daily business, telling us that in some places, life and work went on as usual.

A comparison of the small-town and urban scenes is suggestive. In smaller places we see largely intimate scenes —people stopping on the street to chat or loafing in front of the store—while in the cities individuals tend to become anonymous members of crowds and to be overshadowed by buildings and signs. Because so many Kentuckians now live in urban rather than rural environments (a majority since 1970) and develop friendships with neighbors and co-workers rather than with an extended family, these images speak to us in an important way. They show us our urban cultural heritage in the same way that our family albums show us our family heritage.

Opposite: Walking to market. Jackson, September 1940. MARION POST WOLCOTT.

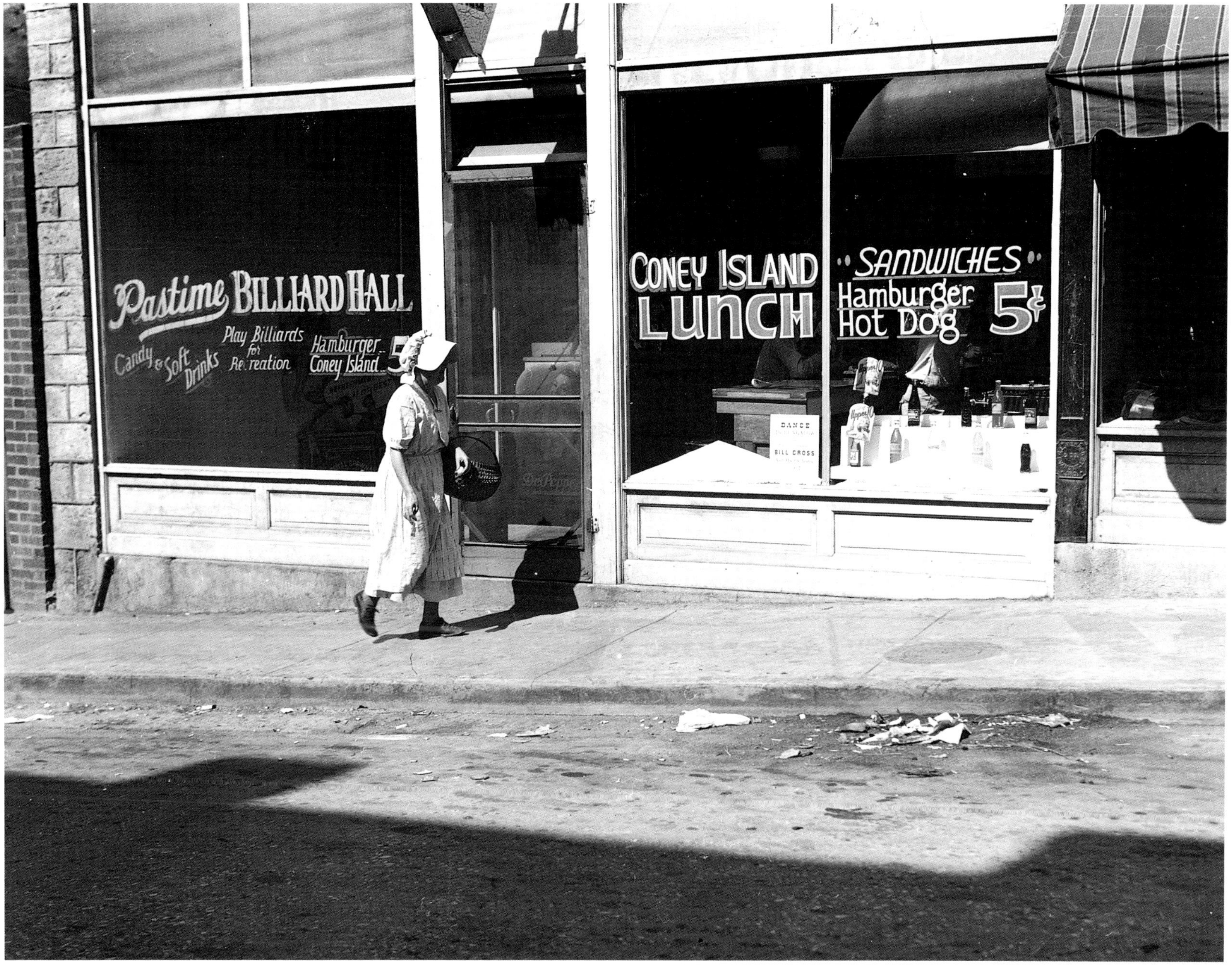
Pastime BILLIARD HALL
Candy & Soft Drinks
Play Billiards for Recreation
Hamburger
Coney Island
CONEY ISLAND LUNCH
SANDWICHES
Hamburger
Hot Dog
5¢
DANCE
BILL CROSS
Dr Pepper

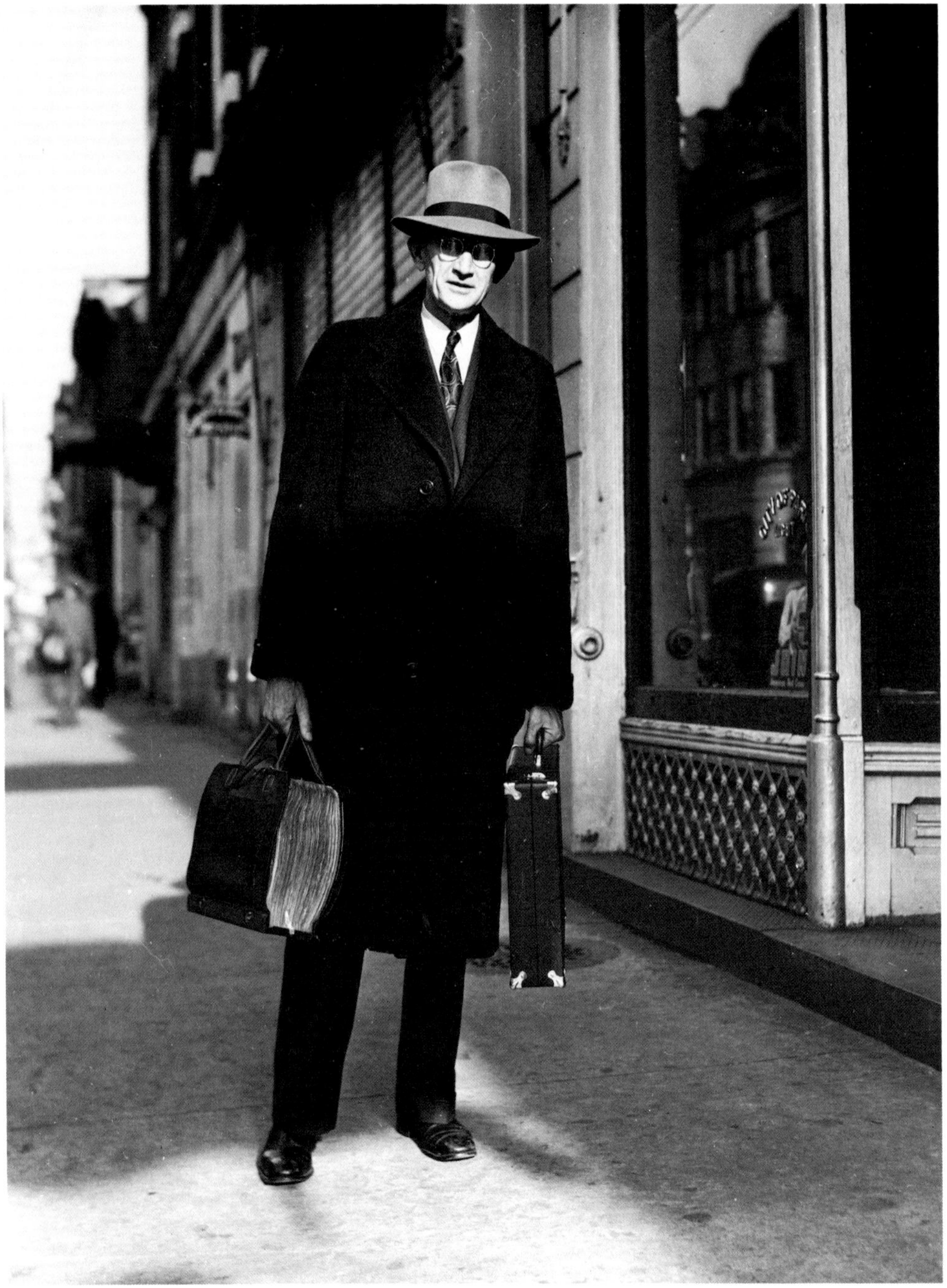

A traveling salesman. Paris, November 1940. JOHN VACHON.

Opposite: Street scene, Middlesboro. October 1935. BEN SHAHN.

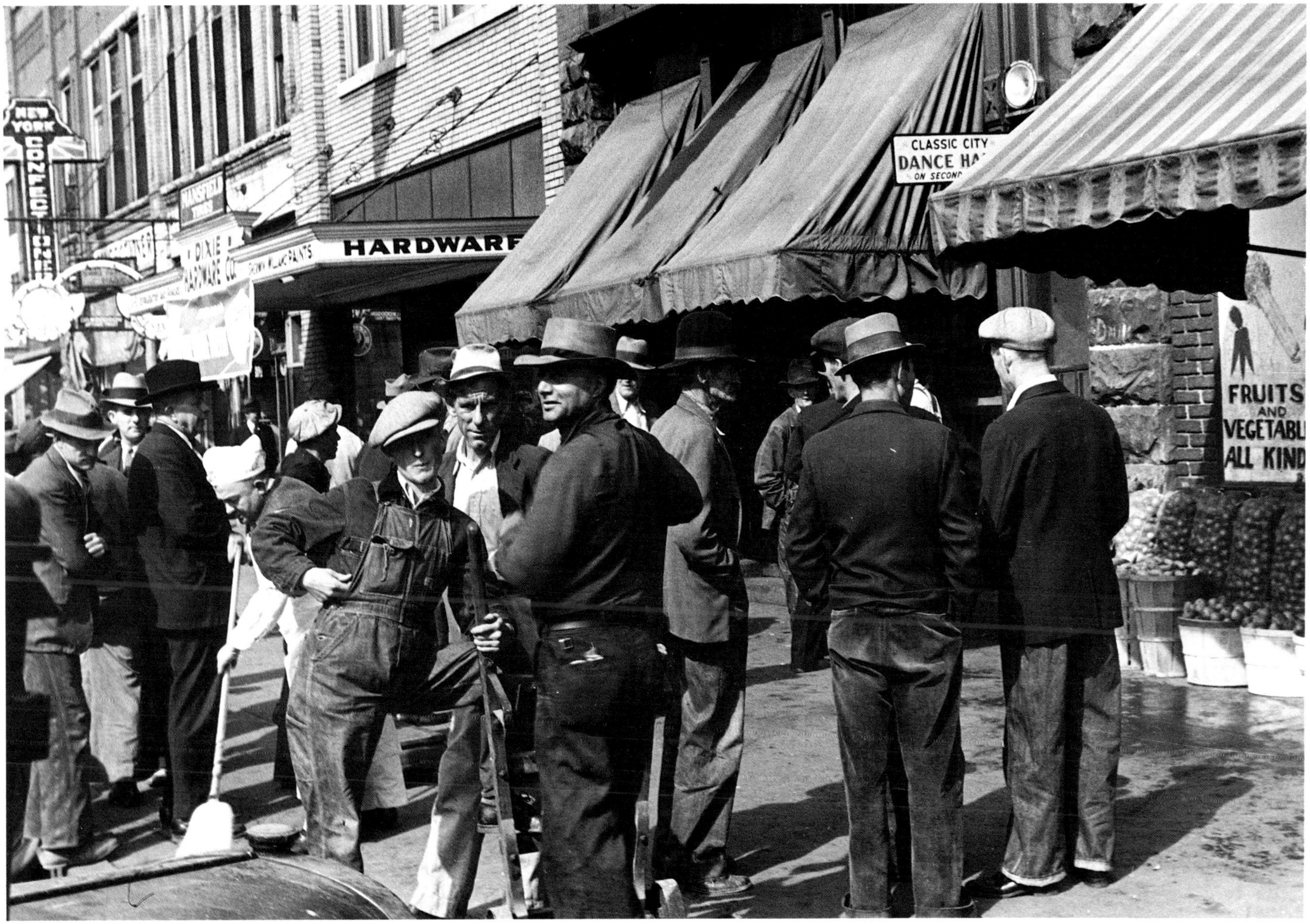
NEW YORK
CONFECT
DIXIE HARDWARE CO.
MANSFIELD
HARDWARE
CLASSIC CITY
DANCE HA
ON SECOND
FRUITS
AND
VEGETABL
ALL KIND

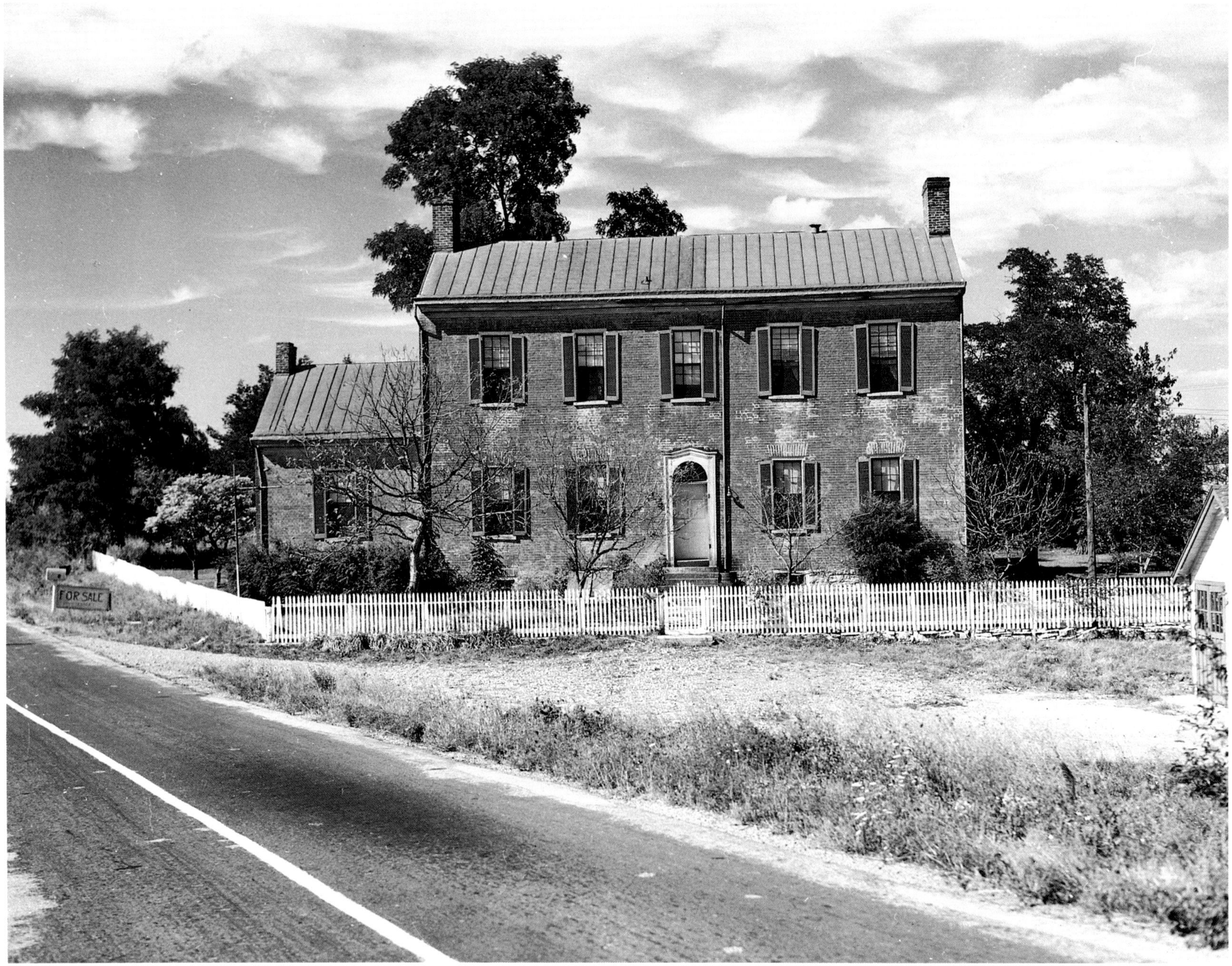
FOR SALE

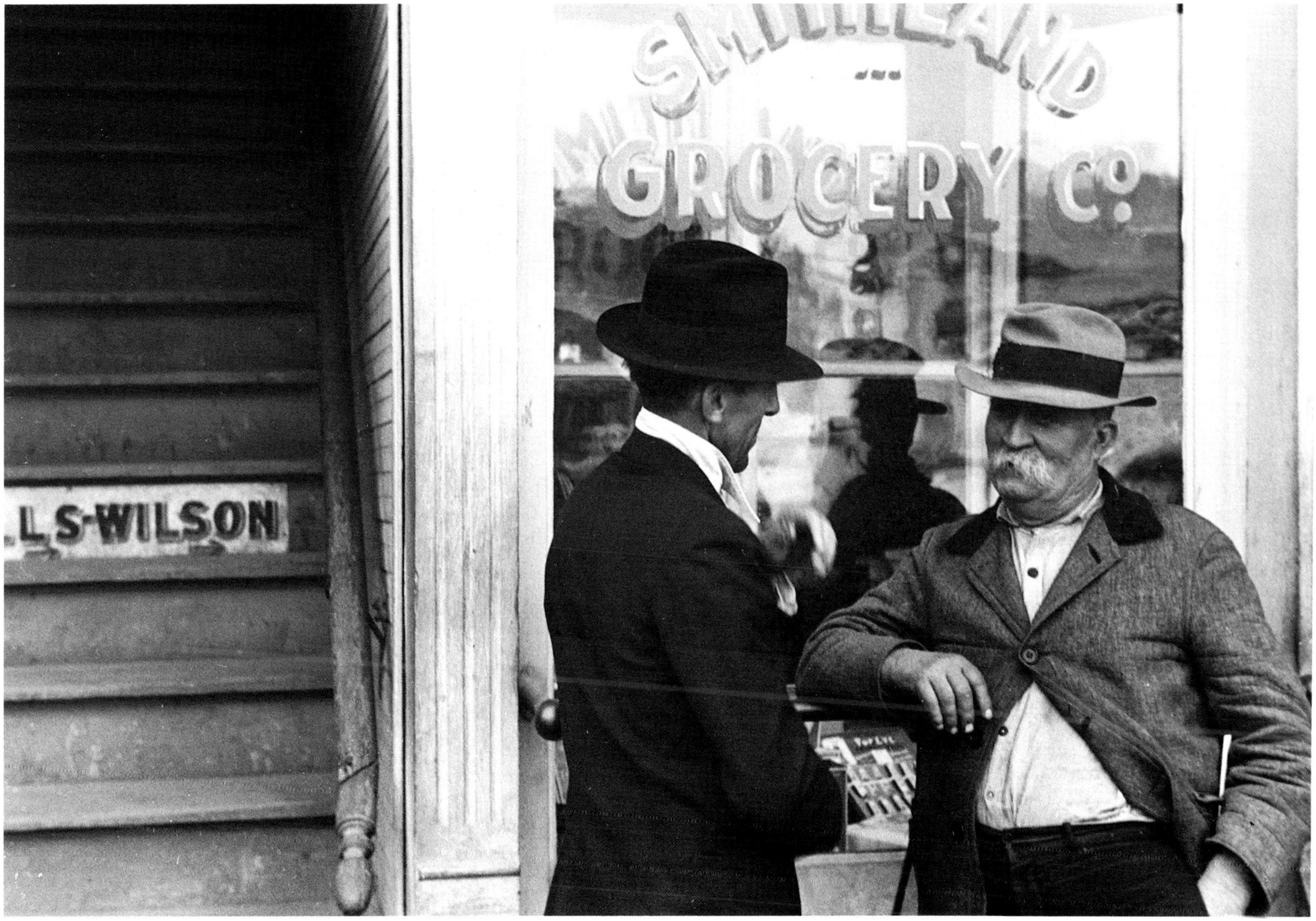

Outside the store. Smithland, October 1935. BEN SHAHN.

Opposite: A brick I-house offered for sale near Bardstown, August 1940. MARION POST WOLCOTT.

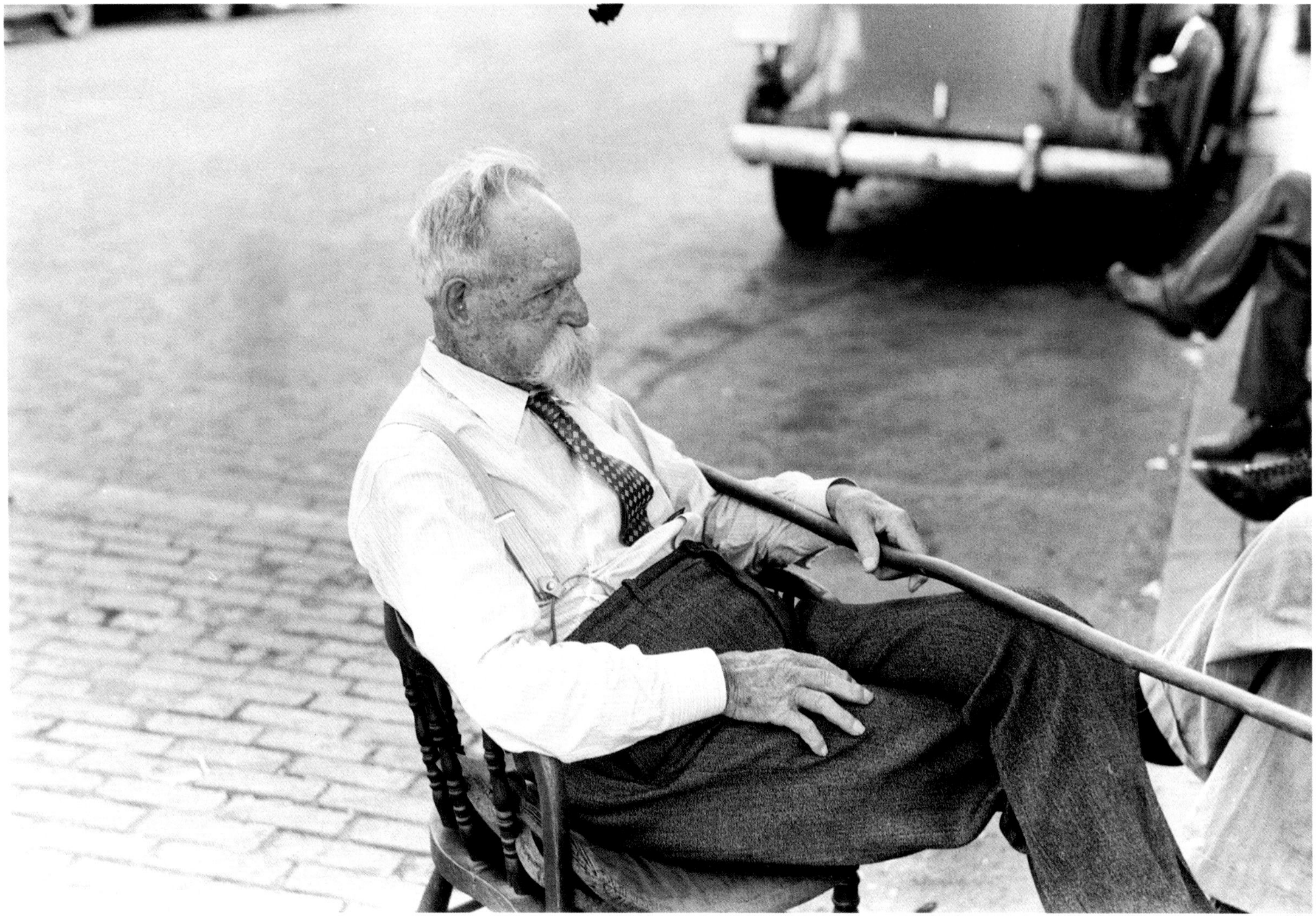

A "Kentucky Colonel" in front of the Woodford County Courthouse. Versailles, September 1940. MARION POST WOLCOTT.

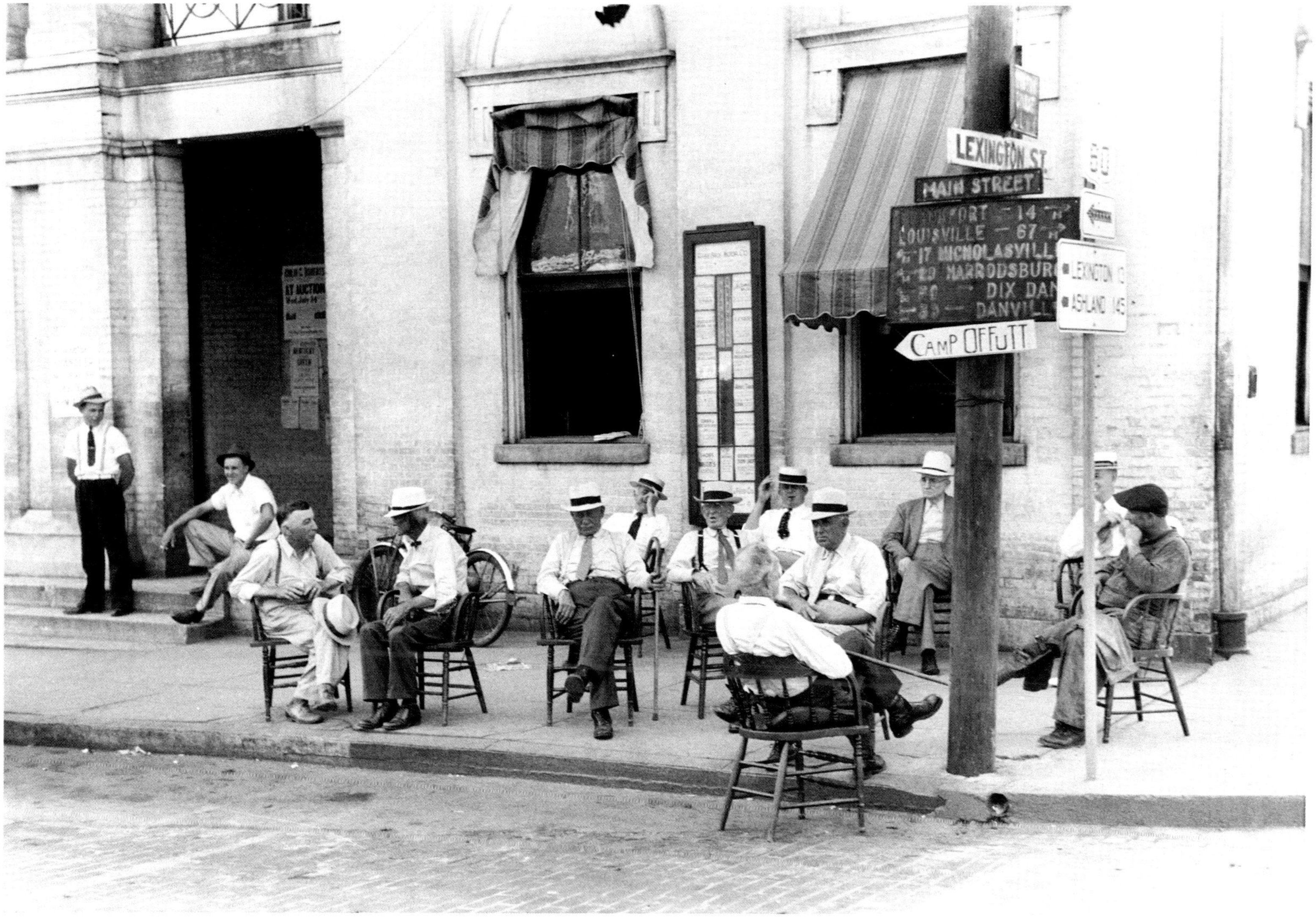

In front of the courthouse, Saturday afternoon. Versailles, September 1940. MARION POST WOLCOTT.

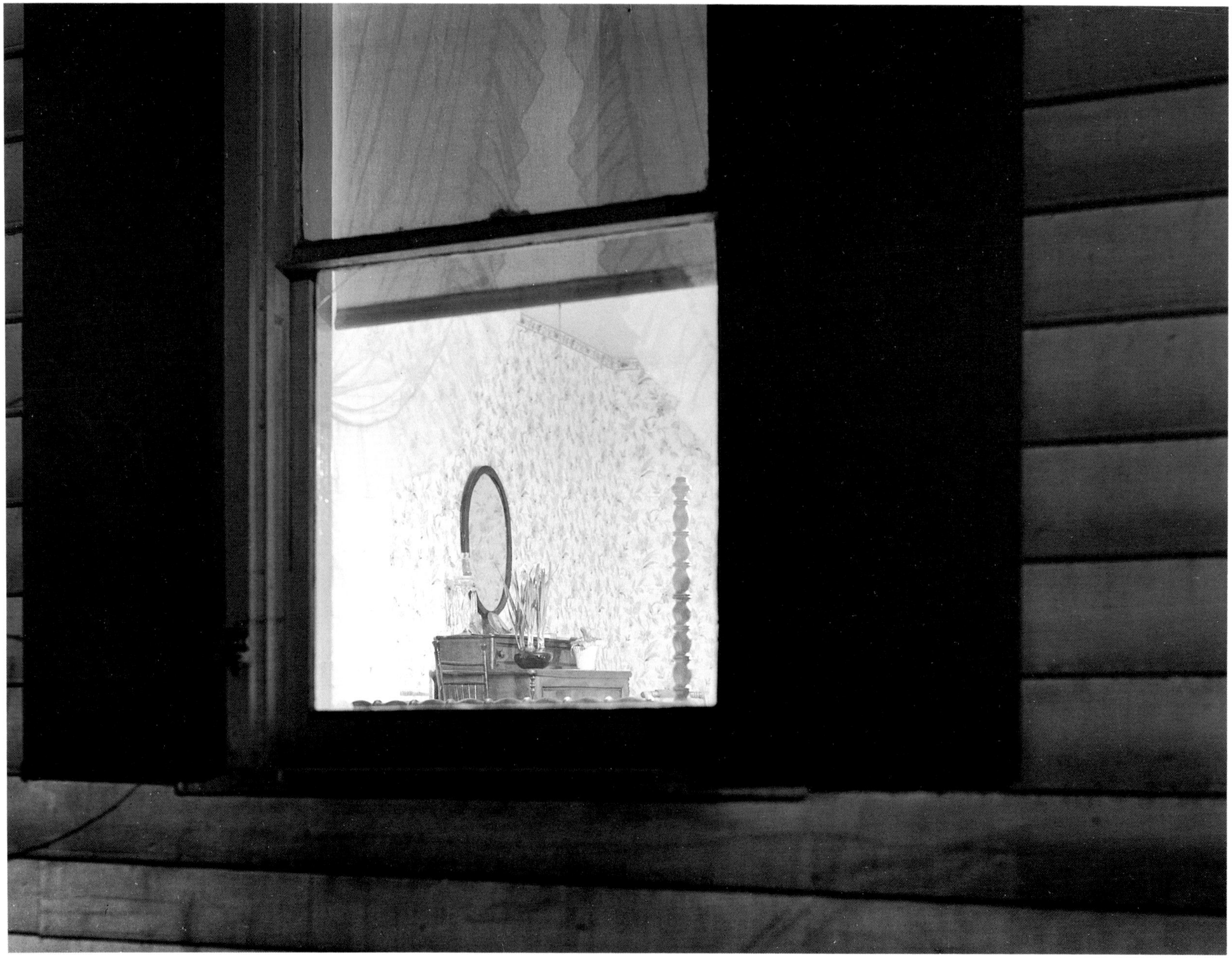

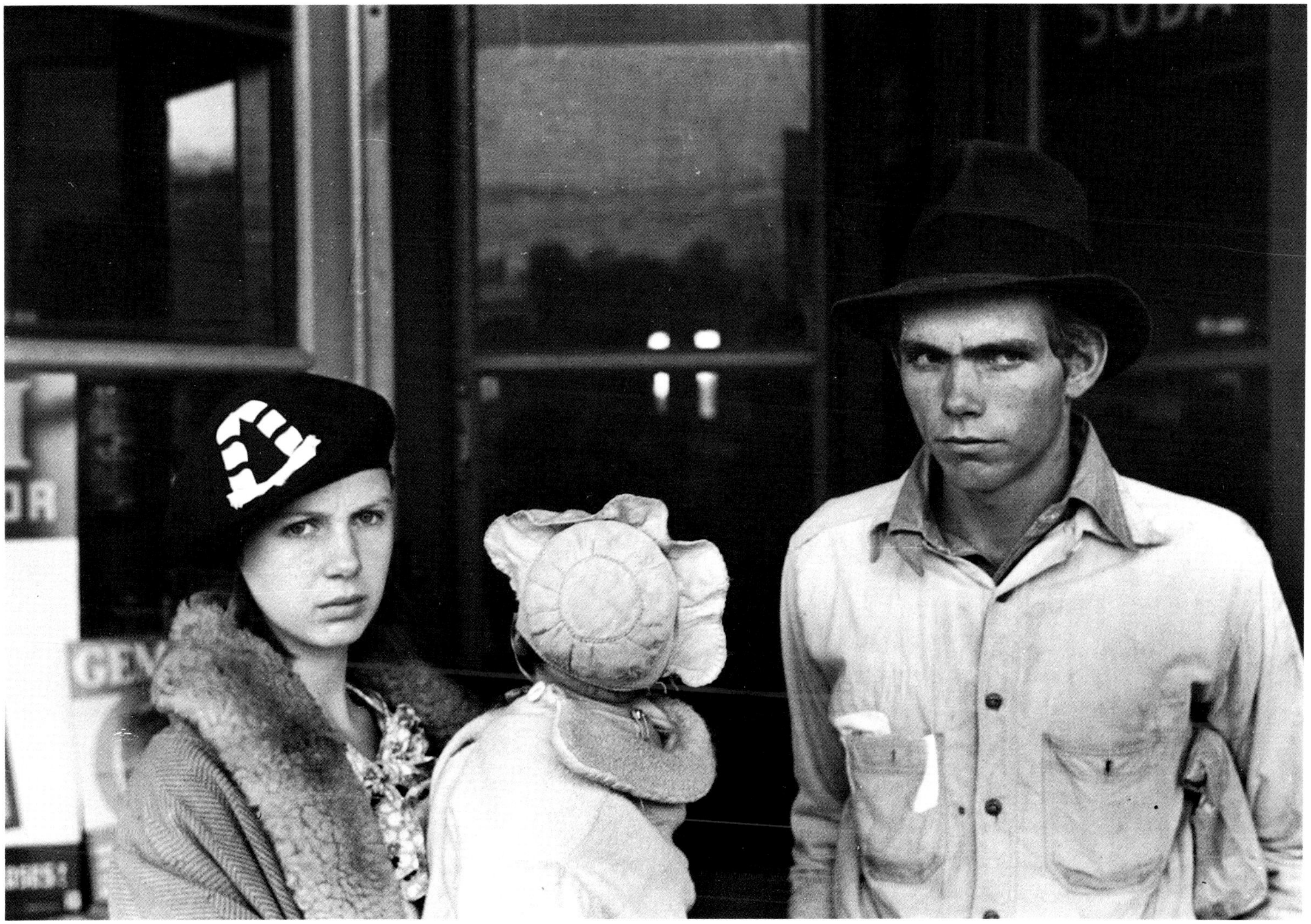

Man, woman, and child. Smithland, October 1935. BEN SHAHN.

Opposite: Scene through a window. Bardstown, November 1940. JOHN VACHON.

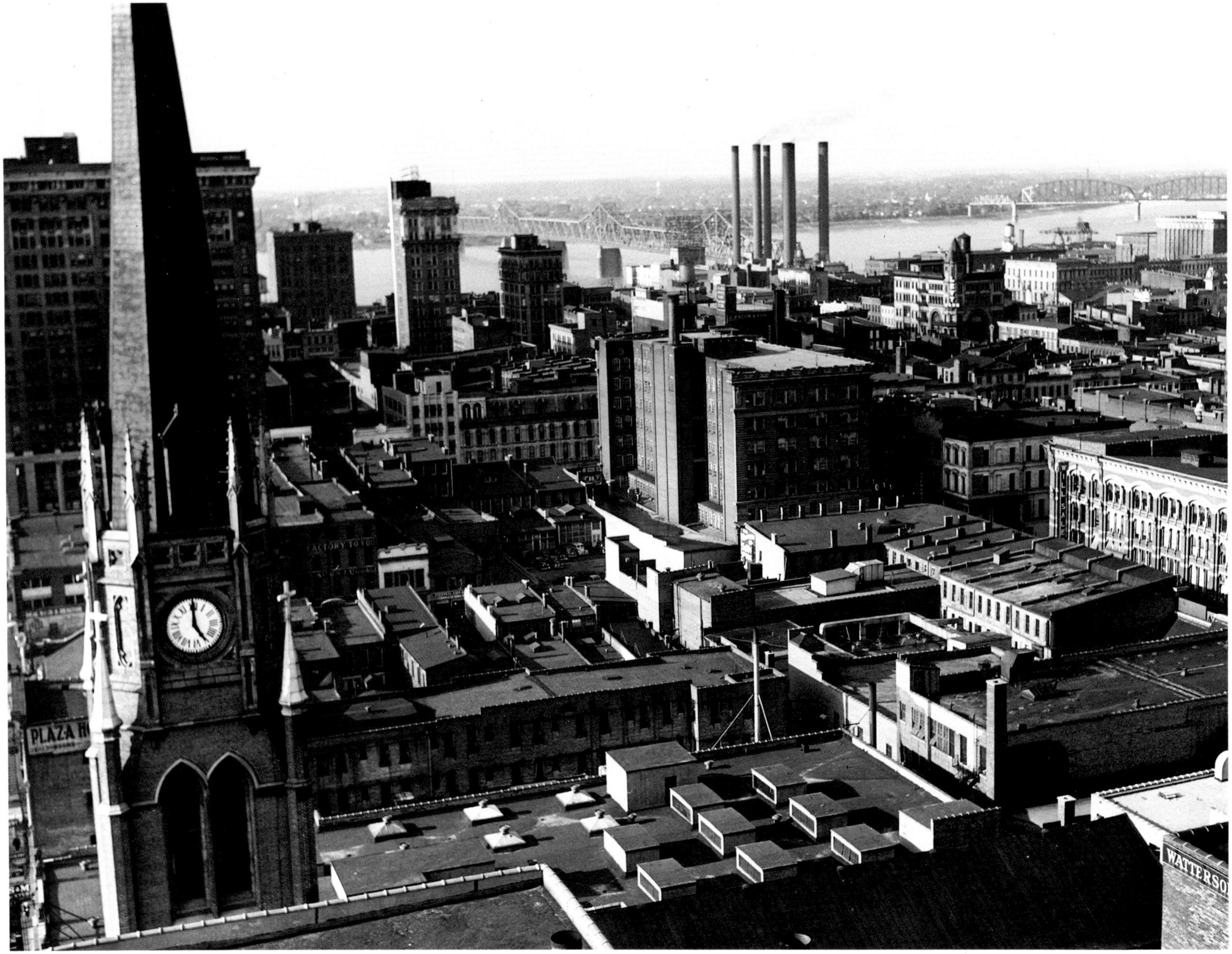

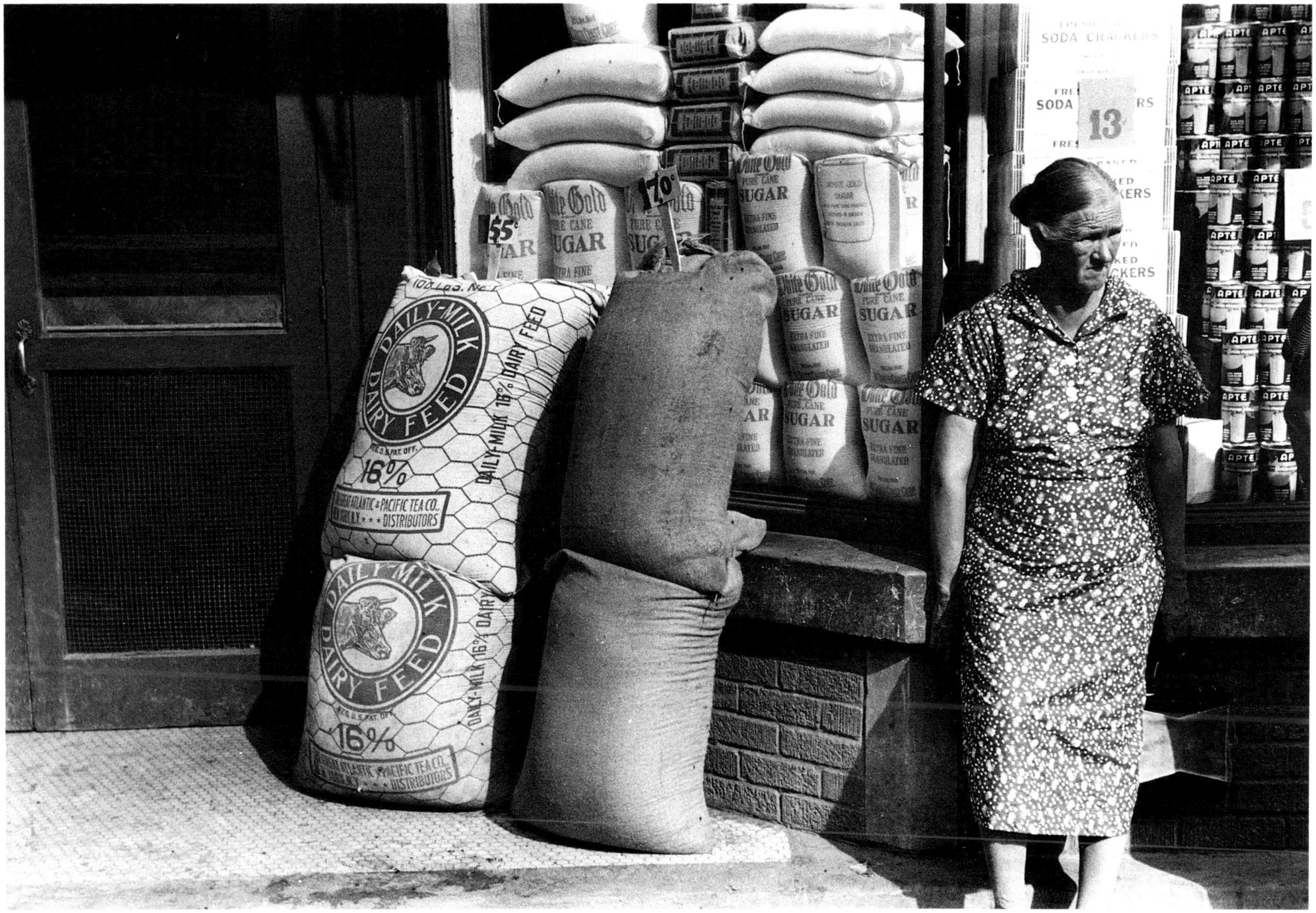

Outside the grocery store. Jackson, September 1940. Marion Post Wolcott.

Opposite: The Louisville business district with the Ohio River in the background. May 1940. Marion Post Wolcott.

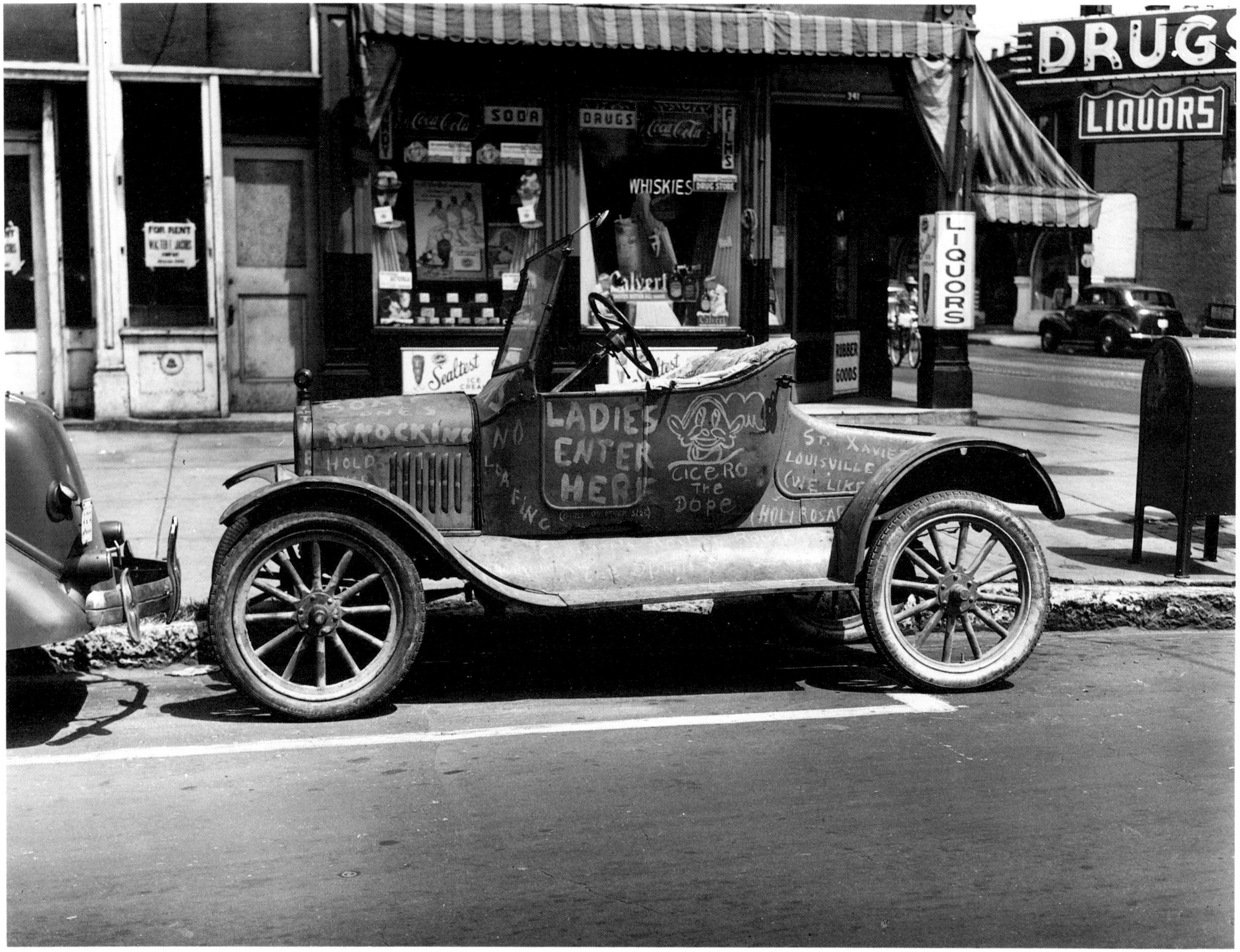

The Hepcats' jalopy. Louisville, August 1940. Marion Post Wolcott.

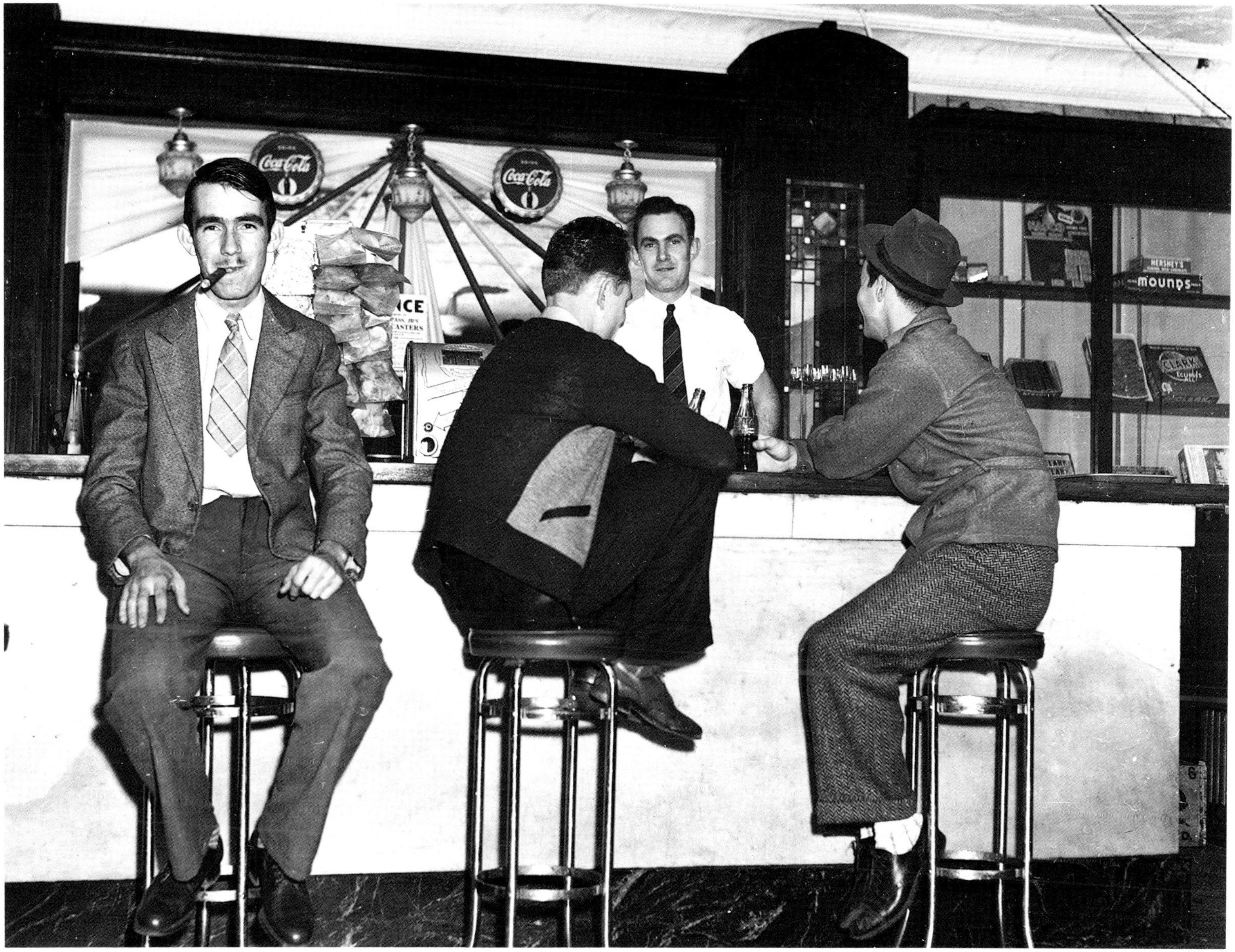

The "boys" at the soft drink parlor in a dry county. Central City, November 1940. JOHN VACHON.

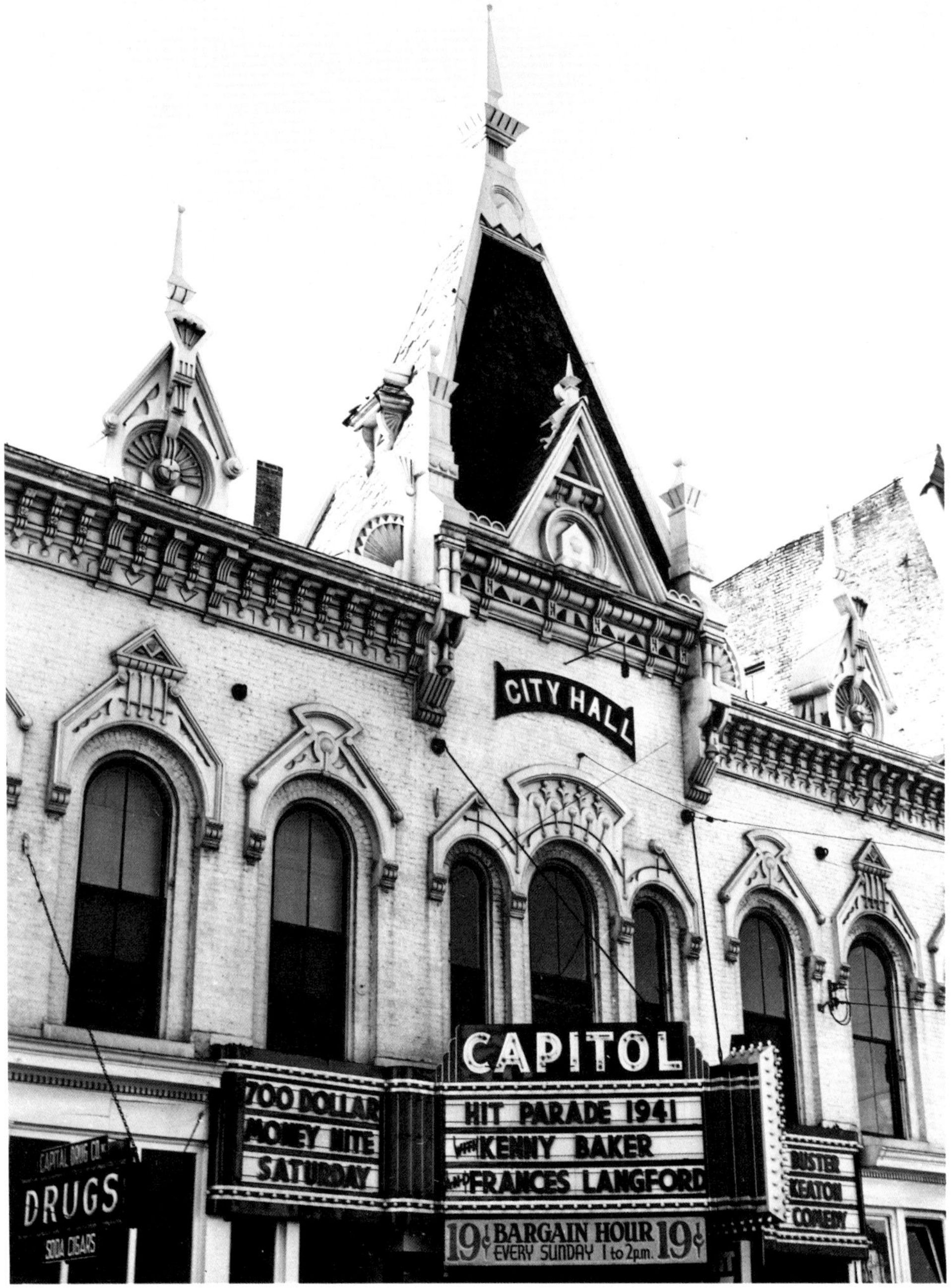

The Capitol Theatre, Frankfort. November 1940. JOHN VACHON.

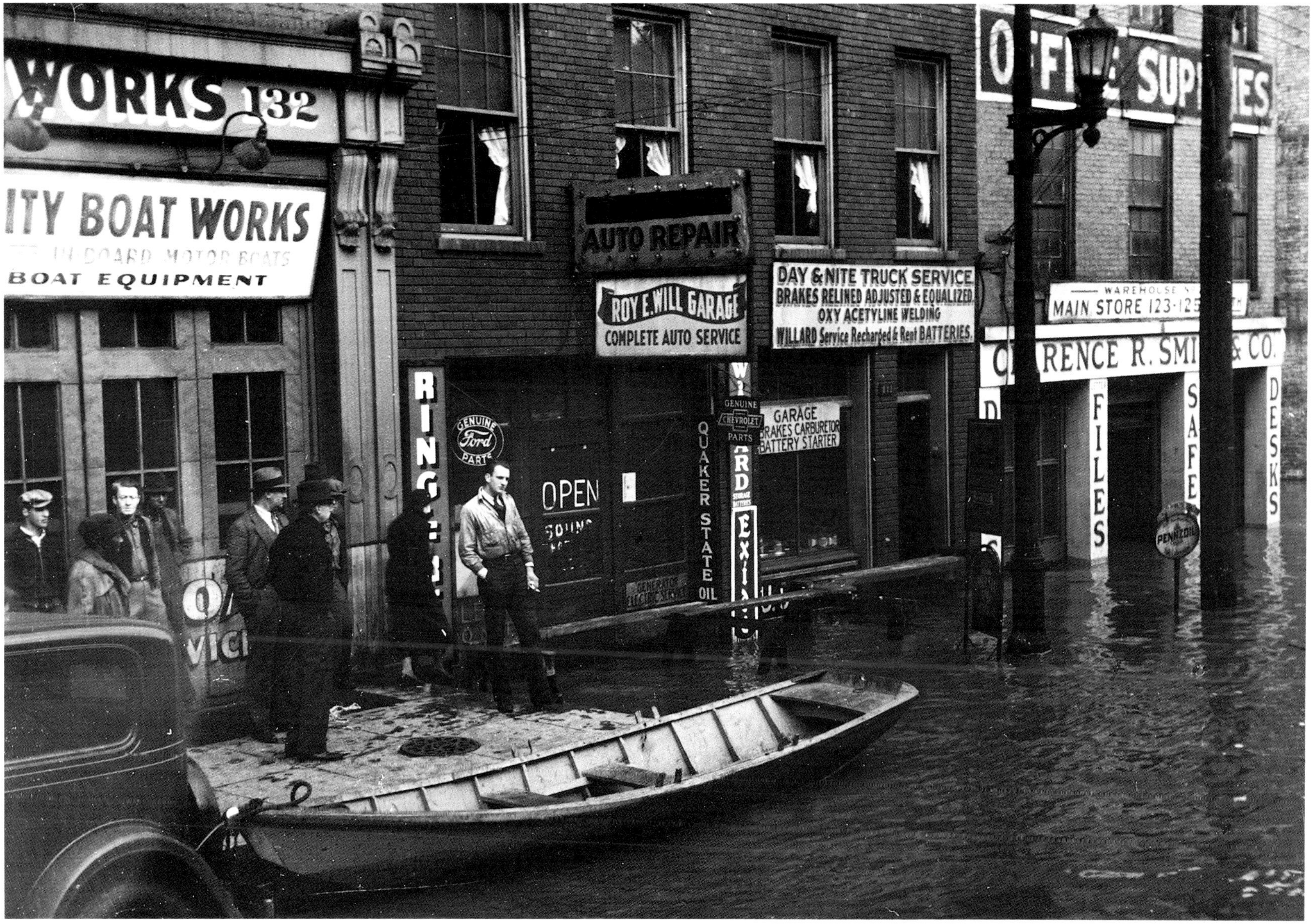

The Ohio River floods the streets of Louisville in March 1936. The following year would bring an even more disastrous flood. CARL MYDANS.

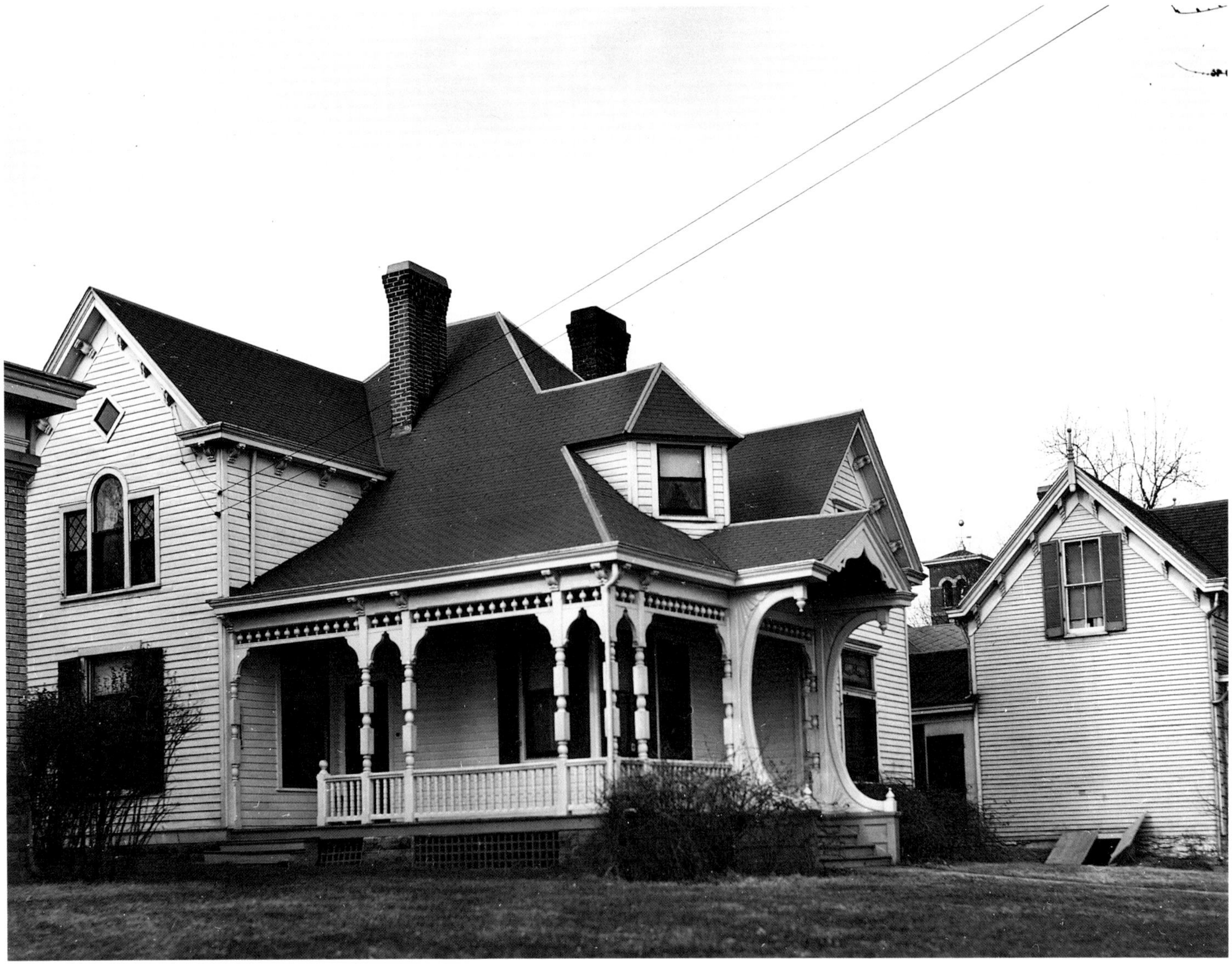

A "pattern-book" house in Paris. November 1940. John Vachon.

Opposite: Exchanging greetings on the bridge. Jackson, September 1940. Marion Post Wolcott.

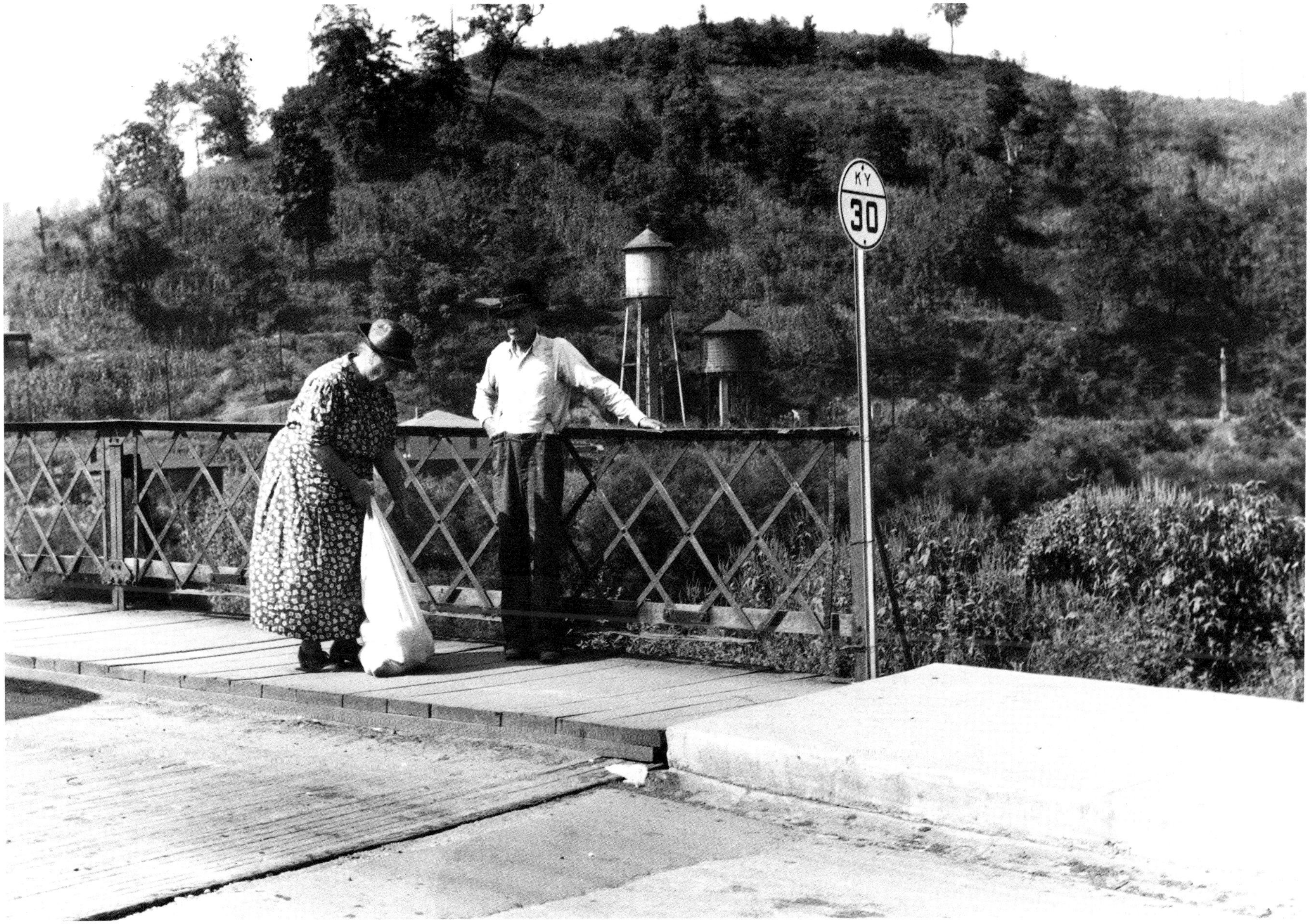
KY
30

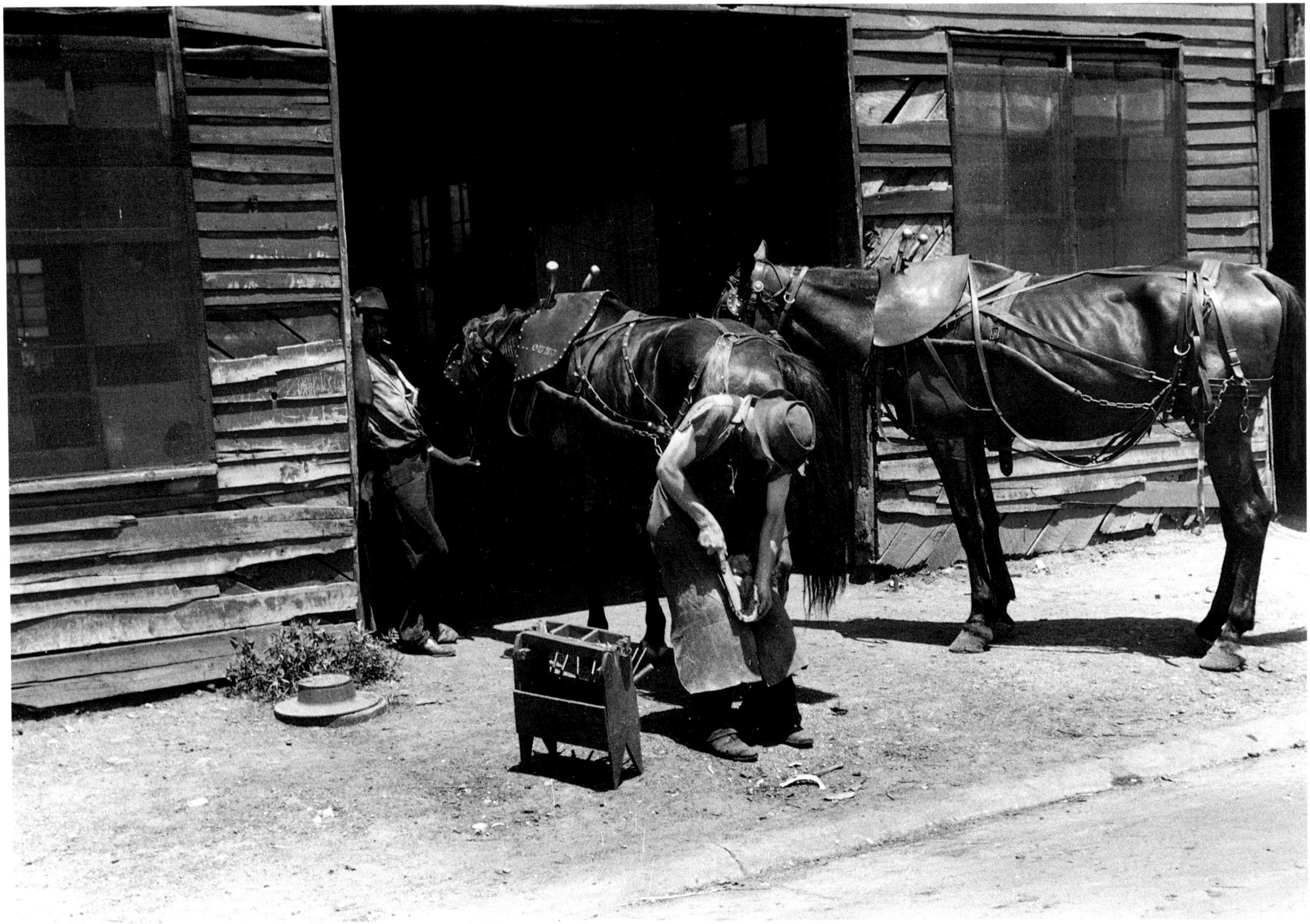

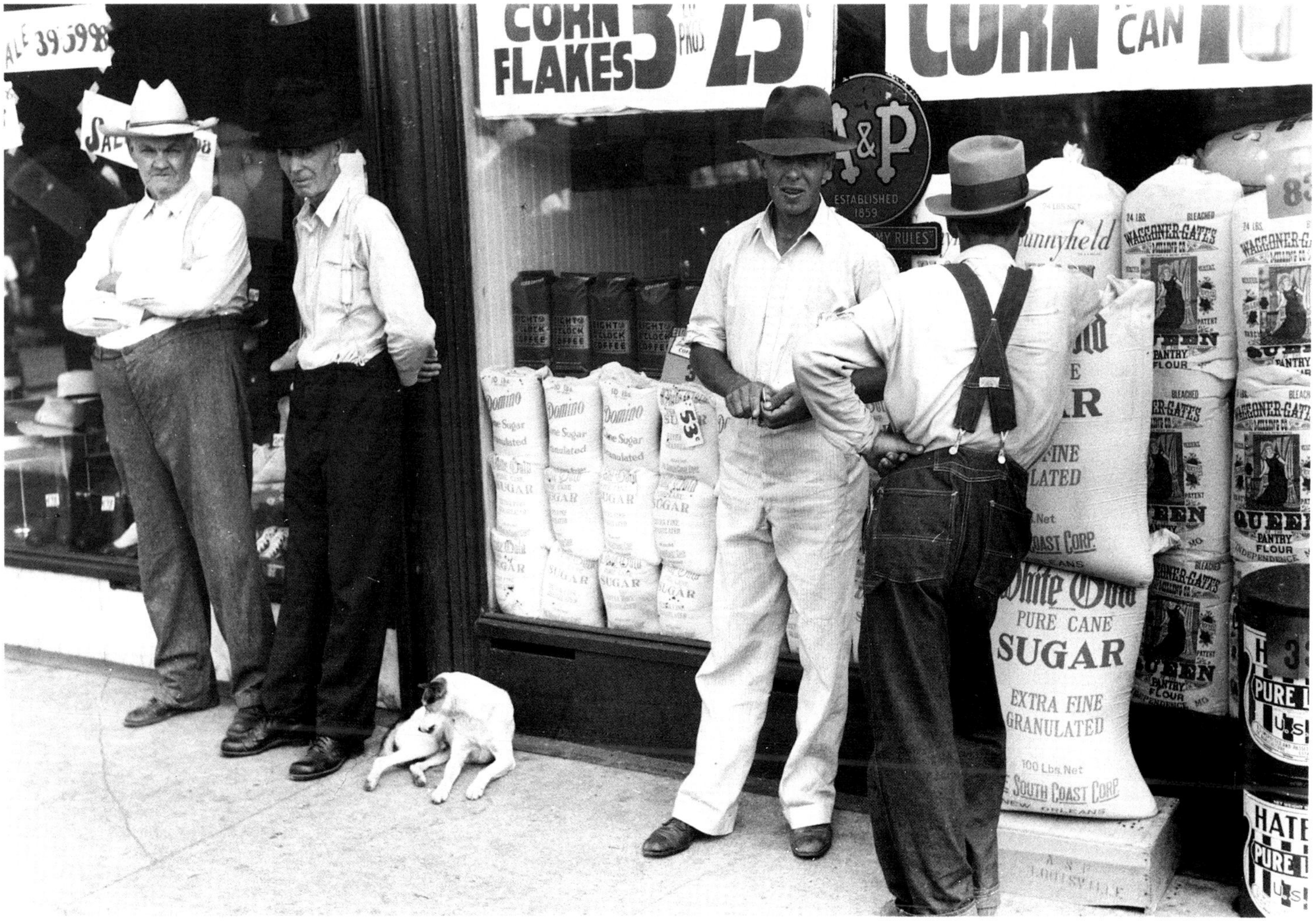

Saturday afternoon at the A&P. Cave City, July 1940. Marion Post Wolcott.

Opposite: A blacksmith at work. Russellville, July 1940. Marion Post Wolcott.

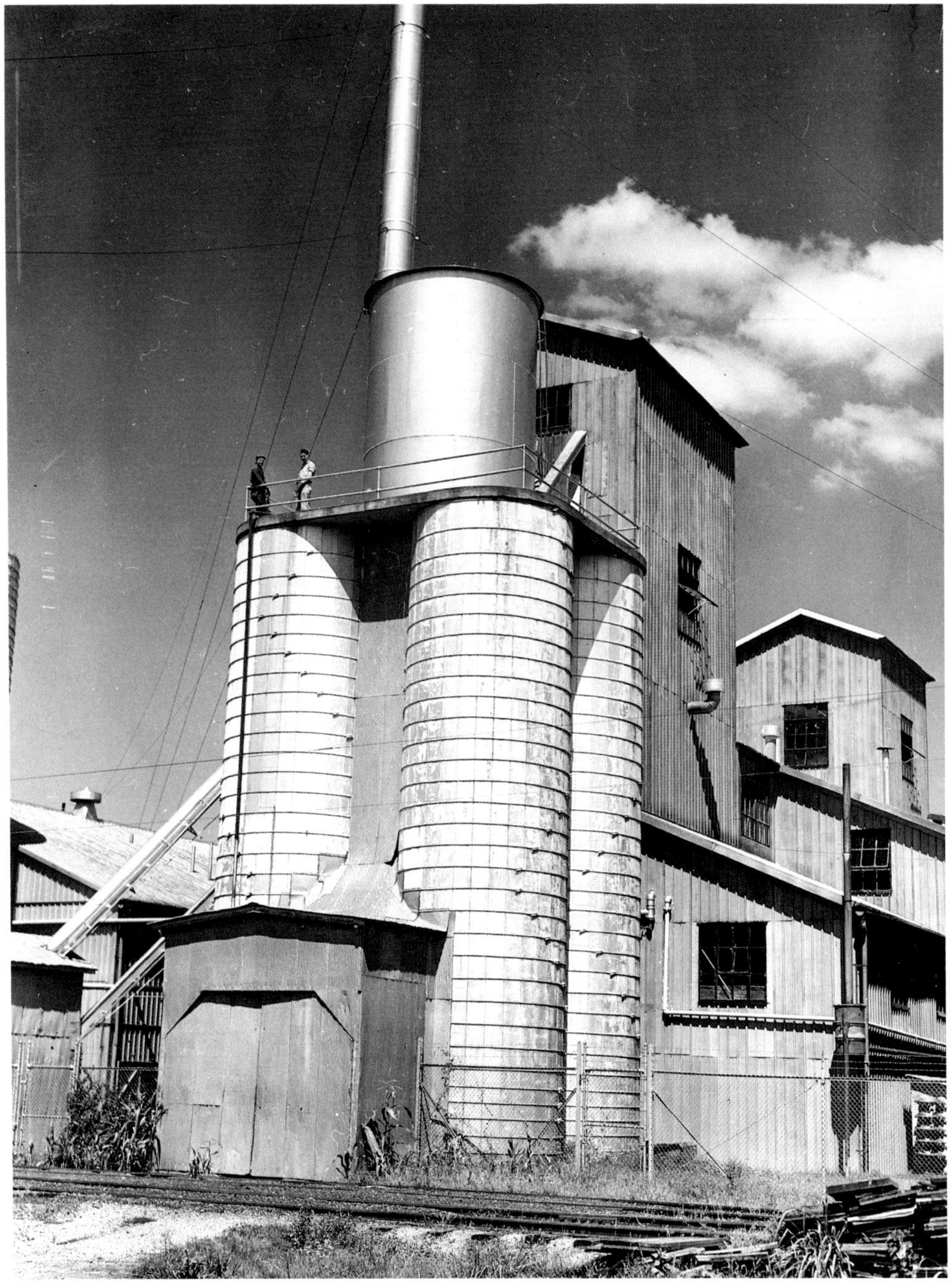

A bourbon distillery near Bardstown. July 1940. MARION POST WOLCOTT.

Opposite: The signs of a "wet" county. South-central Kentucky, July 1940. MARION POST WOLCOTT.

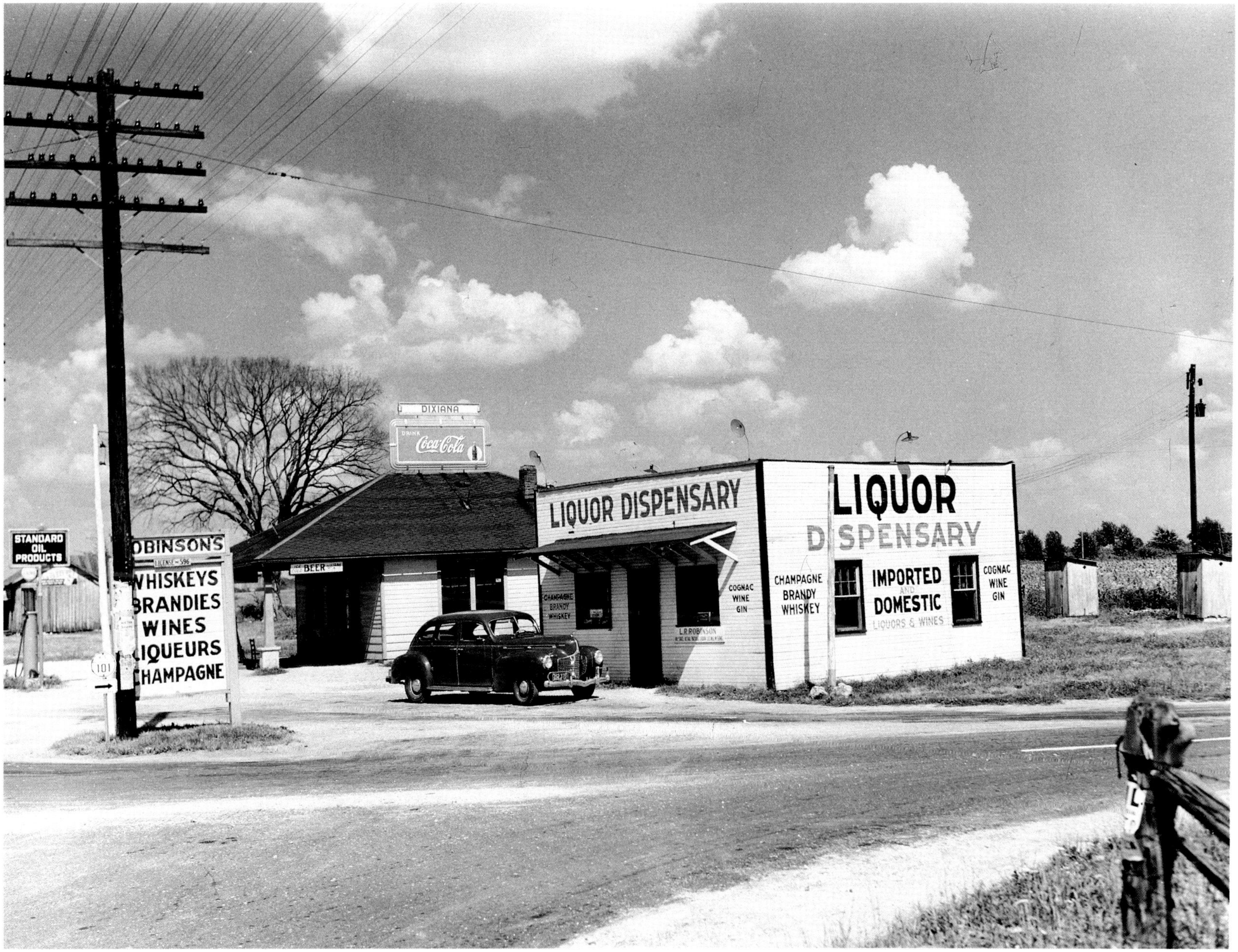
DIXIANA
DRINK Coca-Cola
STANDARD OIL PRODUCTS
OBINSON'S
WHISKEYS
BRANDIES
WINES
LIQUEURS
CHAMPAGNE
BEER
LIQUOR DISPENSARY
CHAMPAGNE BRANDY WHISKEY
COGNAC WINE GIN
L.R. ROBINSON
LIQUOR
DISPENSARY
CHAMPAGNE BRANDY WHISKEY
IMPORTED AND DOMESTIC LIQUORS & WINES
COGNAC WINE GIN
101

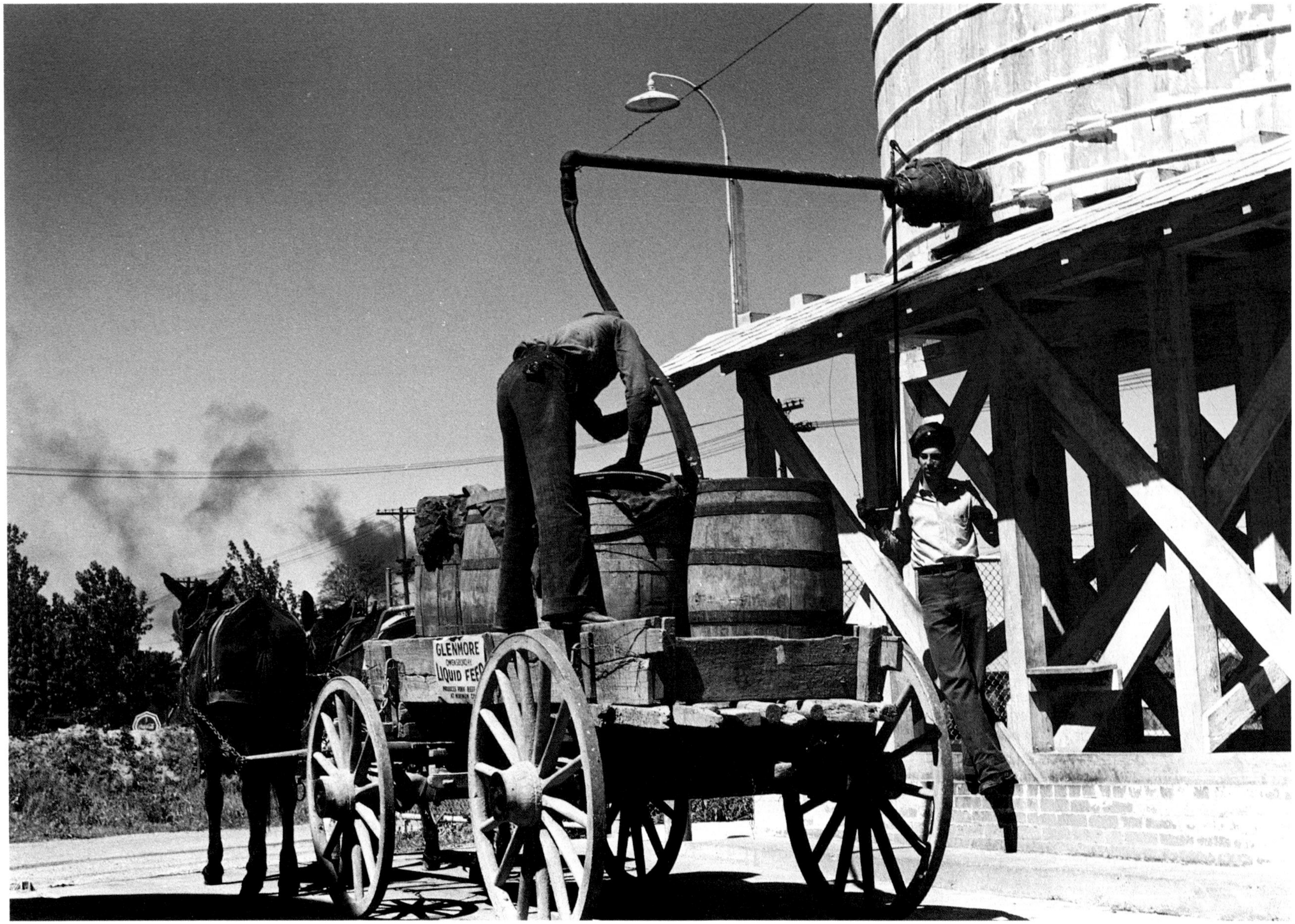

Liquid-feed corn mash, an alcohol by-product, is loaded onto a truck from tanks at a distillery. Owensboro, May 1938. Russell Lee.

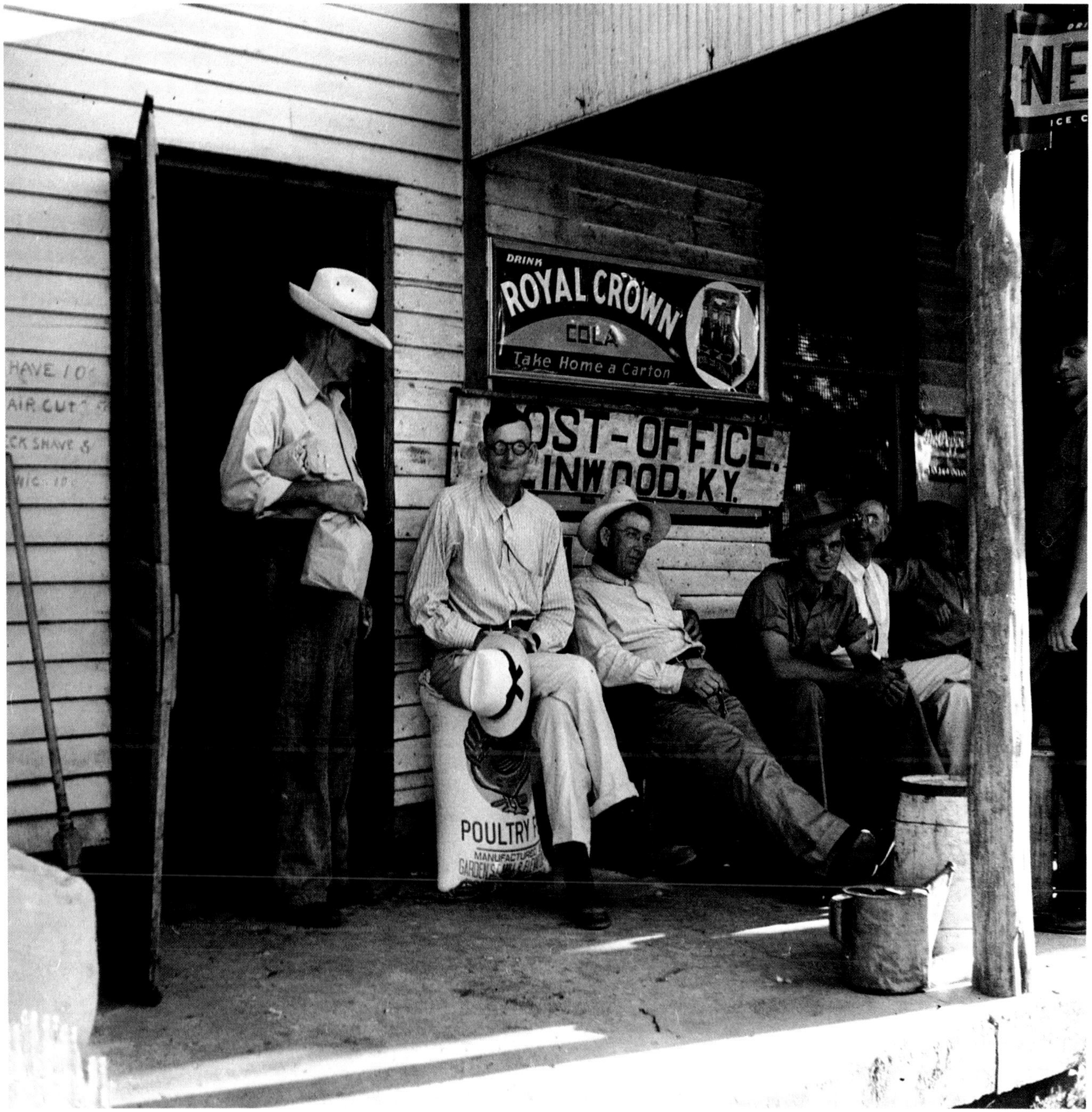

Farmers exchange news in front of the Post Office. Linwood, July 1940.
MARION POST WOLCOTT.

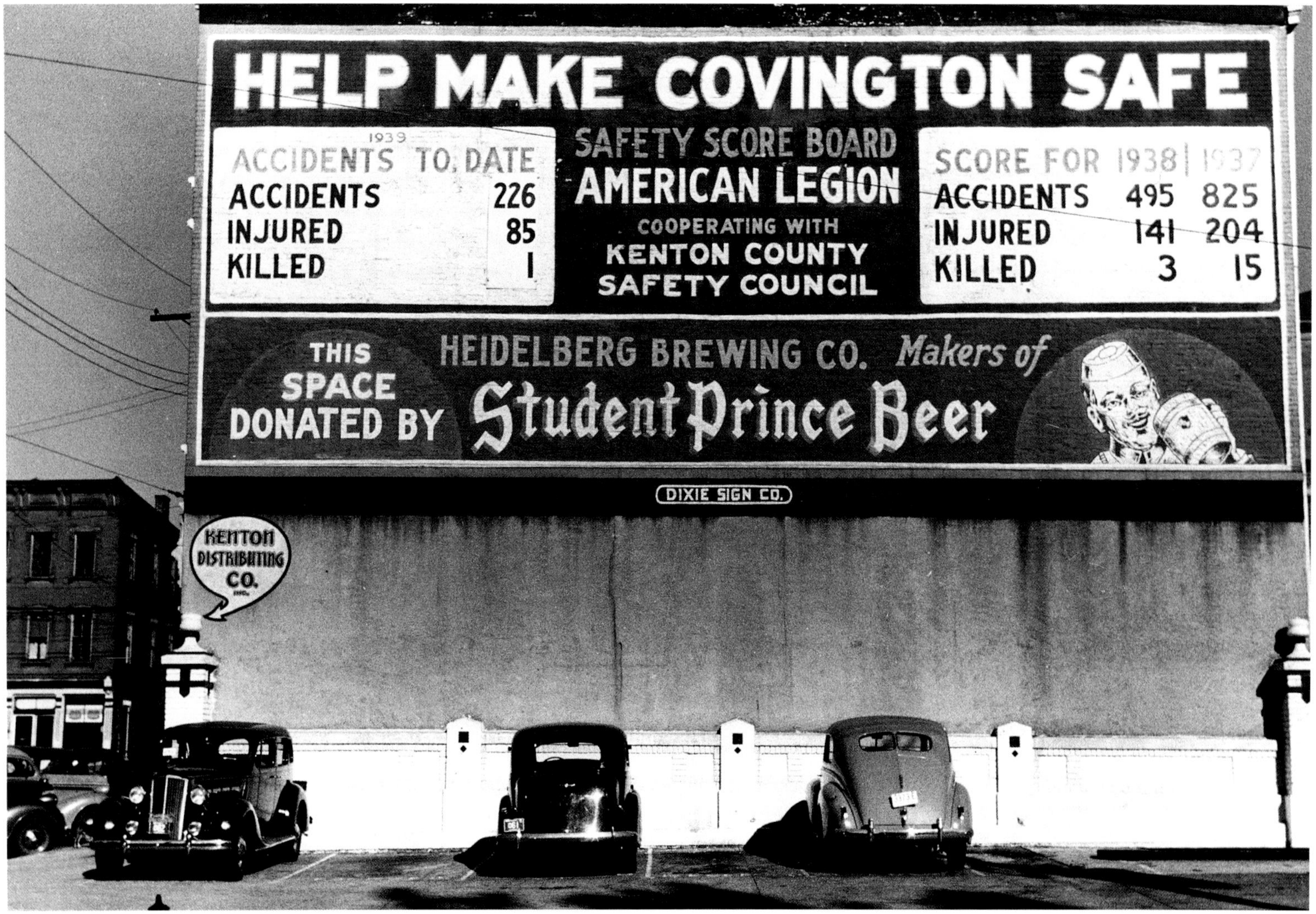

A Covington parking lot. September 1939. JOHN VACHON.

Opposite: The spirit of the times. Covington, September 1939. JOHN VACHON.

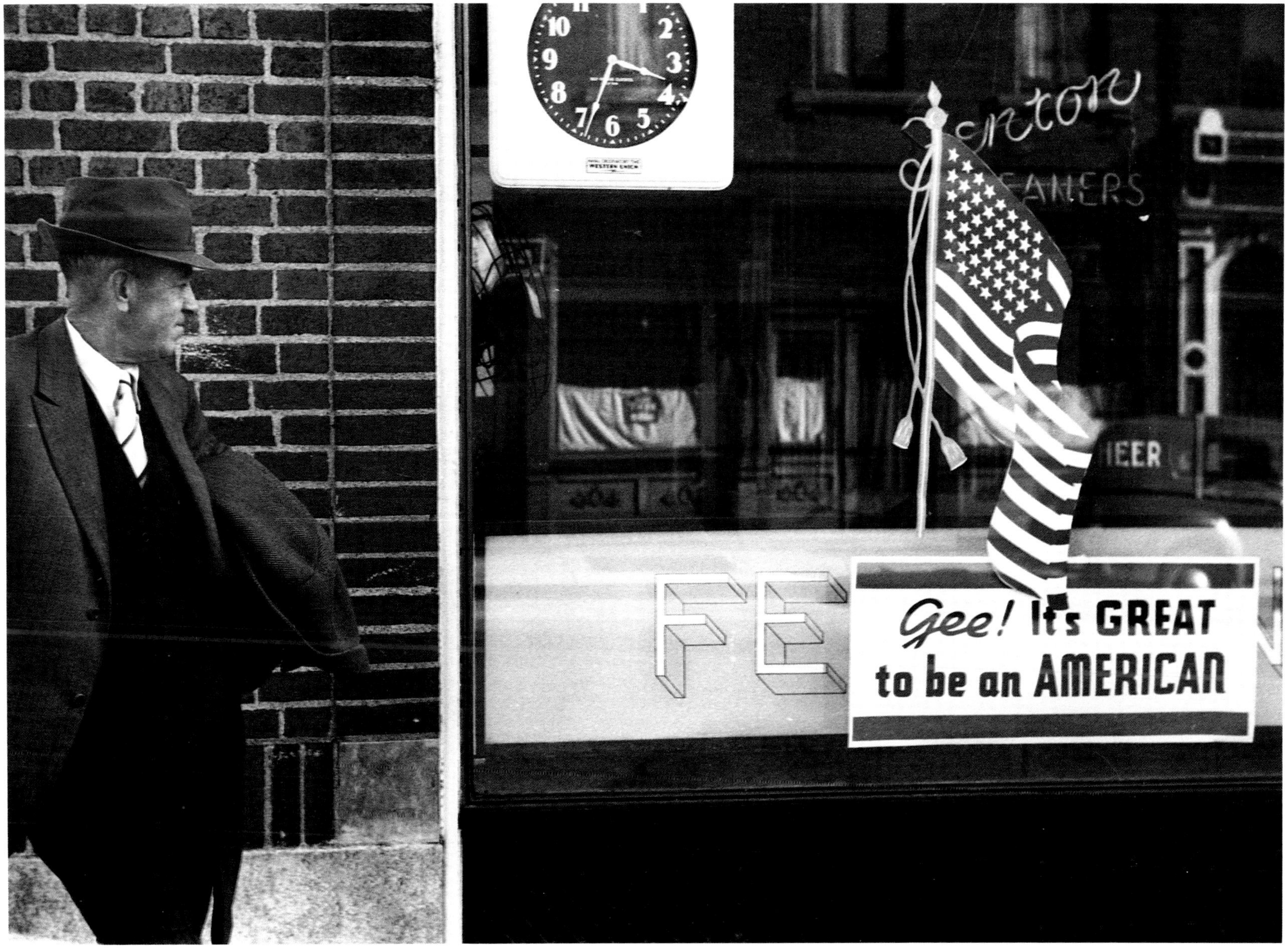
Gee! It's GREAT
to be an AMERICAN

The hazards of travel by car. Near Jackson, September 1940. MARION POST WOLCOTT.

Transportation

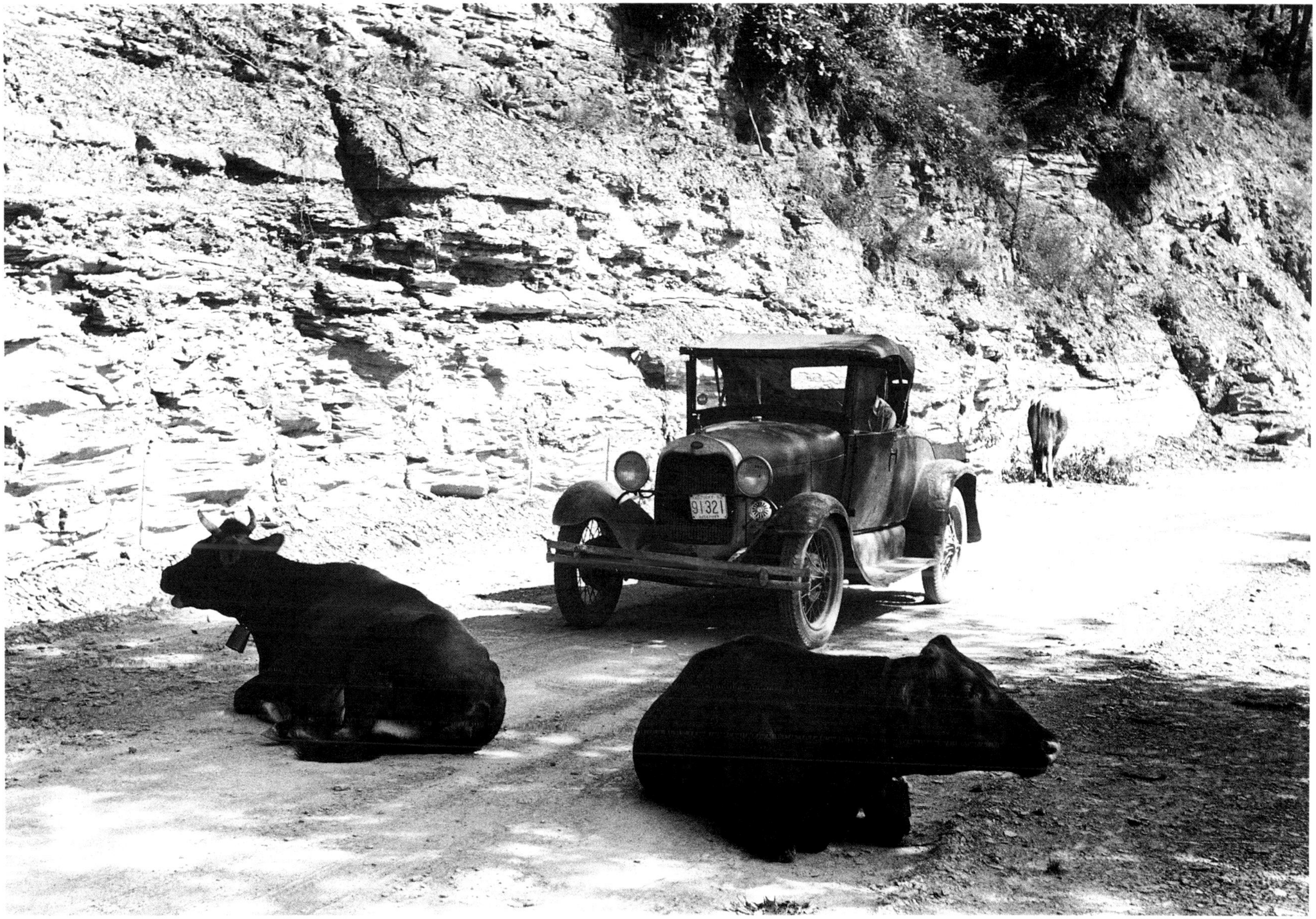

THE FSA PHOTOGRAPHERS who worked in Kentucky were not experts in the history of the region and none had traveled extensively in the state. Essentially they were tourists, "just visiting." Much of what they saw and recorded in these photographs was along or close to the state's major highways. Because their time in any one area was short and their task large, they photographed what they could on their relatively brief trips. They traveled throughout the state on what were considered good roads for their day, including fifteen federal highways. The diversity of the FSA photographs attests to the photographers' ability to "get around" by car in most sections of the state. The photos also show other transportation modes, from footpower to river boats.

Marion Post Wolcott, with personal contacts in Eastern Kentucky, was able to photograph subjects that could not have been reached by means of highways. Writing to Stryker from Louisville in late July 1940, she described the difficulties of a trip recently taken by a *Courier-Journal* photographer and a writer: "They spent 2 weeks and most of the time was consumed walking (where one couldn't take the car) & fording streams & getting out of ditches & up creek beds. It's slow going & the people not too friendly if you're a foreigner & you don't know anybody. In other words—slow going."

But on September 9, during her own journey into Eastern Kentucky with her new-found friend Marie R. Turner, she herself was able to report a more successful assignment: "They are having all these religious meetings & 'memorials' too, some of them coming for miles on foot & horseback. I'm getting children walking to school up creek beds & teachers riding for miles—the mail carried by horseback, etc. people carrying heavy sacks of supplies, & so much else." She was delighted with these images, despite continuing transportation difficulties of her own, which she fully documented in pictures and text. The photo of Wolcott fording a stream by auto says much about the dedication of the FSA photographers to their mission.

Opposite: The photographer's car, stuck in the South Fork of Quicksand Creek. Breathitt County, September 1940. MARION POST WOLCOTT.

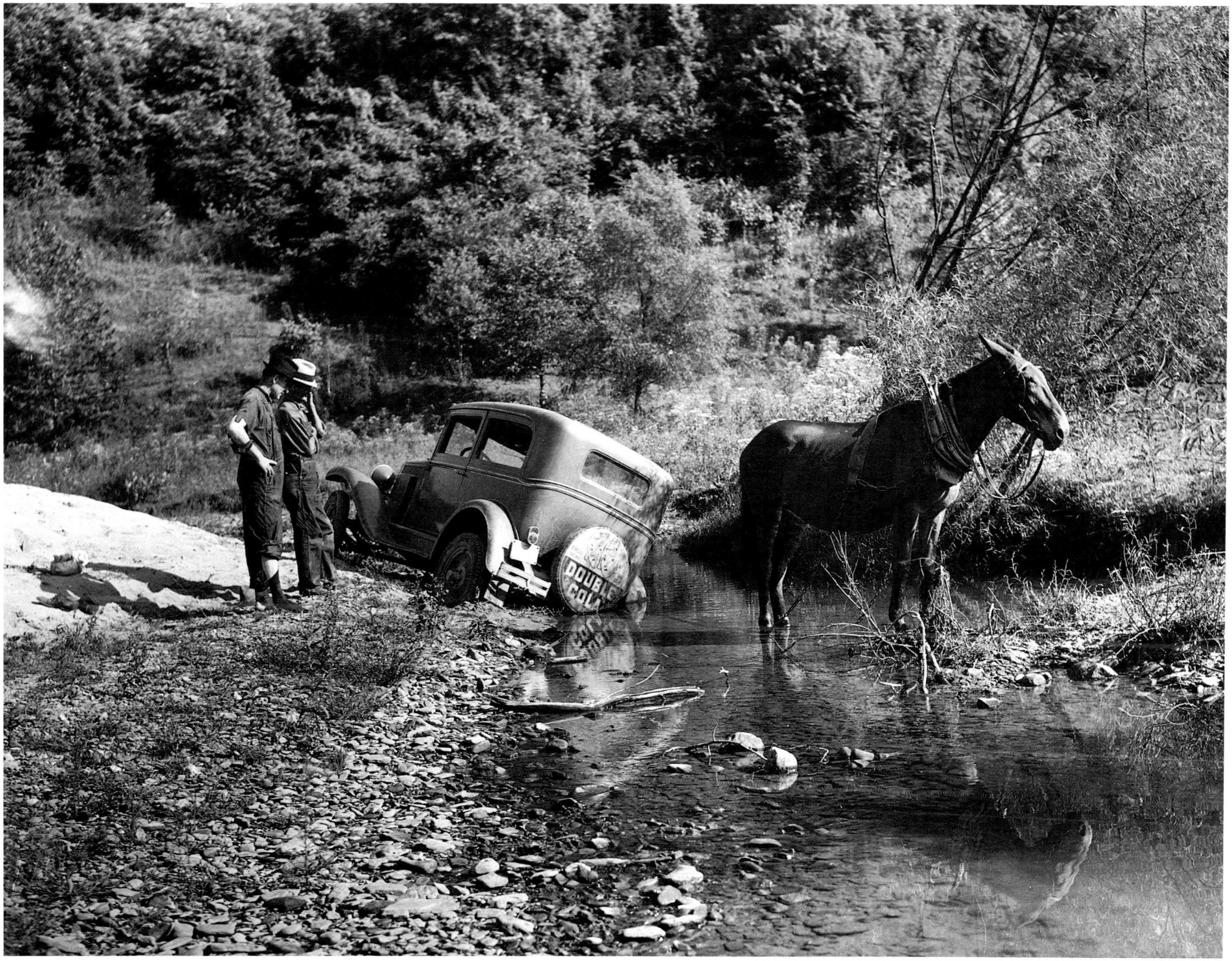

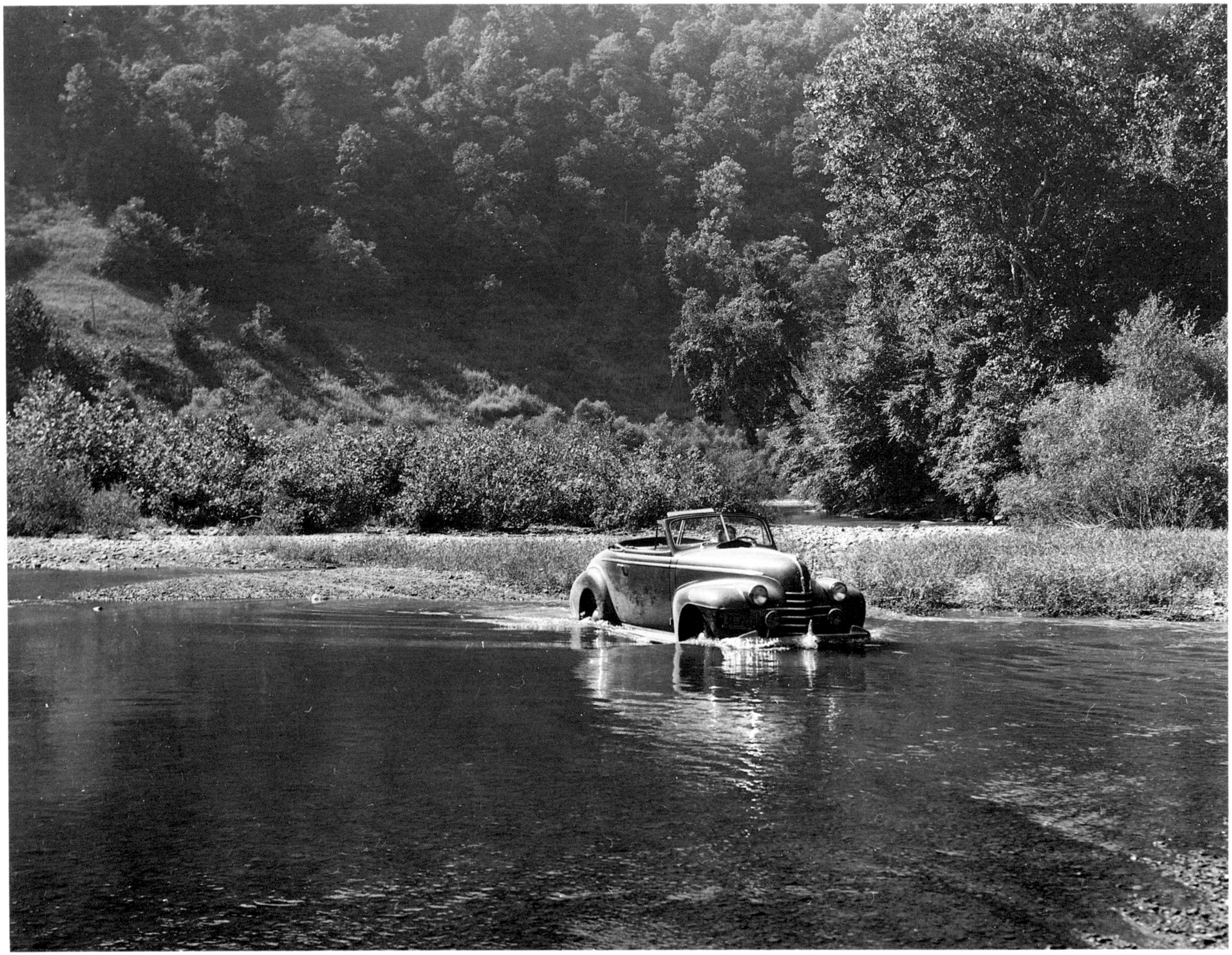

Fording the Morris Fork of the Kentucky River in Breathitt County. August 1940. Marion Post Wolcott.

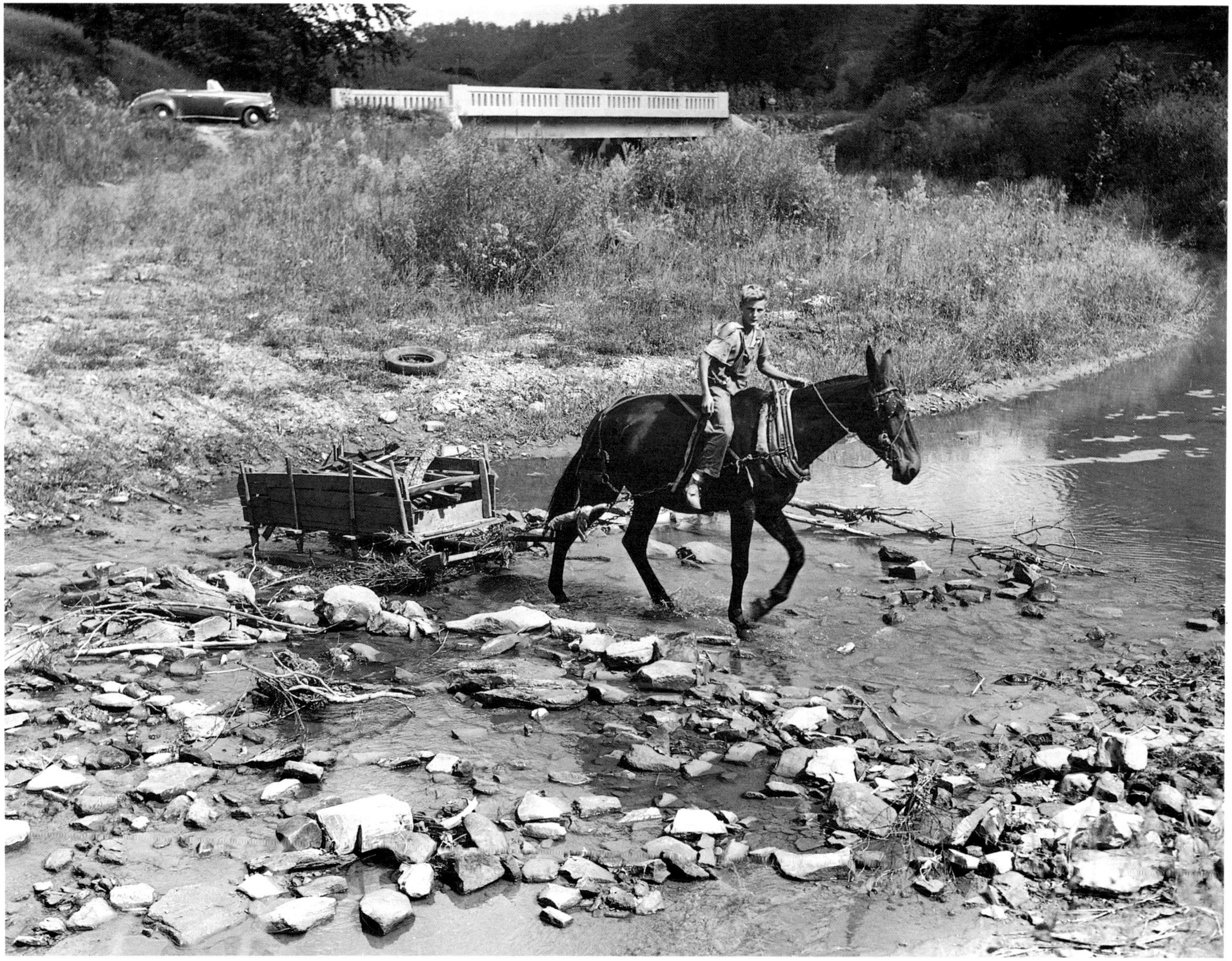

A mountain boy hauls wood across the creek with a mule and sled. Near Jackson, September 1940. MARION POST WOLCOTT.

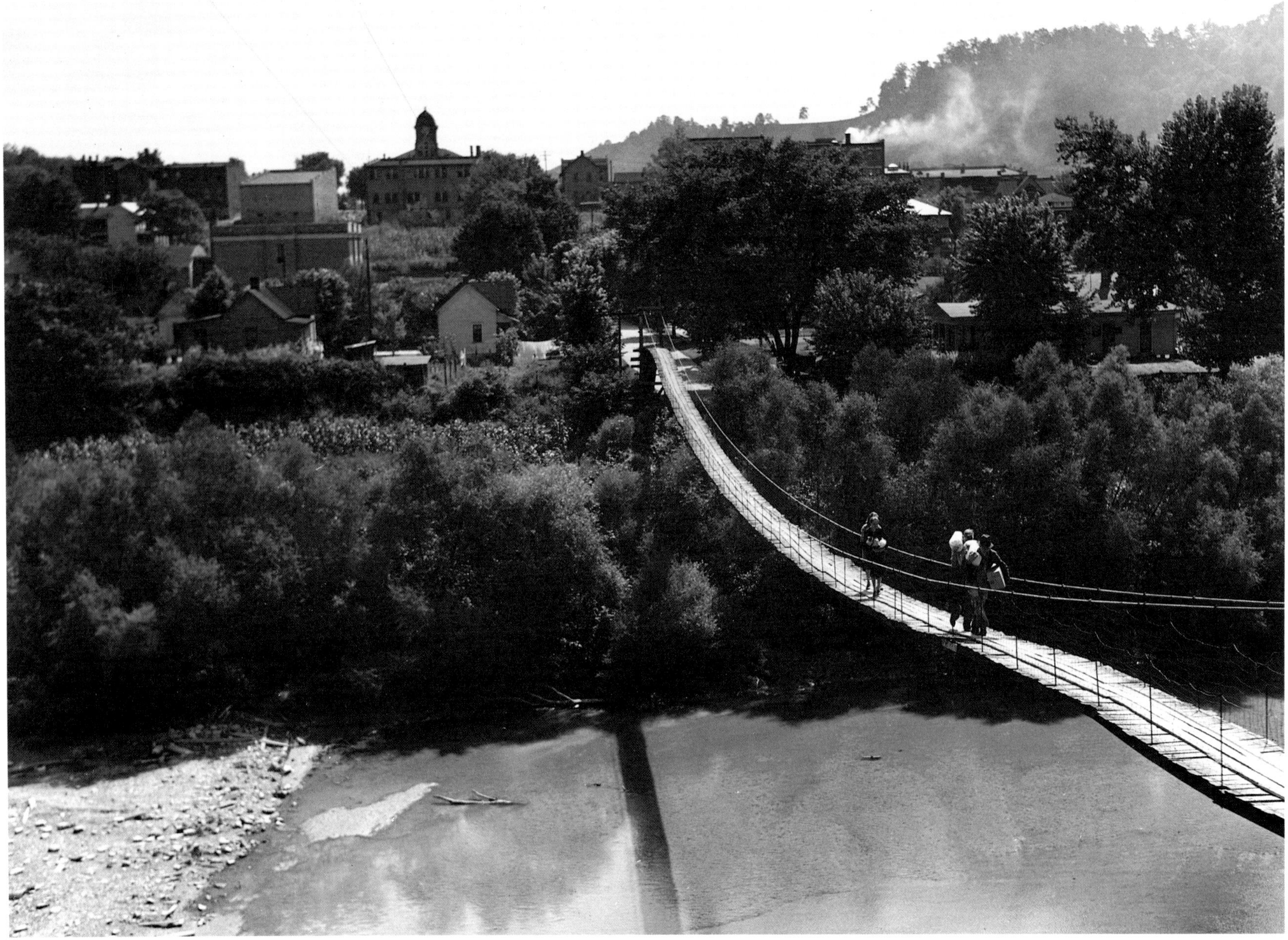

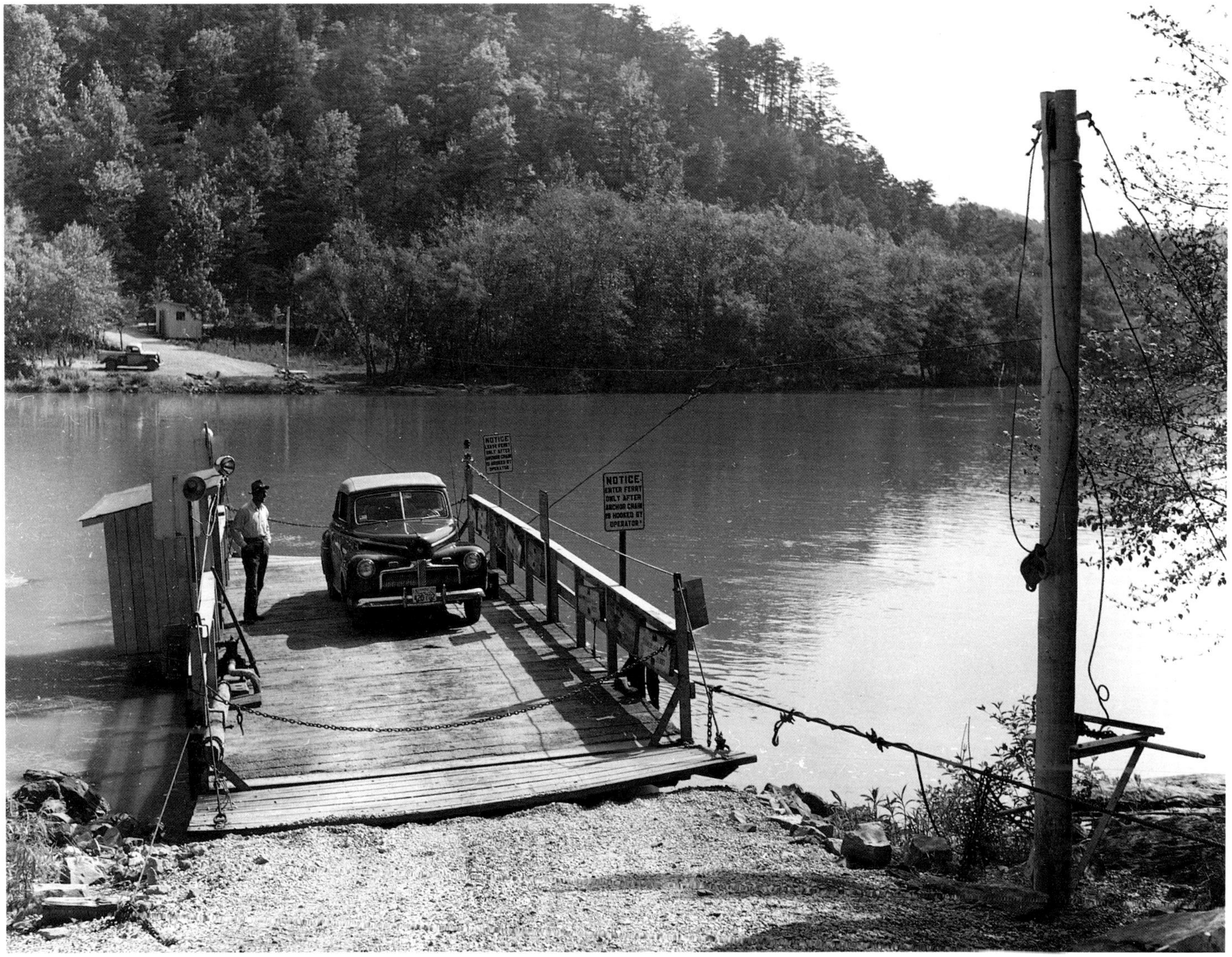

A free cable ferry across the Cumberland River along state highway 90. McCreary County, June 1943. HOWARD HOLLEM.

Opposite: Crossing the swinging bridge in Jackson. September 1940. MARION POST WOLCOTT.

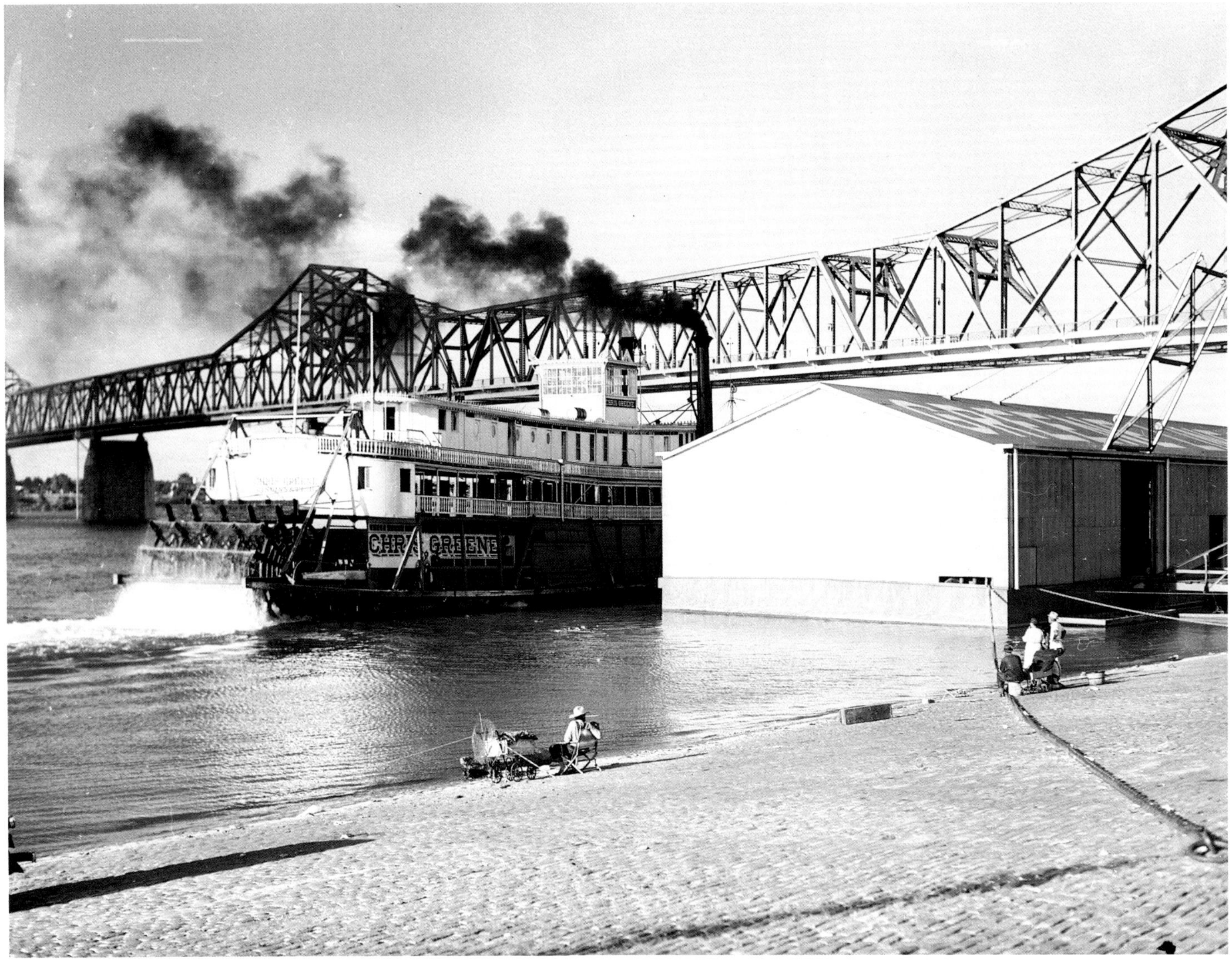

The stern-wheeler Chris Greene leaves the dock at Louisville. July 1940. MARION POST WOLCOTT.

Opposite: Tourist cabins near Cave City. July 1940. MARION POST WOLCOTT.

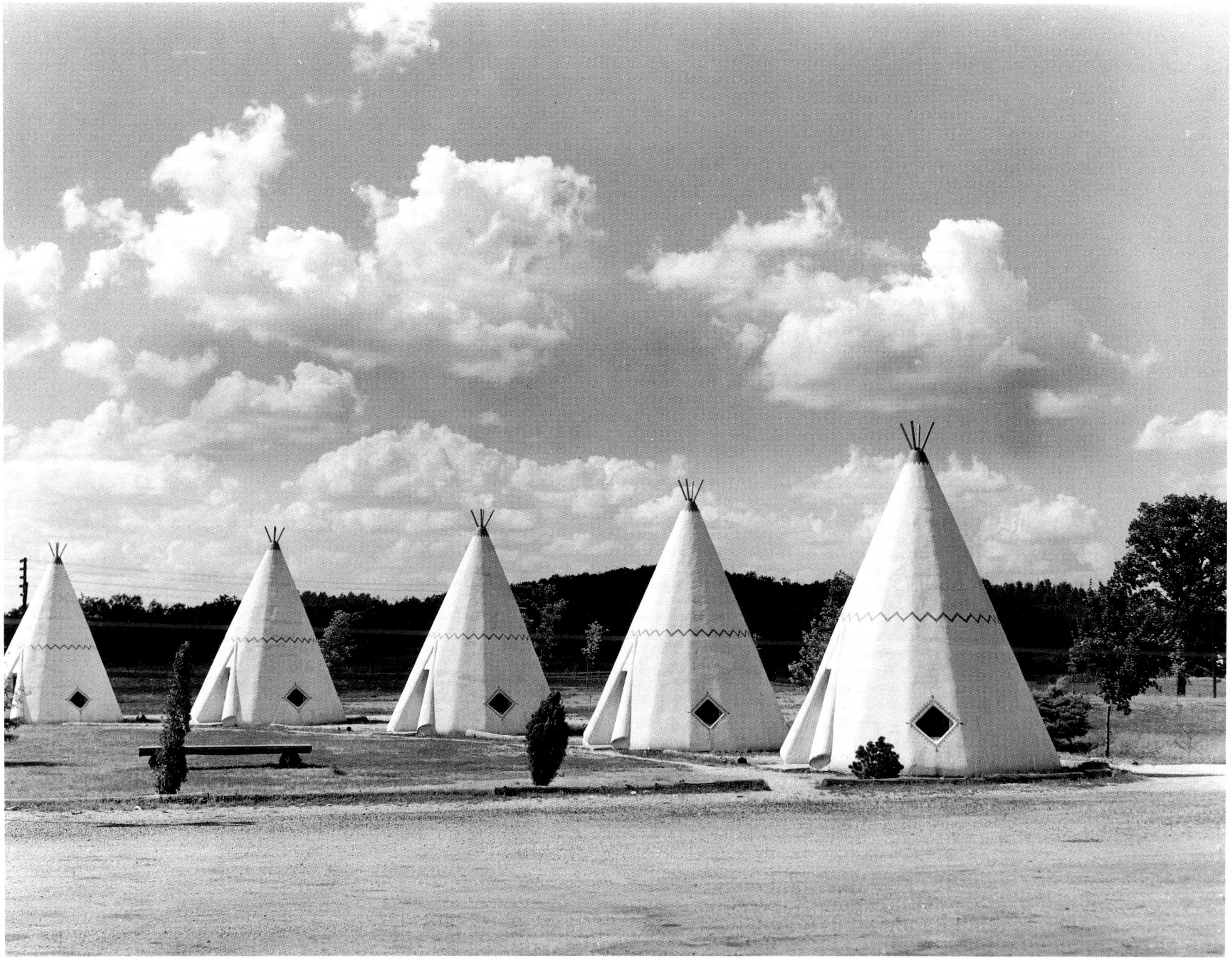

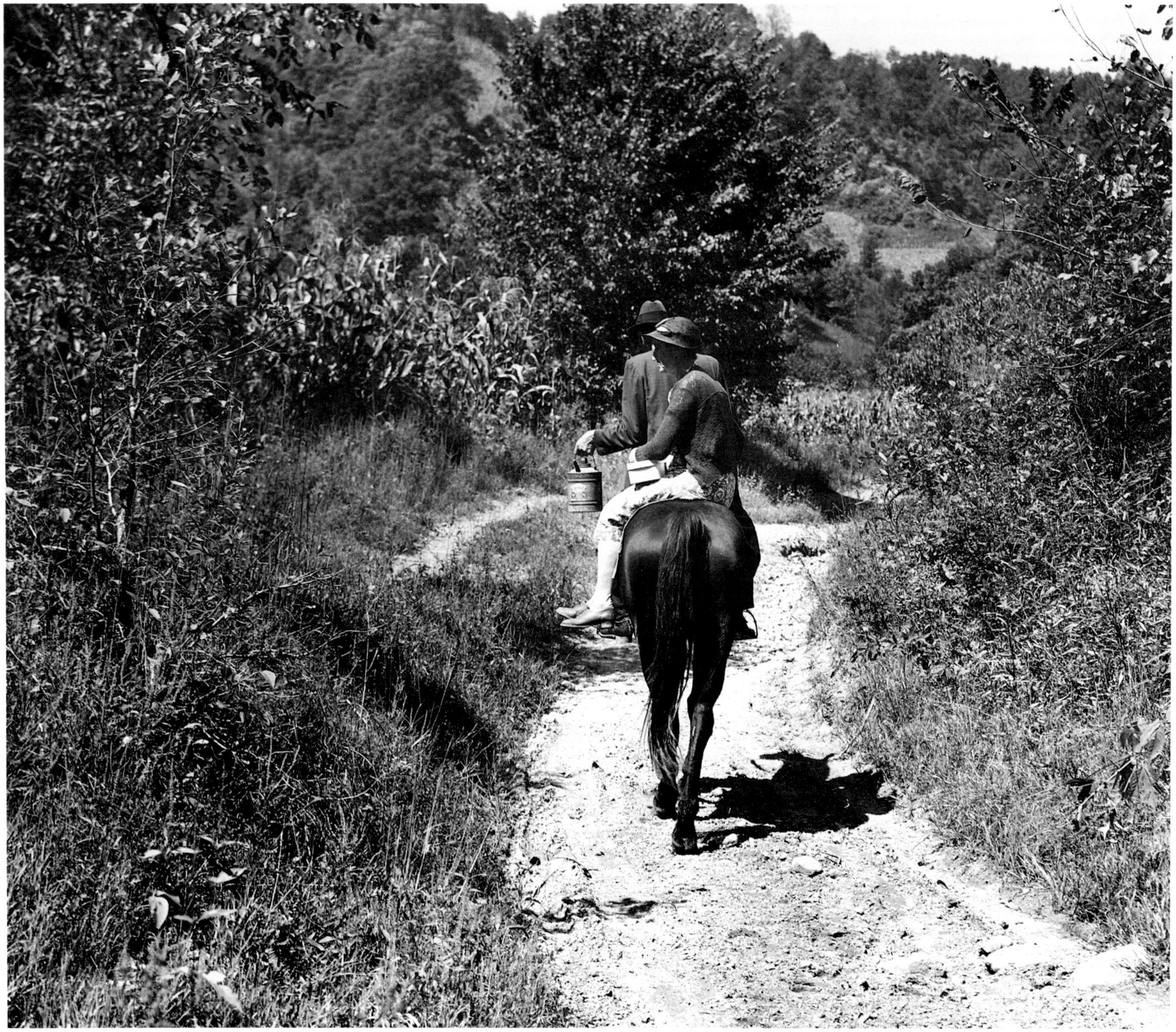

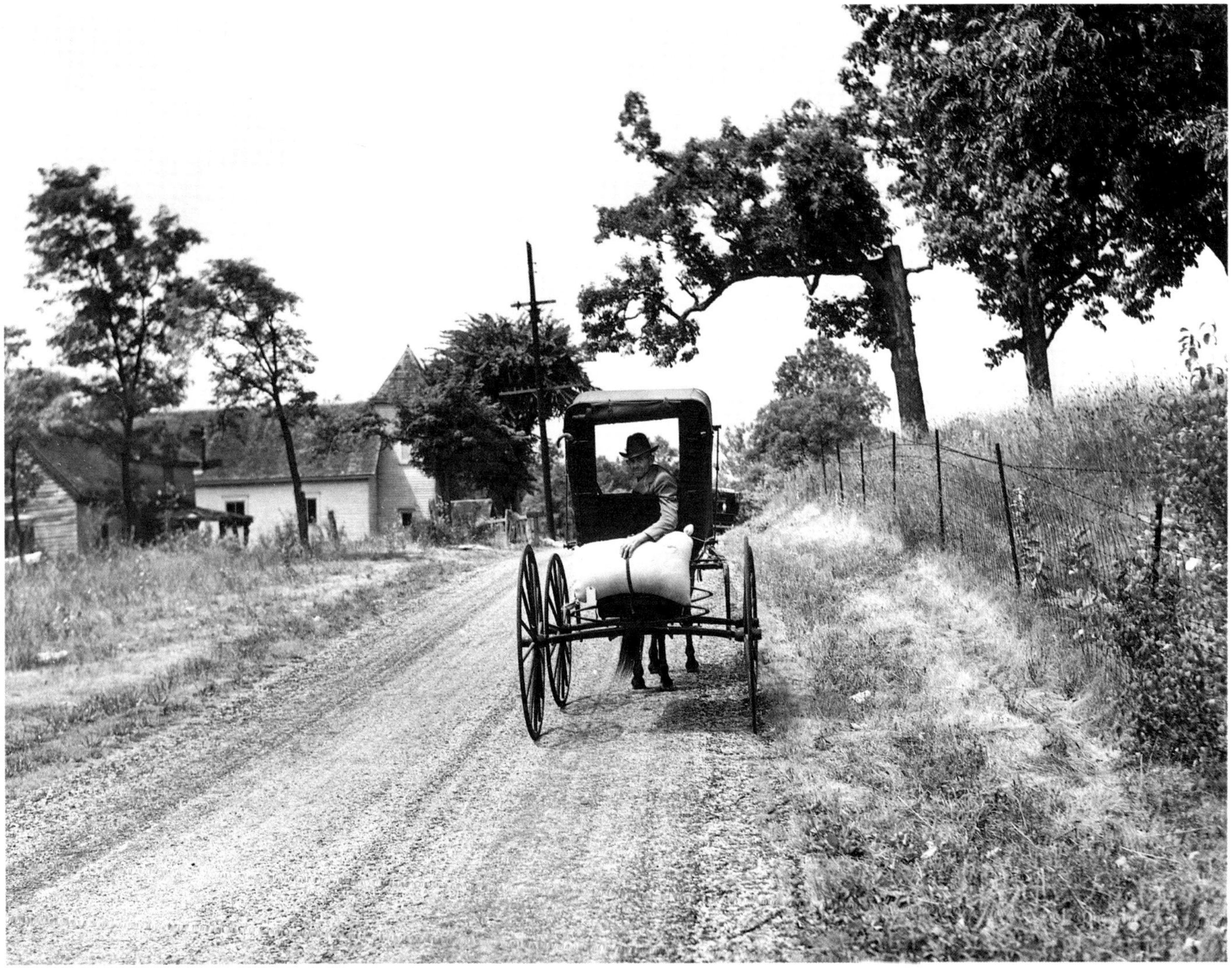

A farmer takes home a bag of feed. Near Lexington, July 1940. MARION POST WOLCOTT.

Opposite: Bringing home groceries by horseback. Breathitt County, September 1940. MARION POST WOLCOTT.

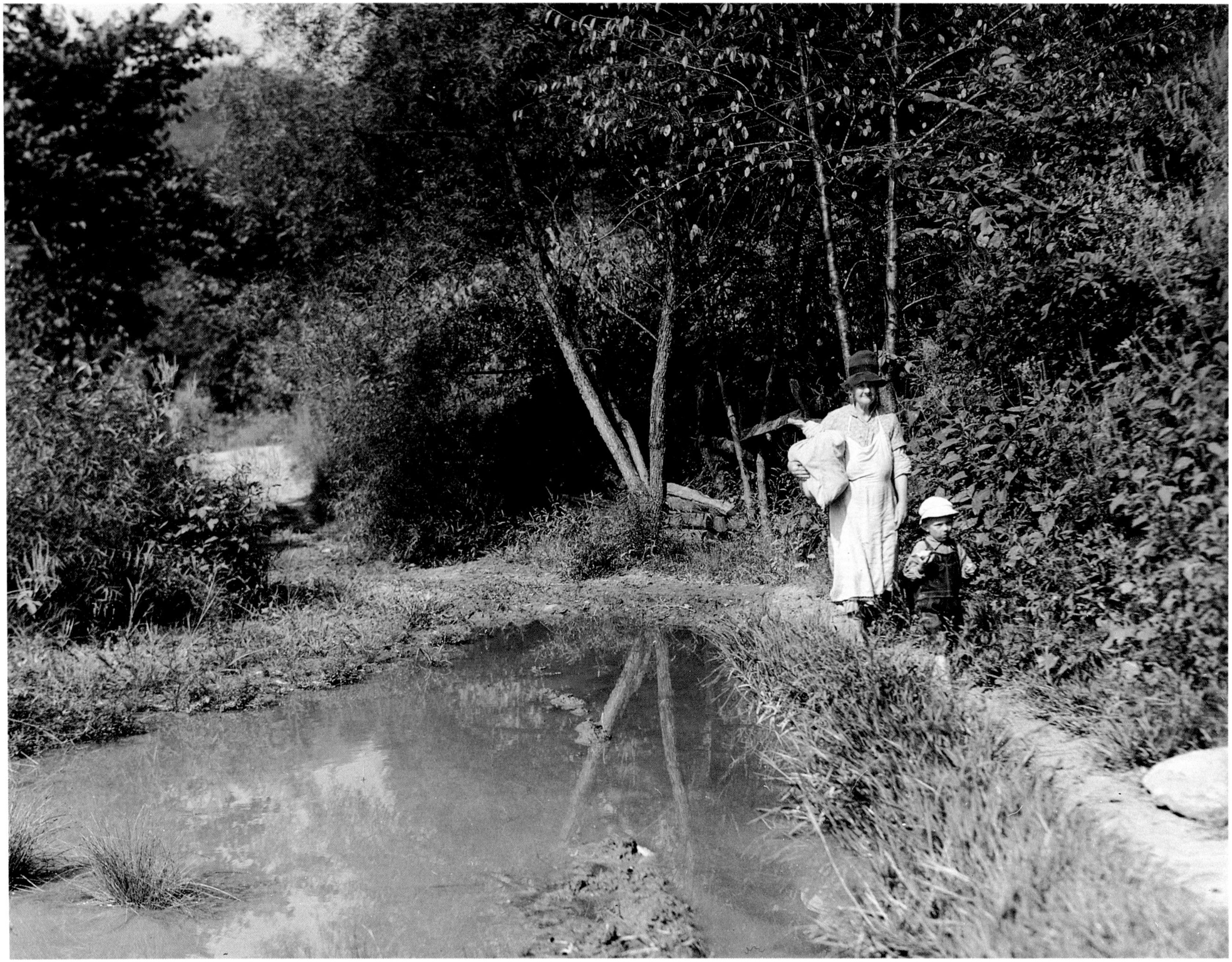

Carrying home supplies from the store on Burton's Fork. Breathitt County, September 1940. MARION POST WOLCOTT.

Coal miners with lunch pails. Jenkins, October 1935. BEN SHAHN.

Coal Mining

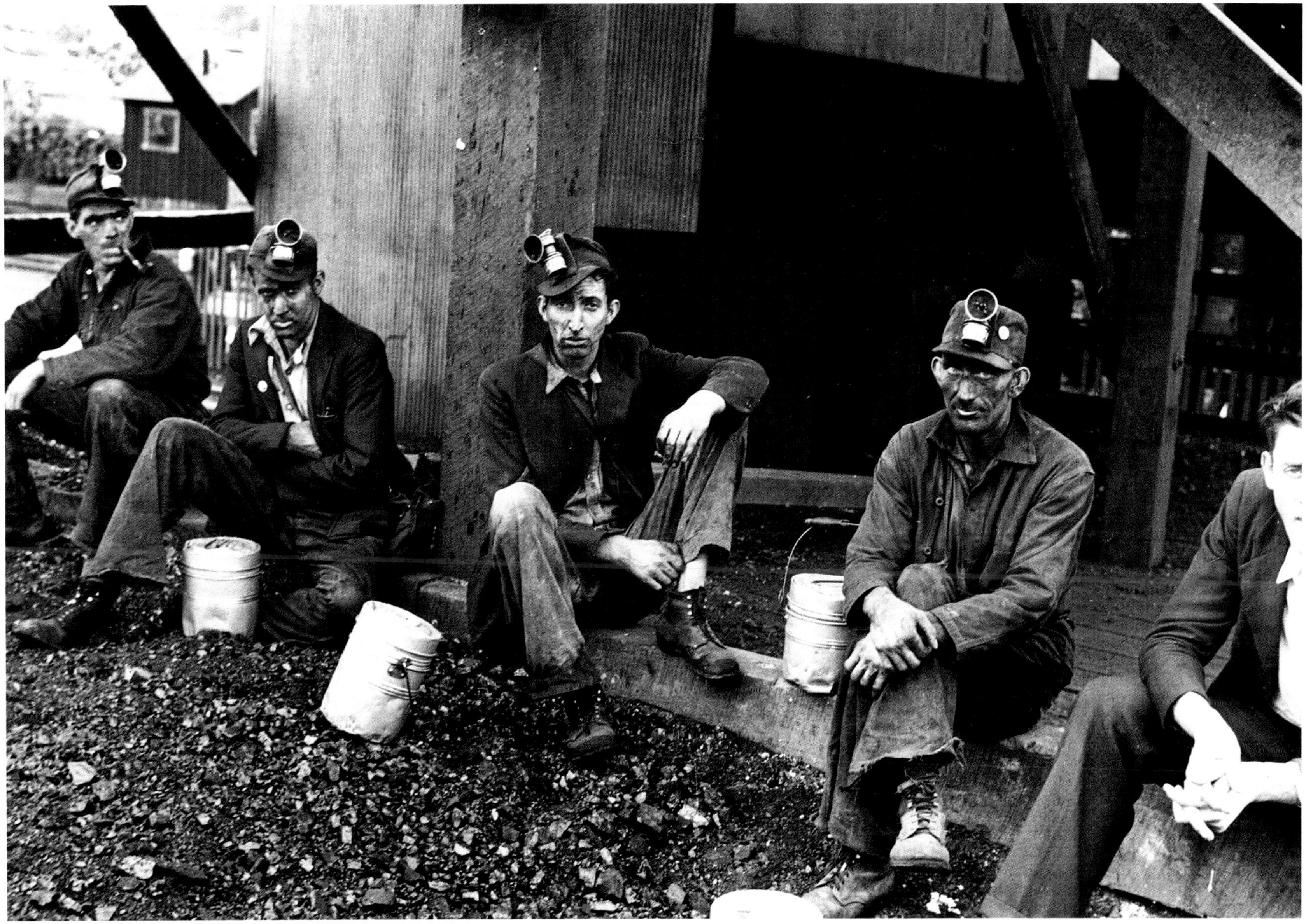

KENTUCKY TODAY is the nation's leading producer of bituminous coal, with mines in two regions, the mountains of Eastern Kentucky and the Western Coal Field. It is therefore both surprising and regrettable that the FSA archives contain so few photos of the Kentucky coal industry or of life in the mining camps that dotted the coalfields.

In the autumn of 1935 Ben Shahn took several dramatic portraits of coal miners in Eastern Kentucky. Arthur Rothstein took a few photos in the same area in 1938, showing mine exteriors. No further FSA work was done in Kentucky until Marion Post Wolcott's trips there in 1940. In the meantime, an extensive photo documentation of coal mining had been completed in the southeastern United States and other parts of the country. This may account for the dearth of FSA coal mining photos from the Commonwealth.

Although we lack in-depth studies of mining operations or of life in a Kentucky mining town, we do see the range of activities associated with the industry as they could be viewed from above ground. The subjects presented here range from large commercial operations to the "raising" of coal for home use in Breathitt County. And the grime-covered faces of Shahn's weary coal miners tell us much about their work and its effect on their lives.

Opposite: A truck loaded with coal heads down the mountain. Between Jackson and Campton, September 1940. MARION POST WOLCOTT.

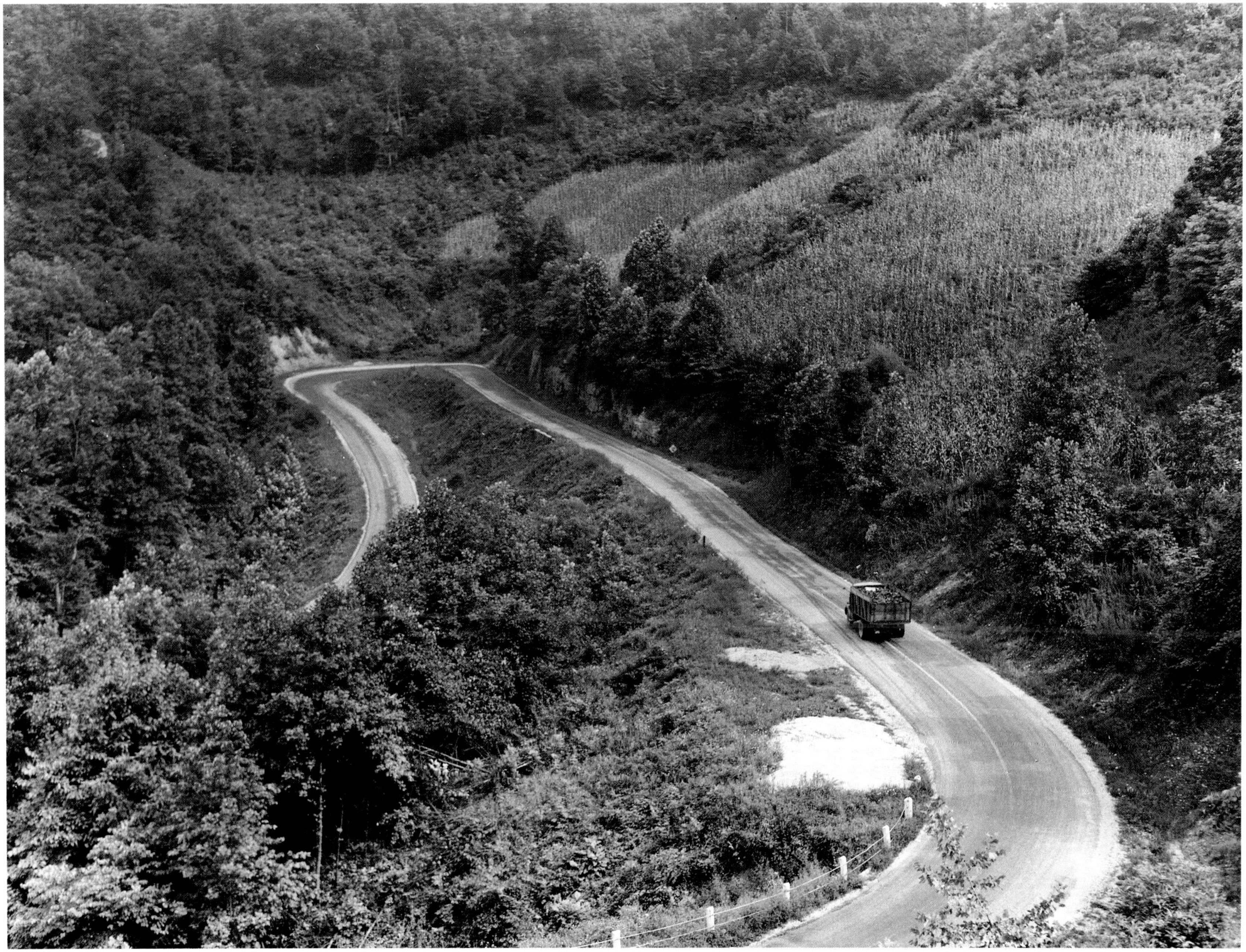

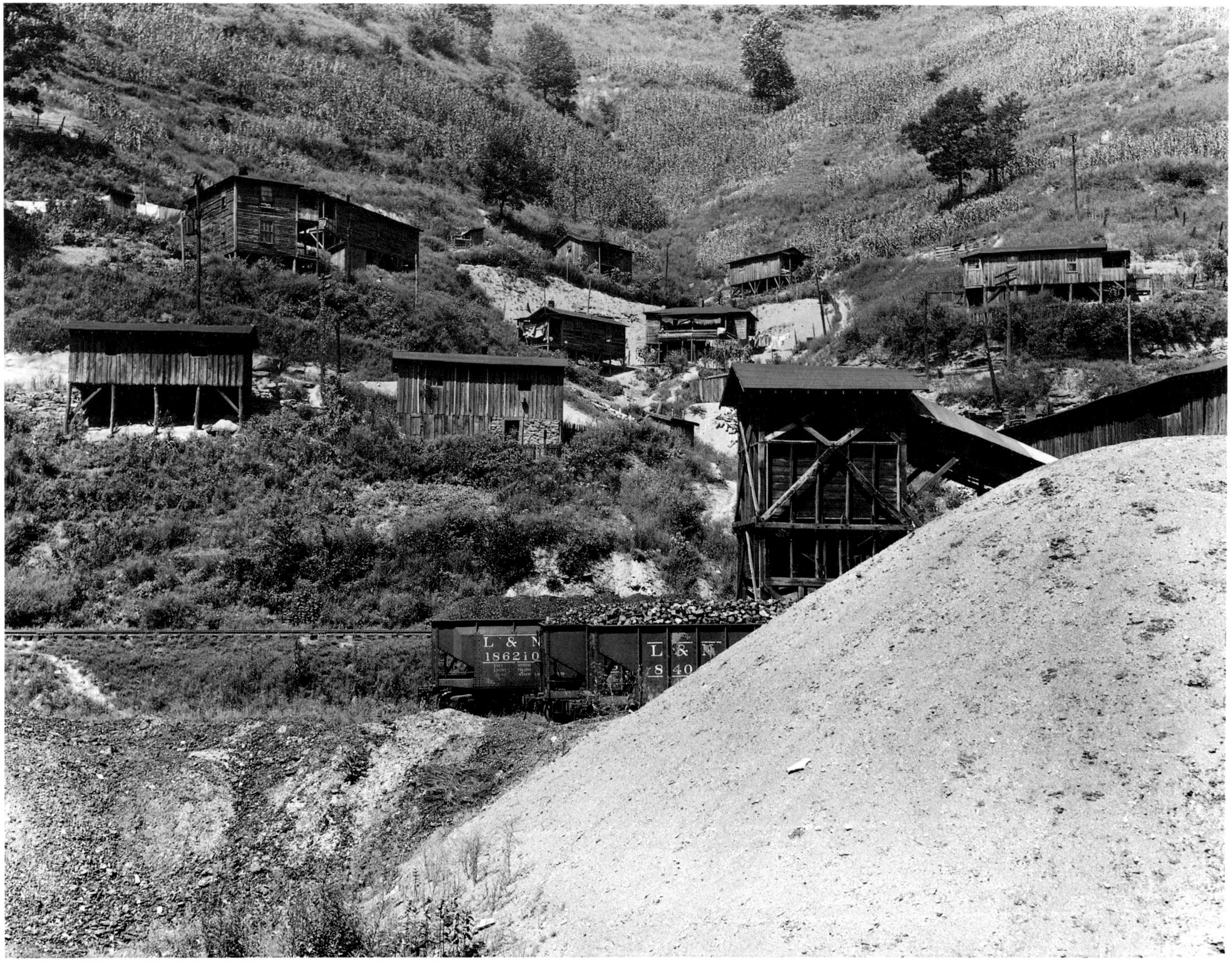
L & N
186210
L & N

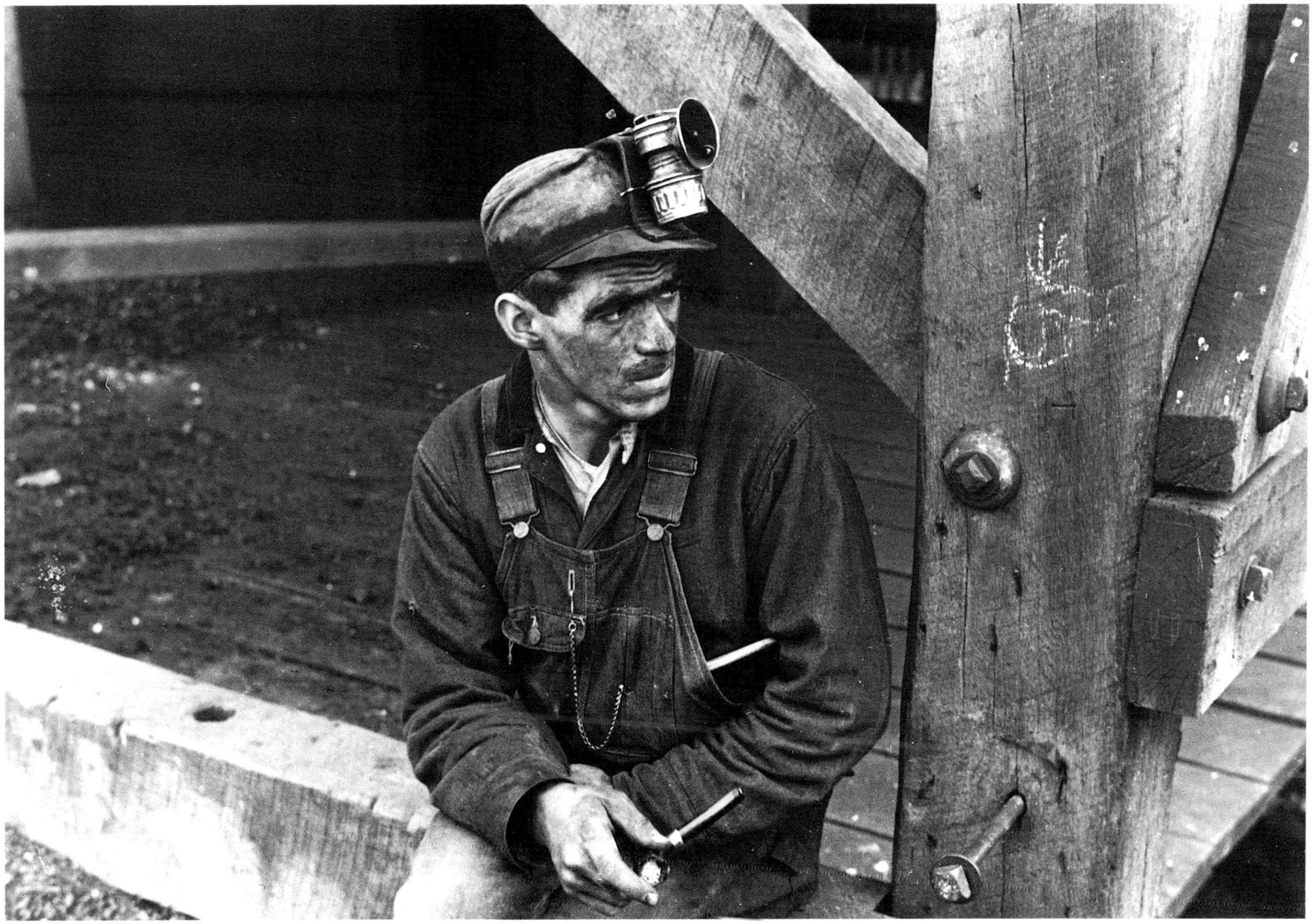

A coal miner. Jenkins, October 1935. Ben Shahn.

Opposite: A coal camp near Hazard. September 1940. Marion Post Wolcott.

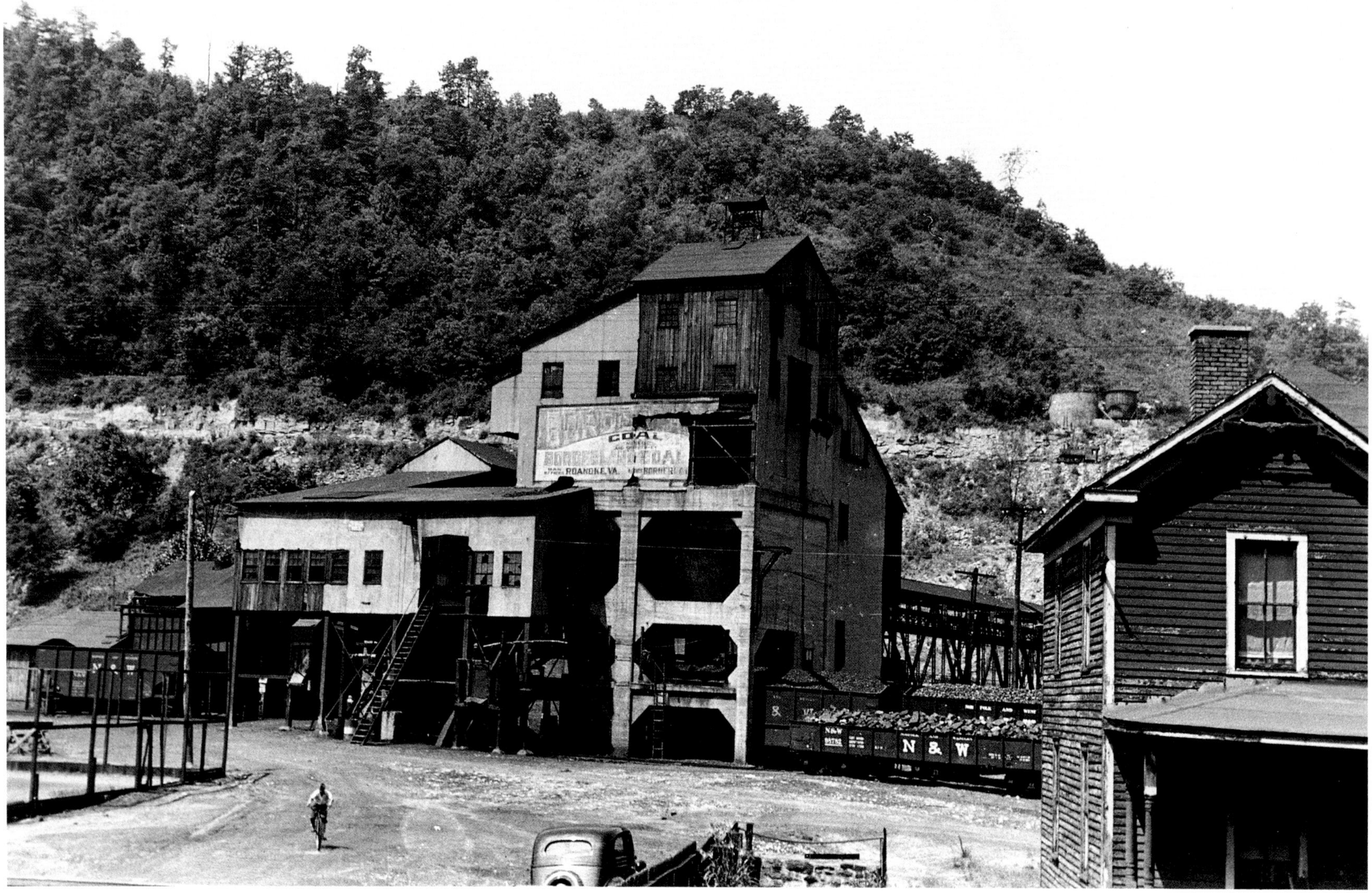

A Floyd County coal mine. May 1938. ARTHUR ROTHSTEIN.

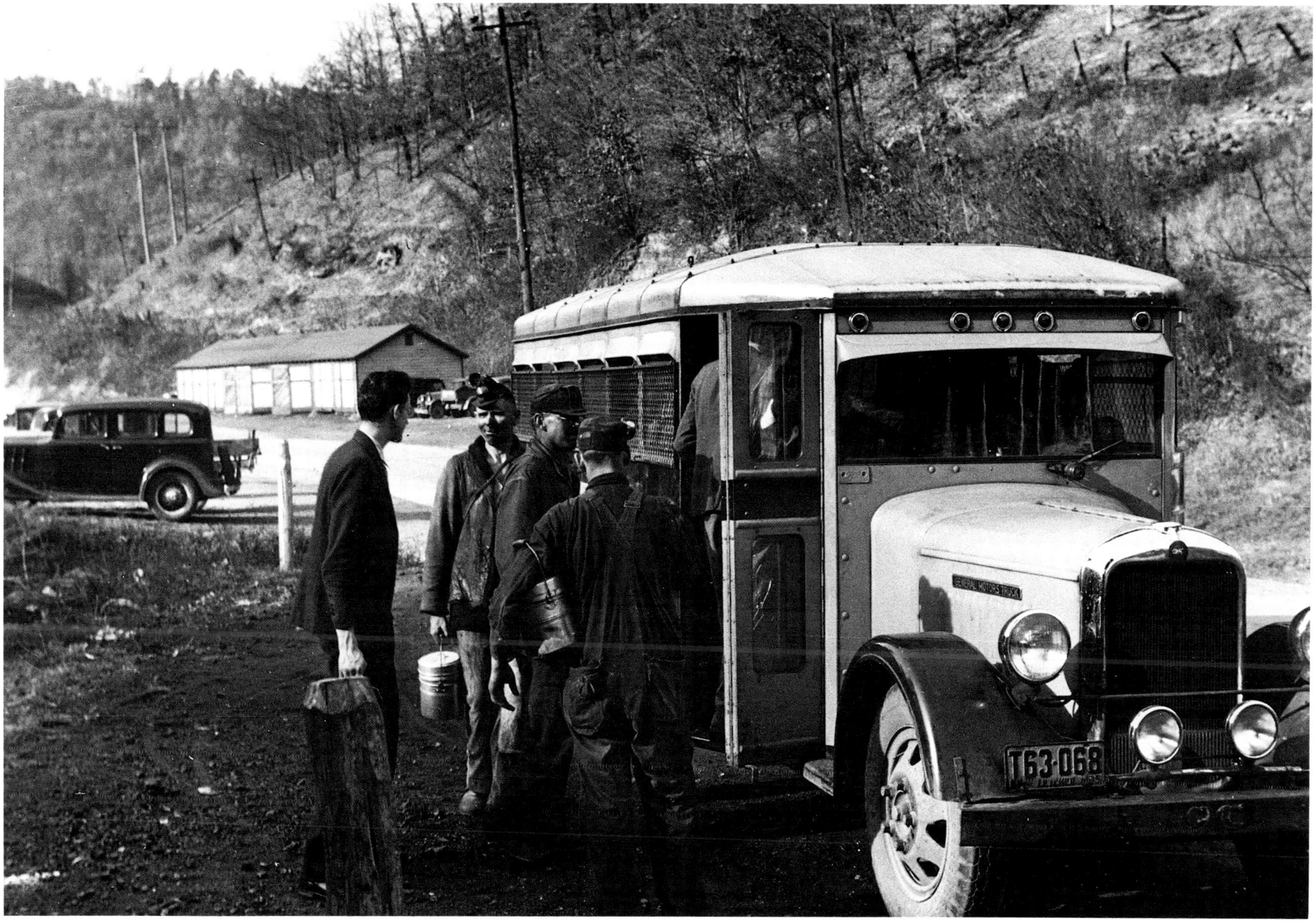

Miners headed for the pit. Jenkins, October 1935. BEN SHAHN.

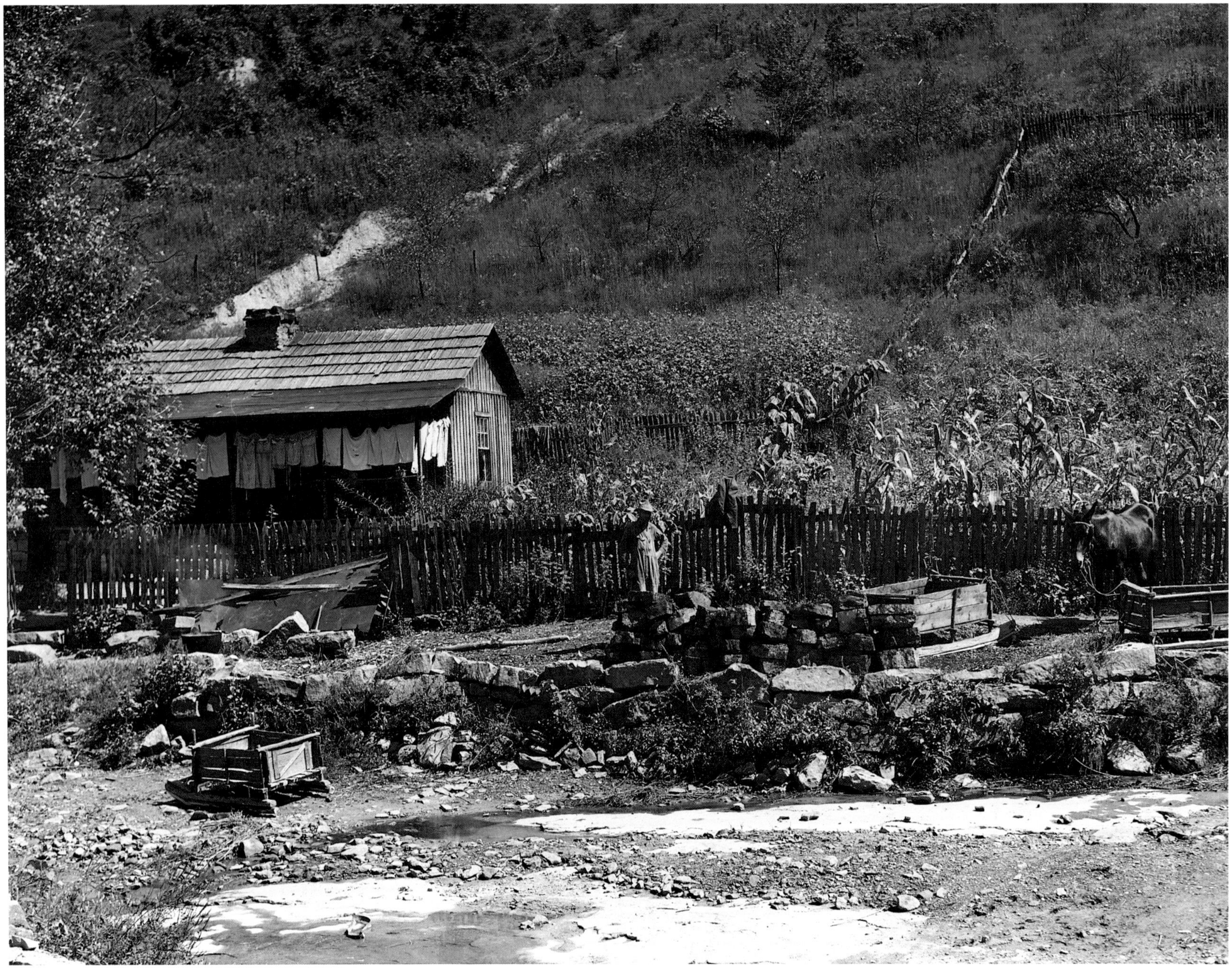

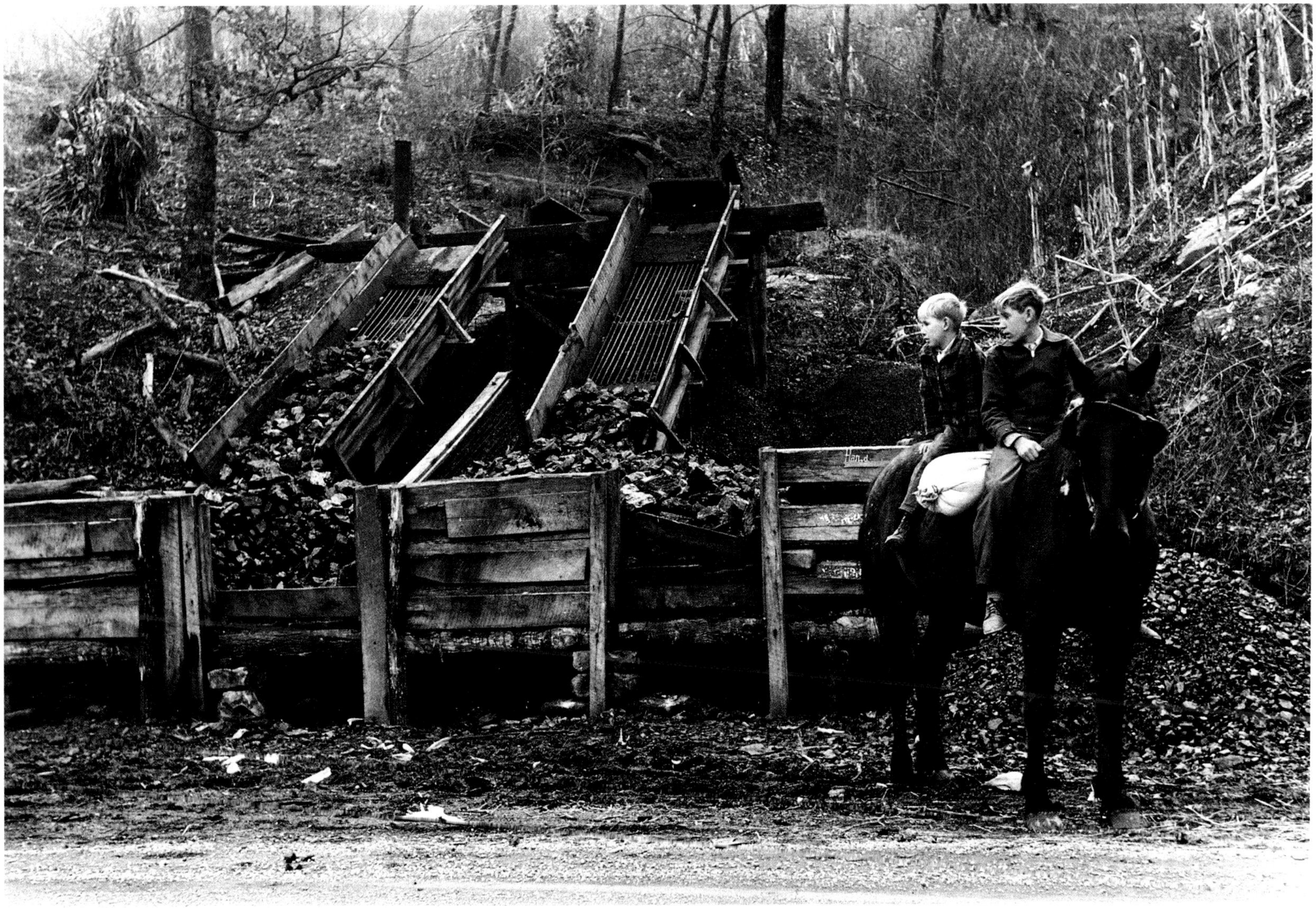

The children of Tommy Abner beside their coal tipple. Near Barbourville, November 1940. MARION POST WOLCOTT.

Opposite: Bright-burning candle, or cannel, coal "raised" by a mountaineer from the hill behind his home for use as winter fuel. Breathitt County, August 1940. MARION POST WOLCOTT.

Workers prepare bronze heads for surface condensers to be used by the Army in marine boilers. Louisville, January 1942. ALFRED PALMER.

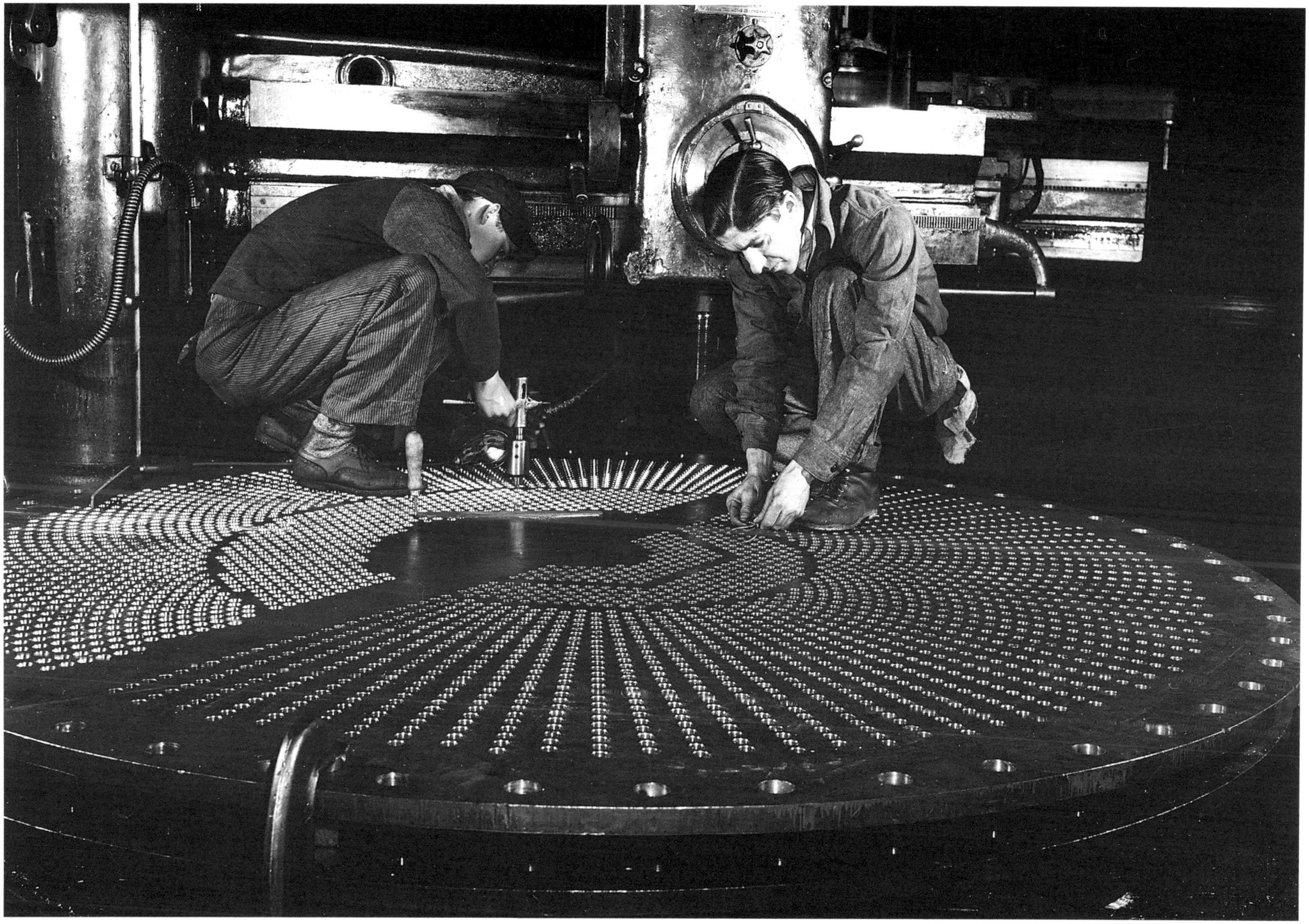

IN THE EARLY 1940s, as the United States geared up for war, the process of industrialization and mechanization that was already under way in Kentucky was greatly speeded up. Civilians heeded the call to support the boys overseas. Farm workers took factory jobs in the cities, the factories shifted from civilian to military production, and many women took over jobs vacated by men or worked in civilian co-ops to feed and clothe the troops.

By November 1943, the demand for manpower for industry and the military had caused a decrease of 10 percent in the population of Kentucky, with higher percentages of loss in rural areas. Many of the migrants never returned to the farm. Persons living in the area that is now Fort Knox were forced to leave their homes to make way for wartime expansion of the army base, and military camps were established or enlarged in other parts of Kentucky.

One result of these massive population shifts was bus stations crowded with people traveling to find work or, having found it, returning home to see their families. Facilities built in peacetime could scarcely accommodate the herds of humanity now passing through them. These conditions were exacerbated by the rule that soldiers in uniform be given priority over civilians.

The FSA photographs taken by Esther Bubley, Howard Hollem, and Alfred Palmer give us glimpses of a people whose way of life was undergoing rapid change. Many of the transformations we see in progress here were to become permanent. Industrialization, the shift of population to urban areas, and the increasing mobility of Kentuckians in all walks of life not only continued after World War II but accelerated. Perhaps symbolic of this moment in the Commonwealth's history is the photo of a tree—a product of Kentucky's long-established lumbering industry—being converted to gunstocks for a war being fought in distant corners of the world.

Opposite: A halftrack armored car, a familiar wartime sight at Fort Knox. June 1942. ALFRED PALMER.

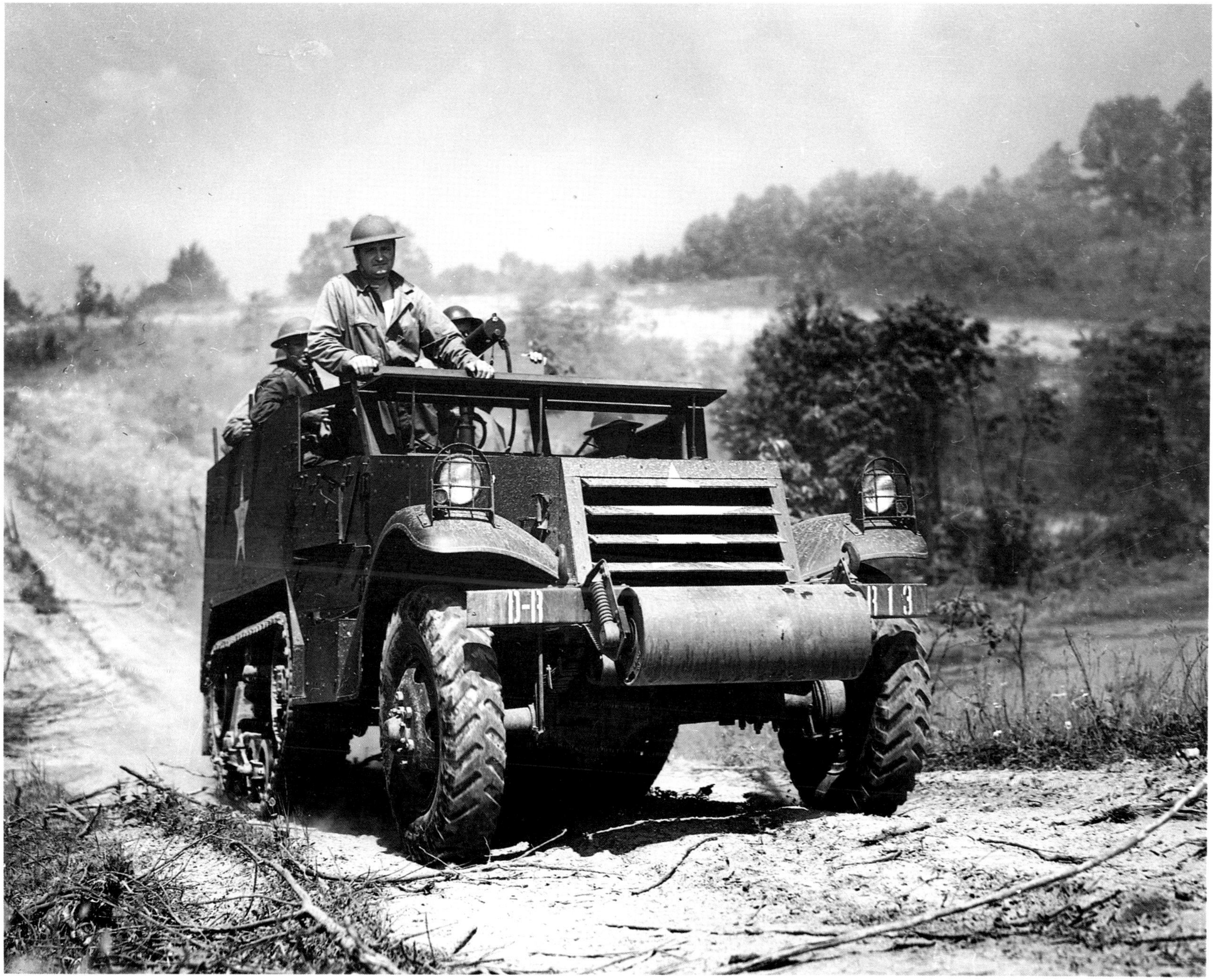
D-R
R13

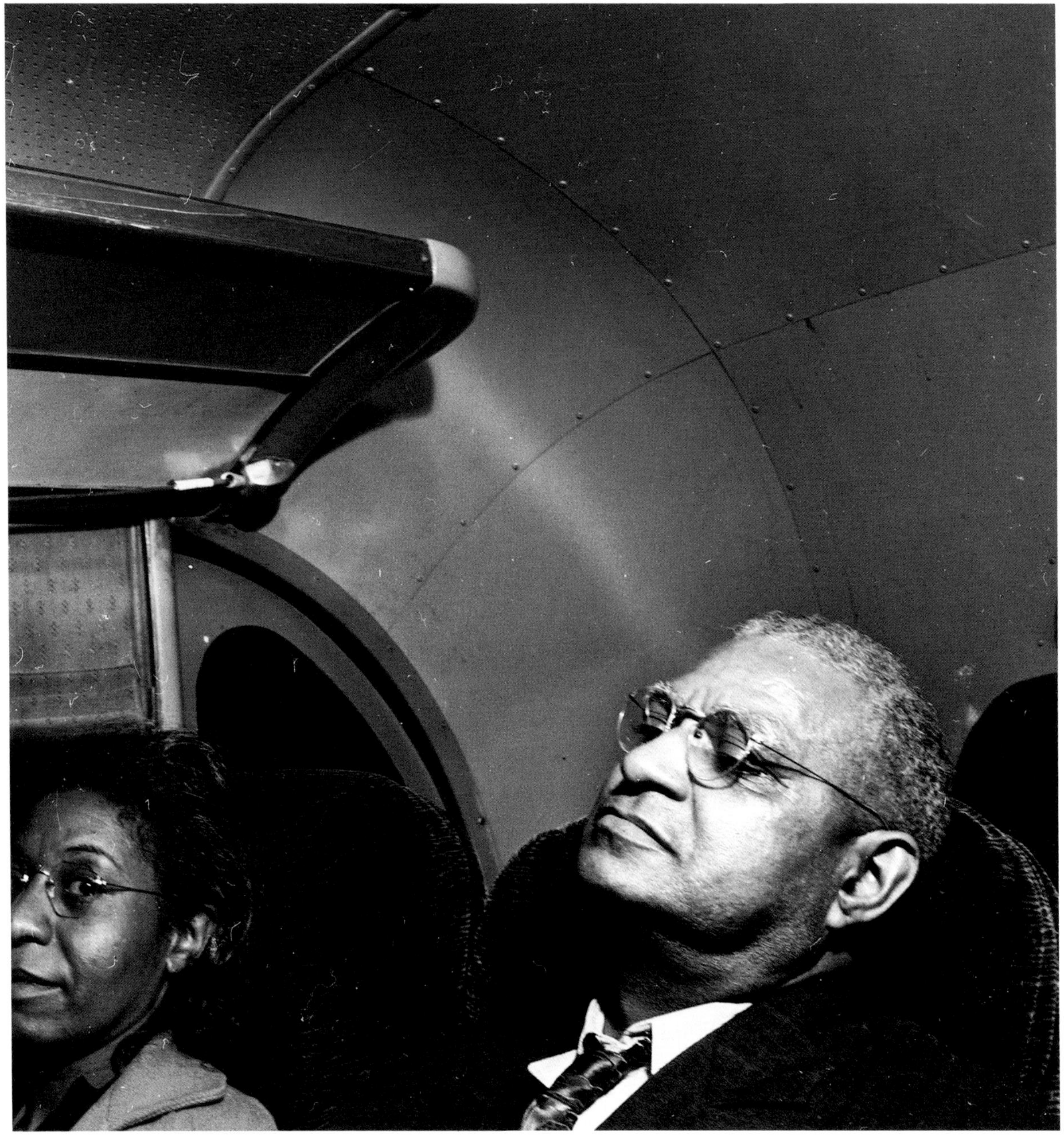

Passengers on a Greyhound bus en route from Louisville to Nashville. September 1943. ESTHER BUBLEY.

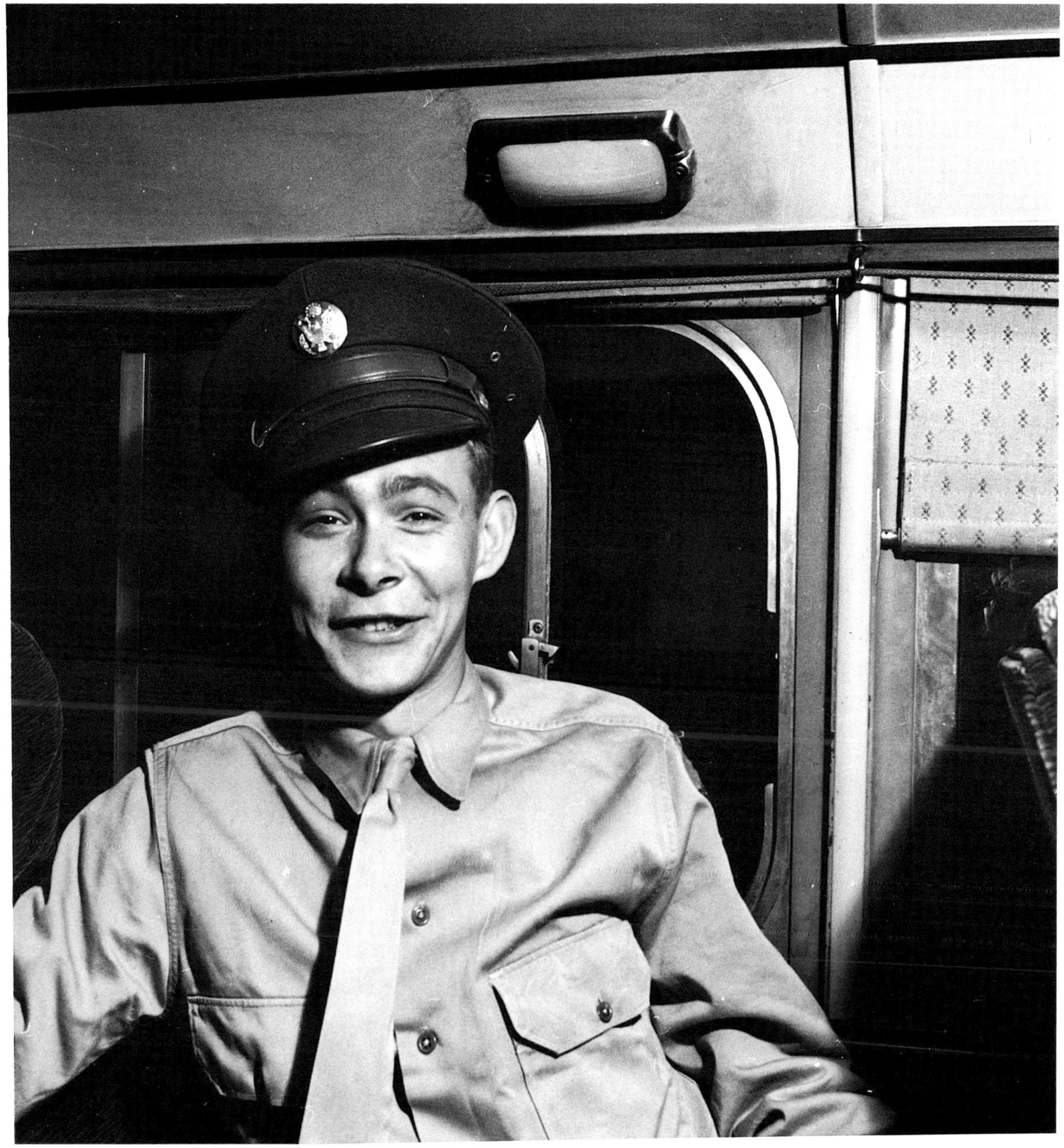

Heading home on furlough.
September 1943. ESTHER BUBLEY.

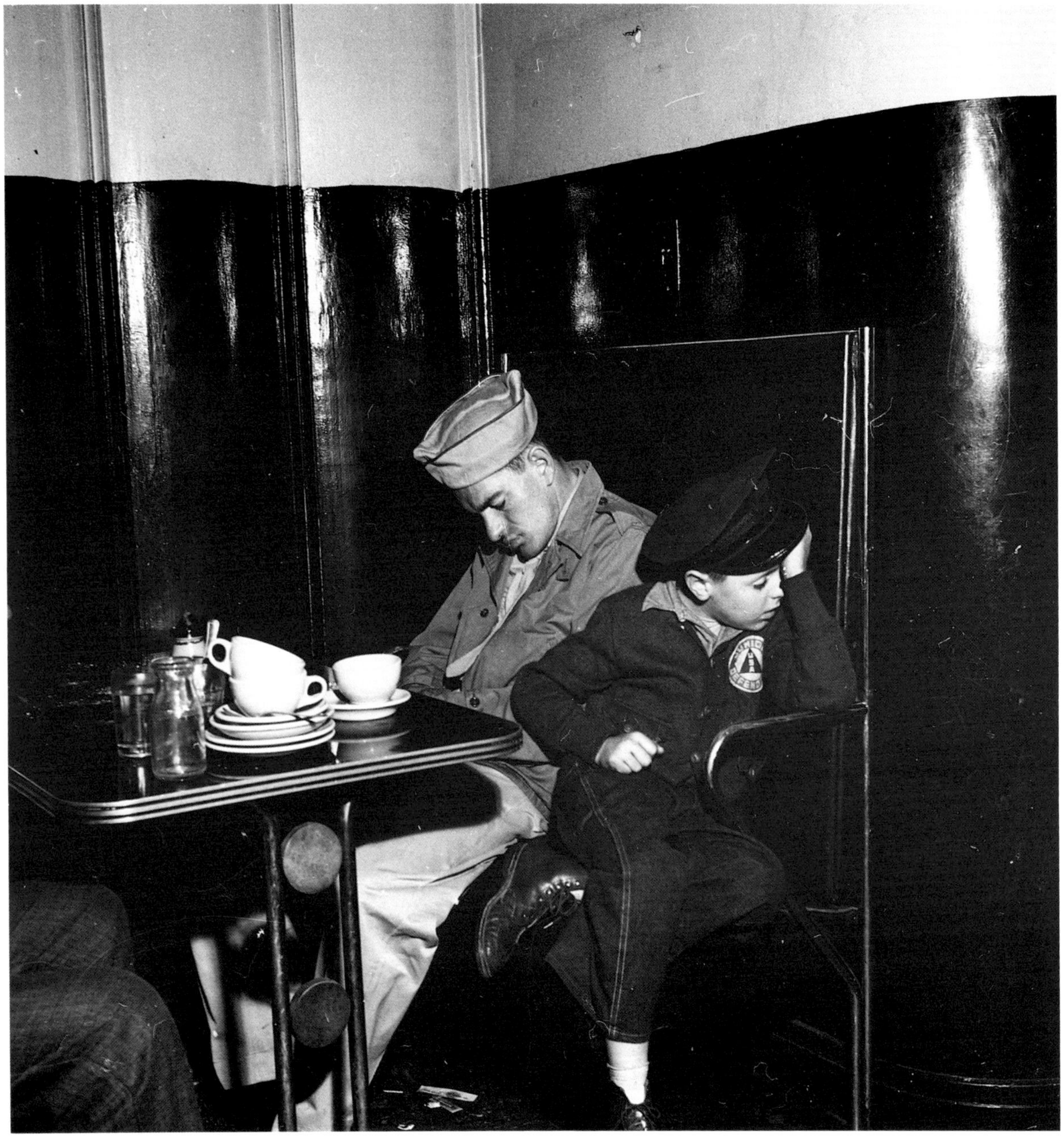

Left and opposite: Bus passengers in the Greyhound terminal at 3 a.m. on a Sunday. Louisville, September 1943. Esther Bubley.

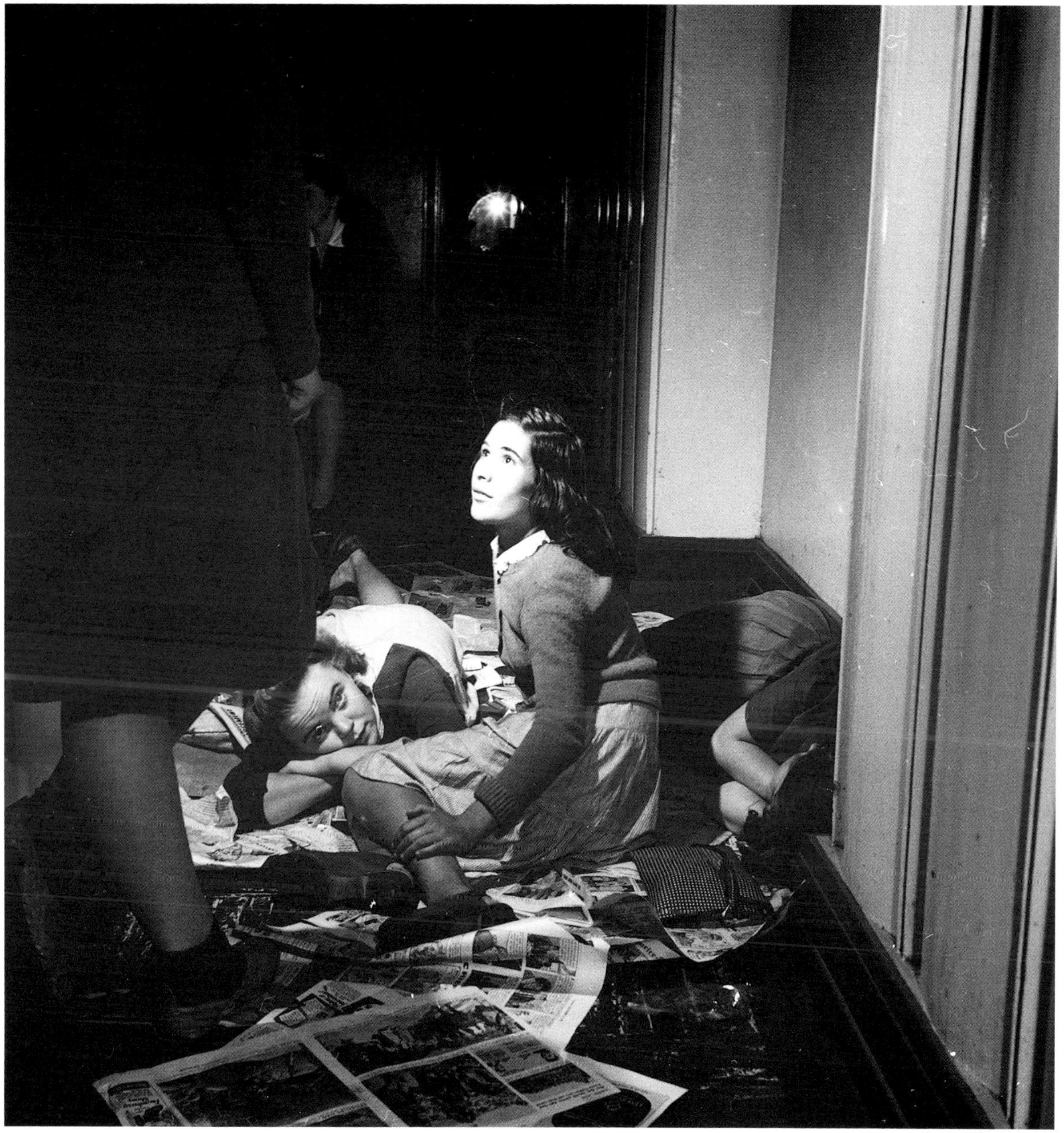

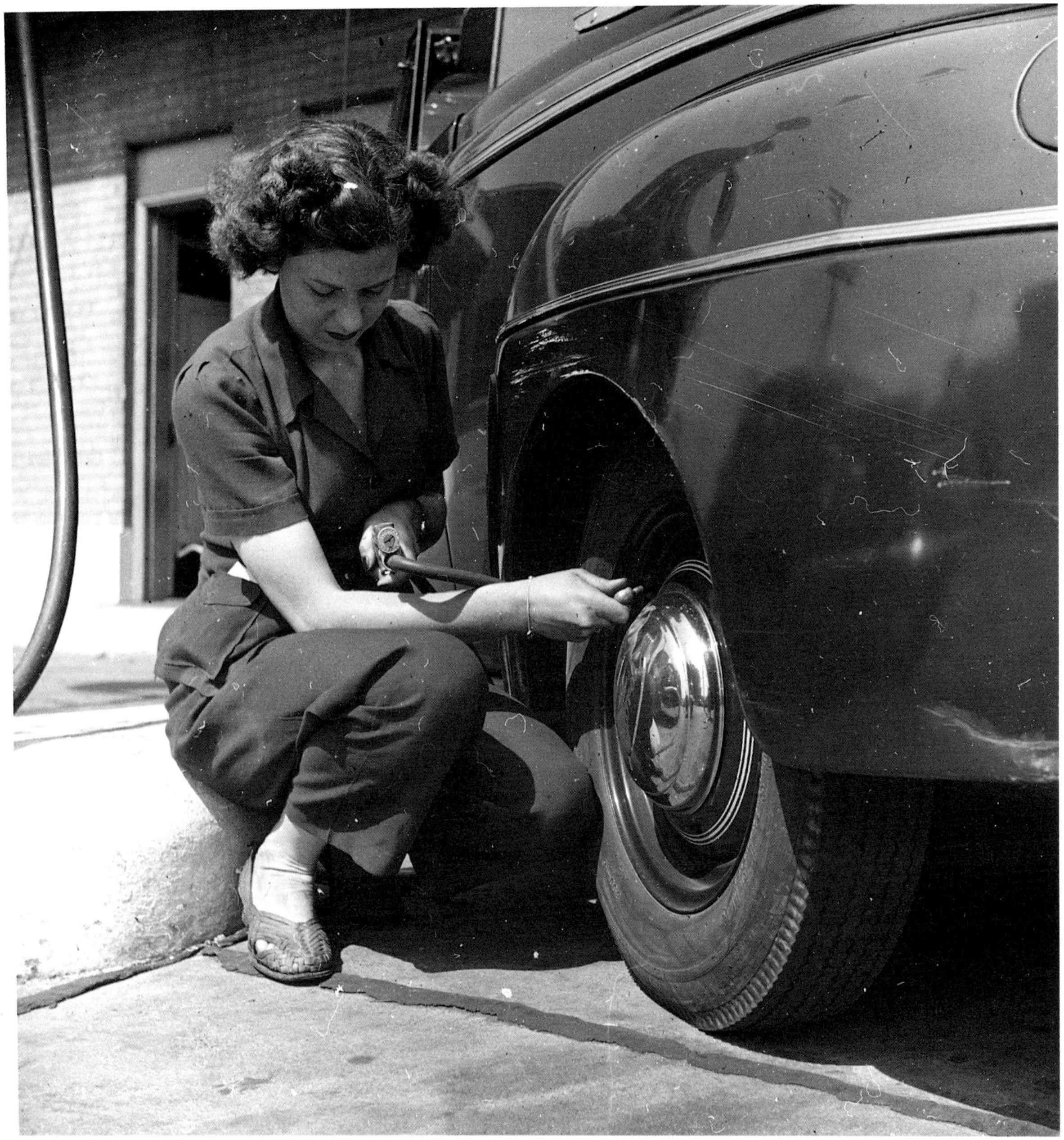

Former beautician Virginia Lively takes on a new occupation during the war. Louisville, June 1943. Howard Hollem.

Opposite: Canning food at a co-op for the war effort. Jeffersontown, June 1943. Howard Hollem.

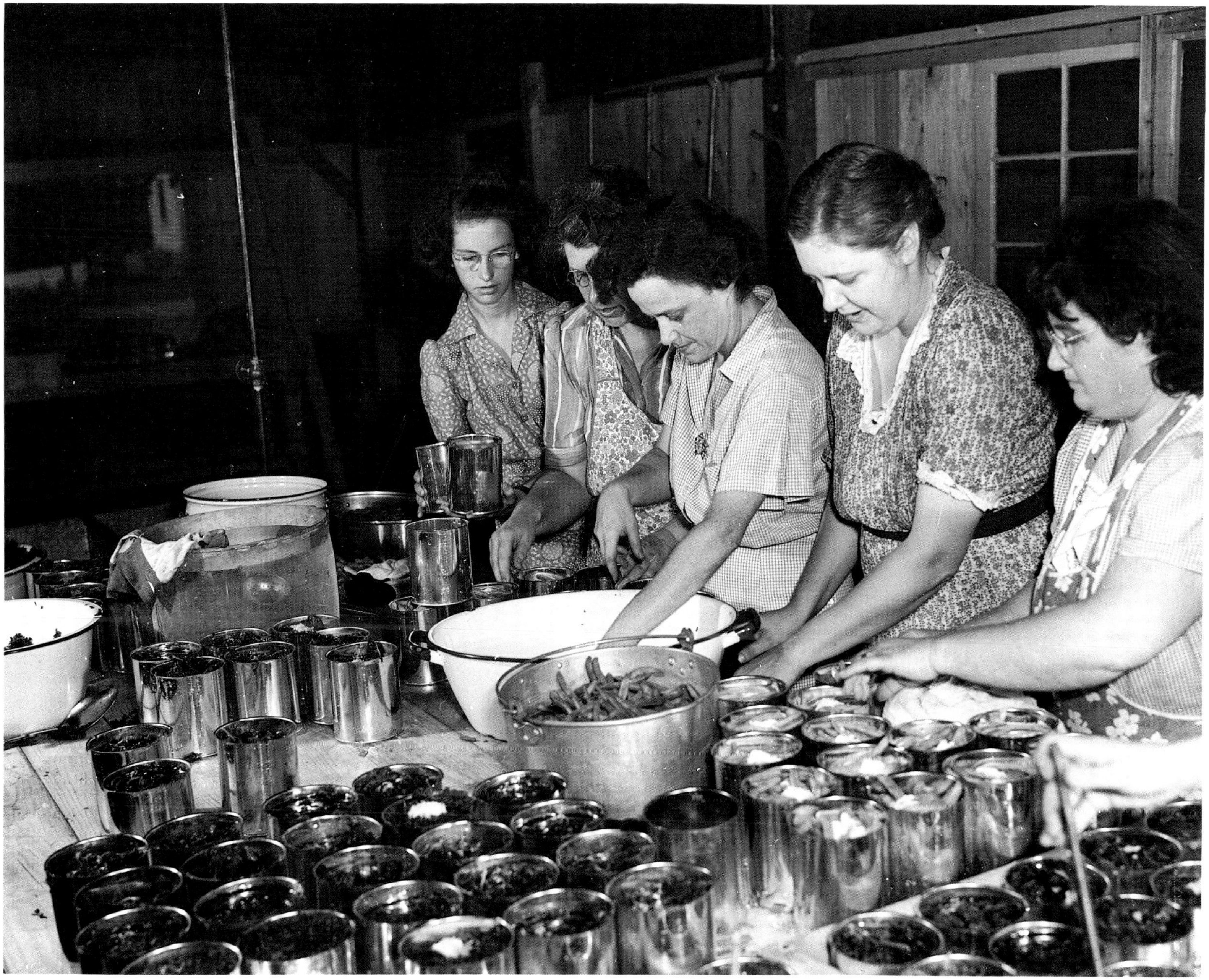

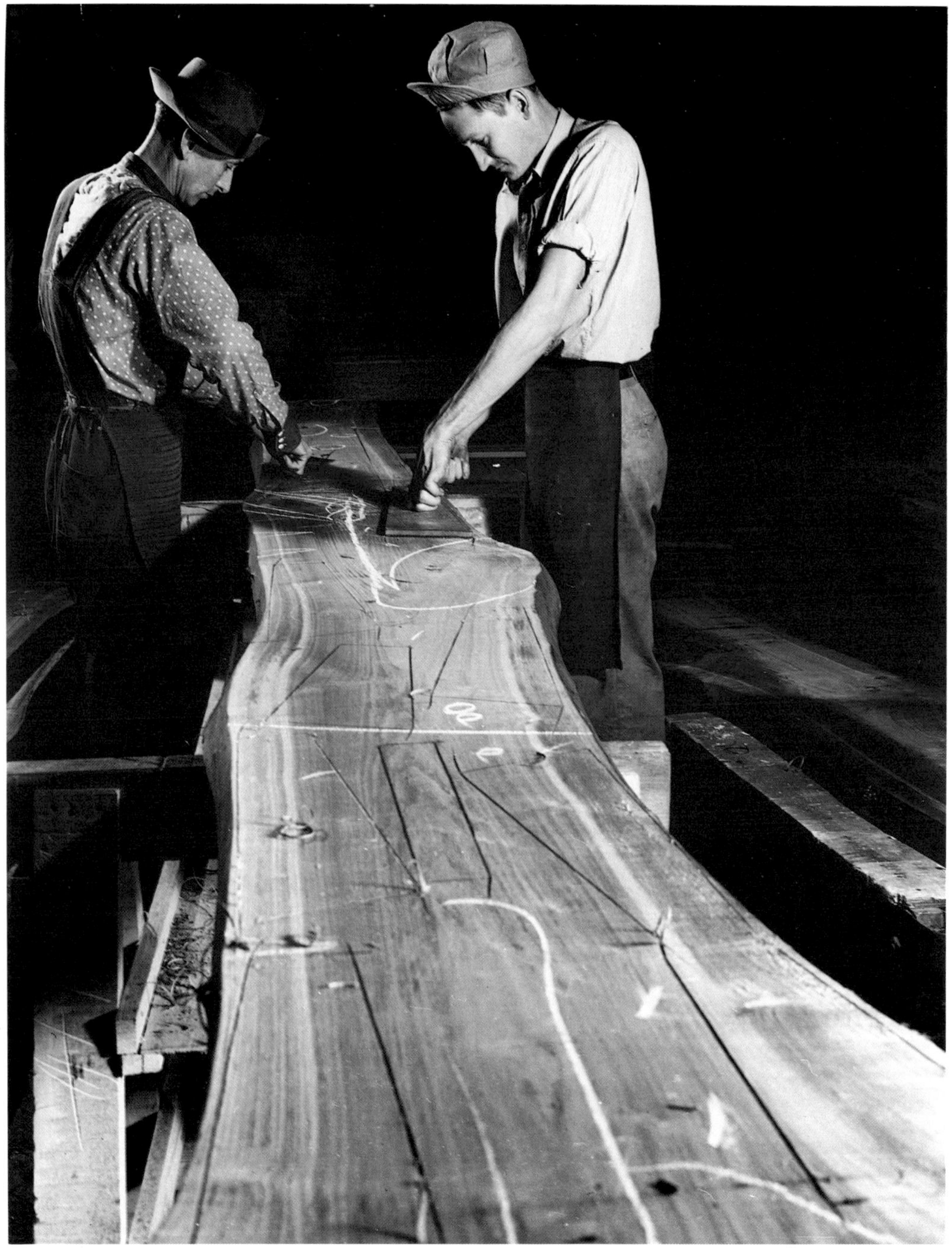

Gun stocks are cut from a slab of walnut that would formerly have become furniture. Louisville, June 1942. ALFRED PALMER.

Opposite: Sewing leg seams in a wartime pants factory. Louisville, June 1941. ALFRED PALMER.

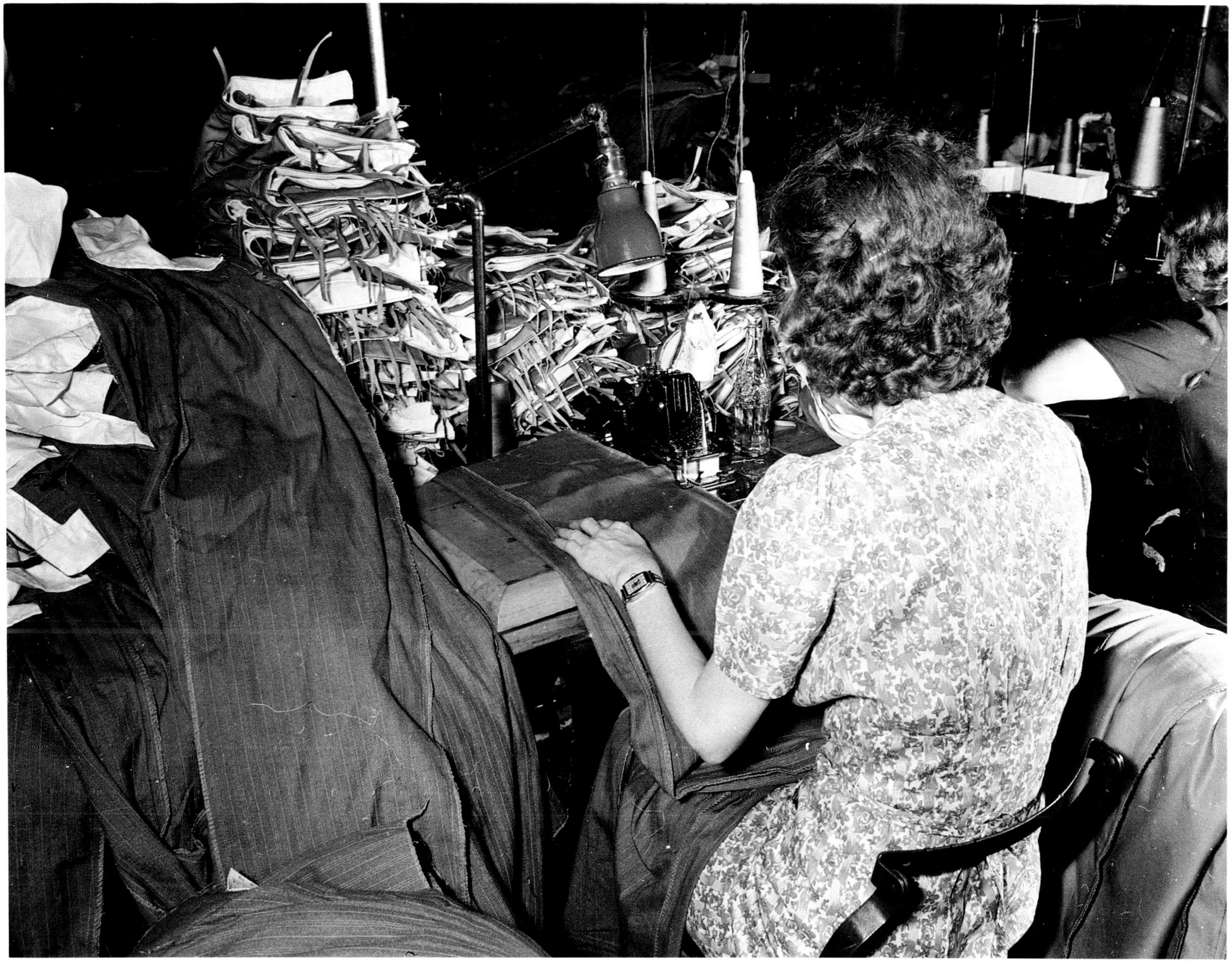

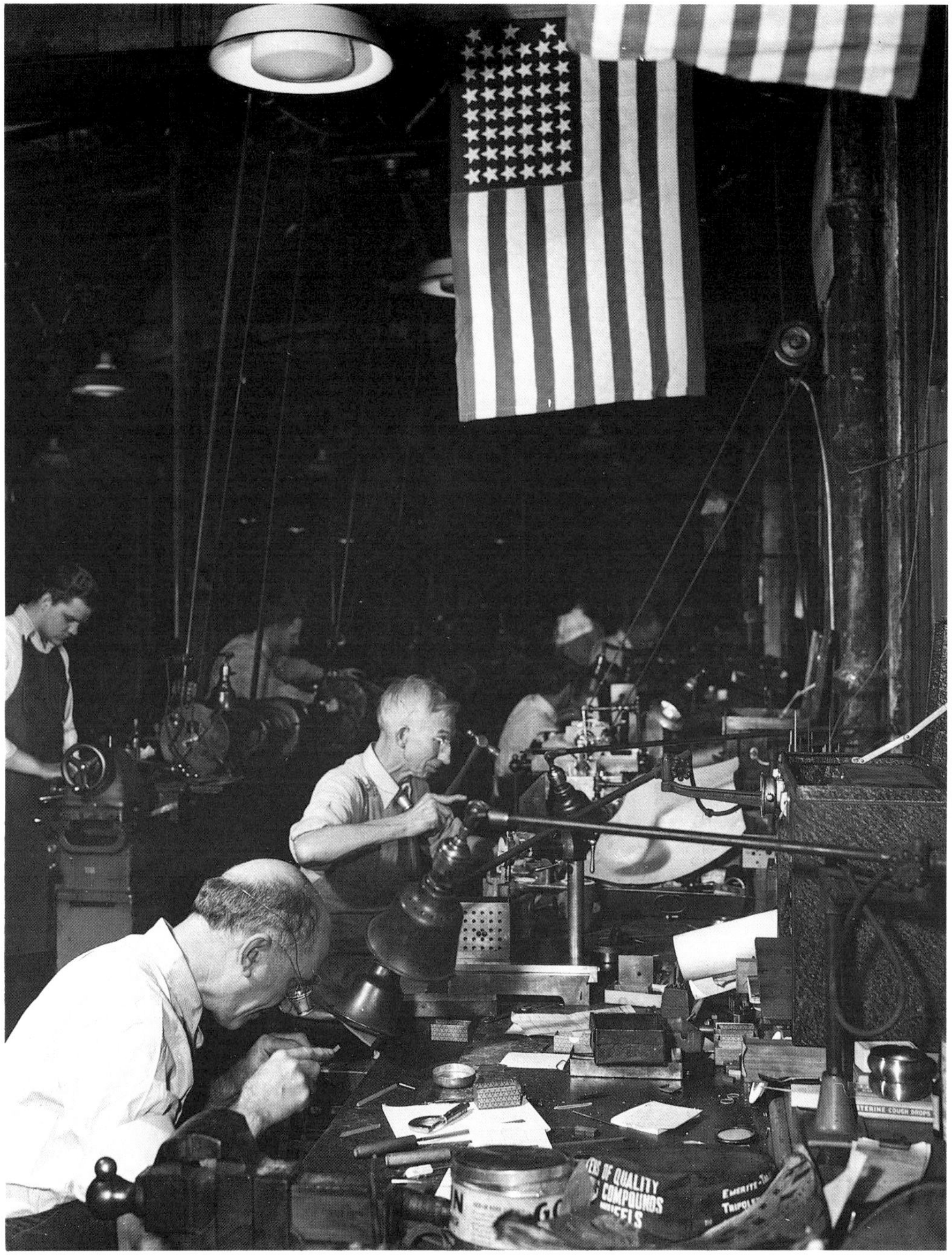

A former watch case factory has converted to turning out gun and radio parts and compass cases for the war effort. Louisville, February 1942. ALFRED PALMER.

Photo Negative Numbers

Page	Negative Number
ii	LC-USF34-55538-E
vi	LC-USF33-30995-M5
viii	LC-USF33-30977-M3
ix	LC-USF33-31095-M1
xii	LC-USF34-55122-D
3	LC-USF33-6138-M3
5	LC-USF33-31080-M5
6	LC-USF34-55784-D
9	LC-USF34-55836-D
11	LC-USF34-56421-D
12	LC-USF34-55768-D
13	LC-USF34-55889-D
14	LC-USF34-55763-D
15	LC-USF34-56387-D
16	LC-USF33-31161-M1
17	LC-USF34-56407-D
18	LC-USF34-55590-D
19	LC-USF34-55551-D
20	LC-USF34-55114-D
21	LC-USF34-55769-D
22	LC-USF33-31026-M2
23	LC-USF34-56110-D
24	LC-USF34-55898-D
25	LC-USF34-55723-D
26	LC-USF34-55598-D
27	LC-USF34-55398-D
28	LC-USF34-55412-D
29	LC-USF34-55365-D
30	LC-USF34-55104-D
31	LC-USF34-61927-D
32	LC-USF34-55439-D
33	LC-USF34-55485-D
34	LC-USF34-2555-D
35	LC-USF33-30973-M4
36	LC-USF34-61786-D
37	LC-USF33-31000-M1
39	LC-USF33-31072-M1
41	LC-USF33-31067-M3
42	LC-USF34-55223-D
43	LC-USF34-55534-E
44	LC-USF33-31060-M4
45	LC-USF33-31074-M2
46	LC-USF33-31038-M2
47	LC-USF33-31118-M4
48	LC-USF34-55849-D
49	LC-USF34-55314-D
50	LC-USF34-55611-D
51	LC-USF34-55208-D
53	LC-USF34-55707-D
55	LC-USF34-55854-D
56	LC-USF34-55690-D
57	LC-USF33-31134-M2
58	LC-USZ62-36225
59	LC-USF34-55696-D
60	LC-USF34-55901-D
61	LC-USF34-55830-D
62	LC-USF34-55691-D
65	LC-USF34-55786-D
67	LC-USF33-31106-M2
68	LC-USF33-31057-M1
69	LC-USF33-31064-M3
70	LC-USF33-30987-M4
71	LC-USF34-55253-D
72	LC-USF33-6079-M5
73	LC-USF33-30941-M1
74	LC-USF34-55111-D
75	LC-USF33-30939-M1
76	LC-USF33-31016-M1
77	LC-USF33-31011-M1
78	LC-USF33-30930-M3
79	LC-USF34-55137-D
80	LC-USF33-30998-M2
81	LC-USF33-30993-M1
83	LC-USF33-11439-M5
85	LC-USF34-55991-D
86	LC-USF34-61910-D
87	LC-USF33-6137-M2
88	LC-USF34-55285-D
89	LC-USF33-6078-M5
90	LC-USF33-30922-M1
91	LC-USF33-30922-M2
92	LC-USF34-61805-D
93	LC-USF33-6077-M2
94	LC-USF34-53762-D
95	LC-USF33-31085-M3
96	LC-USF34-55322-D
97	LC-USF34-61824-D
98	LC-USF34-61812-D
99	LC-USF33-569-M4
100	LC-USF34-61926-D
101	LC-USF33-31081-M5
102	LC-USF33-30965-M3
103	LC-USF33-30960-M2
104	LC-USF34-55115-D
105	LC-USF34-55130-D
106	LC-USF33-11437-M4
107	LC-USF34-55519-E
108	LC-USF33-1674-M2
109	LC-USF33-1674-M3
111	LC-USF33-31133-M4
113	LC-USF34-55773-D
114	LC-USF34-55800-D
115	LC-USF34-55643-D
116	LC-USF34-55622-D
117	LC-USW3-34341-D
118	LC-USF34-55328-D
119	LC-USF34-55218-D
120	LC-USF34-55584-D
121	LC-USF34-55450-D
122	LC-USF34-55746-D
125	LC-USF33-6194-M4
127	LC-USF34-55853-D
128	LC-USF34-55811-D
129	LC-USF33-6194-M3
130	LC-USF33-2765-M1
131	LC-USF33-6196-M5
132	LC-USF34-55578-D
133	LC-USF33-31157-M5
135	LC-USE6-D4138
137	LC-USE5-D6163
138	LC-USW3-37984-E
139	LC-USW3-37960-E
140	LC-USW3-37783-E
141	LC-USW3-37804-E
142	LC-USW3-34327-E
143	LC-USW3-34352-C
144	LC-USE6-D4621
145	LC-USE6-D1105
146	LC-USE6-D3561

Bibliography

Anderson, James C., ed. *Roy Stryker: The Humane Propagandist.* Louisville, Ky.: Photographic Archives, University of Louisville, 1977.

Clark, Thomas D. *A History of Kentucky.* Lexington, Ky.: John Bradford Press, 1960.

———. *Kentucky: Land of Contrast.* New York: Harper and Row, 1968.

Dixon, Penelope. *Photographers of the Farm Security Administration: An Annotated Bibliography, 1930-1980.* New York: Garland, 1983.

Doud, Richard K. Interview with Ben Shahn, Roosevelt, N.Y., April 14, 1964. Transcript at the Archives of American Art, New York, N.Y.

Federal Writers' Project of the Works Progress Administration for the State of Kentucky. *Kentucky: A Guide to the Bluegrass State.* New York: Harcourt, Brace, 1939.

Glassie, Henry. *Pattern in the Material Folk Culture of the Eastern United States.* Philadelphia: University of Pennsylvania Press, 1968.

Hurley, Forrest Jack. *Portrait of a Decade: Roy Stryker and the Development of Documentary Photography in the Thirties.* Photographic editing by Robert B. Doherty. Baton Rouge: Louisiana State University Press, 1972.

———. *Russell Lee, Photographer.* Dobbs Ferry, N.Y.: Morgan and Morgan, 1978.

Karan, P.P., and Cotton Mather, eds. *Atlas of Kentucky.* Lexington: University Press of Kentucky, 1977.

Leuchtenberg, William E. *Franklin D. Roosevelt and the New Deal, 1932-1940.* New York: Harper Torchbooks, 1963.

Meltzer, Milton. *Dorothea Lange: A Photographer's Life.* New York: Farrar, Straus, and Giroux, 1978.

Montell, William Lynwood, and Michael Lynn Morse. *Kentucky Folk Architecture.* Lexington: University Press of Kentucky, 1976.

Odum, Howard W. *Southern Regions of the United States.* [ca. 1936.] New York: Agathon Press, 1969.

Ohrn, Karin Becker. *Dorothea Lange and the Documentary Tradition.* Baton Rouge: Louisiana State University Press, 1980.

O'Neal, Hank. *A Vision Shared: A Classic Portrait of America and Its People, 1935-1943.* New York: St. Martin's Press, 1976.

Raper, Arthur Franklin, and Ira DeAugustine Reid. *Sharecroppers All.* Chapel Hill: University of North Carolina Press, 1941.

Sauer, Carl Ortwin. *Geography of the Pennyroyal.* Frankfort: Kentucky Geological Survey, 1927.

Stryker, Roy E. *Papers of Roy E. Stryker, 1912-1972.* Louisville, Ky.: University of Louisville Photographic Archives, Ekstrom Library. [Microfilm.]

———, and Nancy C. Wood. *In This Proud Land: America, 1935-1943, As Seen in the FSA Photographs.* New York: Galahad Books, 1973.

Vachon, John. "Tribute to a Man, an Era, an Art." *Harpers,* September 1973, pp. 96-99.

Vance, Rupert B. *Human Geography of the South: A Study in Regional Resources and Human Adequacy.* Chapel Hill: University of North Carolina Press, 1932.

Watkins, Charles Alan. "The Blurred Image: Documentary Photography and the Depression South." Ph.D. dissertation, University of Delaware, 1982. Available from University Microfilms, Ann Arbor, Mich.

Wolcott, Marion Post. *Marion Post Wolcott: FSA Photographs.* Carmel, Calif.: Friends of Photography, 1983.

Written Records of the Farm Security Administration, Historical Section—Office of War Information, Overseas Picture Division, Washington Section. Washington, D.C.: Library of Congress, 1984. [Microfilm.]